Sheng

Sheng

Rise of a Kenyan Swahili Vernacular

Chege Githiora

JC JAMES CURREY

James Currey
is an imprint of
Boydell & Brewer Ltd
PO Box 9, Woodbridge
Suffolk IP12 3DF (GB)
www.jamescurrey.com
and of
Boydell & Brewer Inc.
668 Mt Hope Avenue
Rochester, NY 14620–2731 (US)
www.boydellandbrewer.com

British Library Cataloguing in Publication Data
A catalogue record for this book is available on request from the
British Library

ISBN 978-1-84701-207-4 (James Currey cloth)
ISBN 978-1-84701-227-2 (James Currey Africa-only paperback)
ISBN 978-1-84701-208-1 (James Currey paperback)

The publisher has no responsibility for the continued existence
or accuracy of URLs for external or third-party internet websites
referred to in this book, and does not guarantee that any content on
such websites is, or will remain, accurate or appropriate

This publication is printed on acid-free paper

Contents

Illustrations

Preface

This book is the culmination of more than a decade and half of thinking about Sheng, making observations and collecting language data over the same period. I have also benefitted from informal discussions with many individuals and during formal academic workshops, conferences, seminars and lectures. I hope to make a useful contribution to the understanding of the language, culture and society of Kenya in a style accessible to all those interested in the topic: students, sociolinguists, and others in cognate fields such as anthropology, youth culture and (African) urban studies, and educationists, teachers, parents, policy makers and language planners who are grappling with the challenges of multilingualism and language choice in education. Others may just be interested in learning about Sheng, its history, and its relationship to Swahili. This book is also addressed to Sheng speakers and practitioners – *ma-youth wa Kenya* (Kenyan youth), mainly, who are passionate about Sheng, which many refer to as *lugha yetu ya vijanaa* (our (youth) language), and who are eager to see it documented, its commercial potential harnessed, and for it to be given the serious attention it deserves when discussing the language situation of Kenya. I therefore write in the hope that the book may make a difference to lives outside the university.

There is a lot of translation in this book: translating my thoughts into words on paper, poring over translations and interpretation of meanings, and translating them yet again between Sheng, Swahili, English, Gikuyu and Dholuo. It is an energy draining exercise which forces the writer to explain many cultural nuances of the language, but it is necessary to the telling of the Sheng story. It is part and parcel of the sociolinguistic description needed to understand a complex multilingual ecology such as that of Nairobi or Kenya at large. Nevertheless, in filtering and assimilating the 'foreign' and the 'other' (Sheng, Kenya, Swahili, etc.) into the target culture (English), one feels self-conscious, at times, of engaging with excessive 'cultural translation' (Trivedi 2007). Furthermore, linguistic jargon and definitions constitute yet another 'language' which must be translated in order to make the book accessible to a wider readership because some of the discussions take a technical turn in order to accurately explain linguistic phenomena relevant to Sheng. On both levels, this exercise demonstrates the nature of language in actual practice: it is fluid and shifting, it involves shared knowledge of linguistic codes as well as the socio-cultural norms and values which guide the conduct and interpretation of speech in a community of practice. It foregrounds the conceptualization of language as a set of 'ways of speaking', an alternative view to Chomsky's original concept of language as grammar, an abstracted set of rules or norms (Hymes 1974). It also questions the boundaries that have been laid between the names of languages such as Sheng or Swahili, and highlights the importance of history, culture, ideology and power relations in understanding what we call 'language'. This study of Sheng also demonstrates that language is a complex and dynamic system, that a multiplicity of resources is required to navigate the complexity of everyday interaction in any multilingual setting.

Acknowledgements

I have been assisted and shown direction by many Nairobians and Sheng enthusiasts over the many years that I have spent researching the subject. During the most recent fieldwork of January–March 2017, I was ably assisted by a group of Sheng practitioners – young men and women who have a passion for 'their' language, even conducting their own research and writing on Sheng although they are not part of any formal academic institution. Some are actively involved in its documentation, others in its role as the new language of music, media, and advertising. Most of them, however, are ordinary 'youth' of the Eastlands where Sheng adds spice to an otherwise challenging life of high unemployment, crime, and poor and crowded housing. Others are artists and musicians who have taken Sheng to heart and made it integral to their productions. Henry Ohanga, widely known by his stage name Octoppizzo, is a well-known genge (Kenyan Hip Hop) musician, a millennial at 30 years of age and a passionate music artist that I was lucky to interview. He began to rap in Sheng because he realized it was 'the real language that reflected how he actually spoke or communicated with his friends and family' (Interview, Nairobi, March 2017). I was impressed by the diligence, intelligence, creativity and passion of all the young men and women who speak and work with Sheng. The people and spaces in which Sheng is the predominant speech code are a constant backdrop to the discussions in this book: the *mitaa* (neighbourhoods) or housing estates of the Eastlands; the speakers themselves, students, teachers and school settings where I did many interviews, markets, *jua kali* stands, *mama mboga* stalls and corner kiosks. The 'insider' status and detailed local knowledge of the research assistants was invaluable: it provided ease of access to language informants, and enabled the administration of large volumes of questionnaires and the building of (anonymized) profiles of individual Sheng practitioners to give the reader a 'hands on' feeling of the language and its sociolinguistic context. My engagement with young and old Nairobians on the topic of Sheng was also hugely complemented by a network of fellow Kenyan academics and institutions, my familiarity with the city, and knowledge of the nuances of the dynamics of language, culture, history, and society of Nairobi and Kenya.

I have received help, advice, and information of all kinds, formally and informally, from too many people to enumerate, but several require special mention: Abdi Rashid Jibril (Rashidi) my good friend who not only hosted me on some occasions during my research in Nairobi, but also generously shared his expansive Nairobi network of Sheng practitioners, especially those in the music industry such as Octopizzo. Geoffrey Gathu (Jeff) and Duncan Ogweno (Dunkie) of GoSheng Services (www.sheng.co.ke), and Joseph Wambua (Jemedari) a musician and popular host on Citizen Radio for their invaluable assistance in linking me to Sheng people and spaces. They arranged interviews with individuals and groups and assisted me in collecting and recording data and conducting interviews in March 2017 in several locations in Nairobi. They also gave me many words of advice and insights as speakers of Sheng who have some experience in documenting the language, particularly with translations of difficult Sheng passages. 'Big up' to Josphat Mukaya (Jose) who acted as team leader of the field assistants, who included Adam, Waruteere, Kɔii, and Cynthia. I could not have spent such a fruitful research stint in the Eastlands estates of Ofafa and Jericho off Jogoo road, without their help. In London, I am indebted to an in-depth interview with Maxim Anderson, historian and Rastafarian Elder, who helped me understand and interpret the jamaicanisms that are prevalent in Sheng.

I am also grateful to the University of London's School of Oriental and African Studies (SOAS) for periodic weeks of study leave over the years to conduct this research although it was in Term 2, 2017 (January–March 2017) when the book came together as I conducted fresh fieldwork. Thanks to colleagues at SOAS, Professor Friederike Lüpke, who took time to read and comment on the manuscript, Dr Noriko Iwasaki for collating helpful feedback from her group of MA Linguistics students (2018) who attended one of my seminars on Sheng; Dr Farouk Topan and Dr Ida Hadjivayanis for sharing with me their insights on Zanzibari language and culture; Professor Lutz Maarten and Chenjerai Shire for the many conversations about Swahili and Bantu languages; and Elisabeth Kerr for assistance in generating graphs and charts from my research data (Nairobi Data Set 2002–2017). I am most grateful to Carli Coetzee, editor of *Journal of African Cultural Studies* (JACS), for her infectious enthusiasm about this book project, as well as moral and intellectual support. She also arranged permission for me to use some material previously published by JACS. To Lynn Taylor, the commissioning editor at James Currey Publishers for putting this book through all the publishing paces with patience and creativity, and for commissioning two anonymous reviewers whose feedback was critical. I am indebted to academic colleagues and some administrative staff at Kenyatta University's Departments of English and Linguistics, and of Kiswahili and African Languages: Mrs Frashiah Gathogo for organizing space for me to conduct interviews with students; Dr Eunice Nyamasio and Dr Mwangi Gacara for allowing me to interview their MA and BA students at short notice; Dr Chacha Mwita, chairman of the Institute of African Studies at KU, and Dr Fridah Kananah and Dr Hilda Kebeya for hosting the 2016 African Urban Youth Languages (AUYL) Conference at KU, which brought together very many of us involved in research into emerging African speech codes. Of course all errors in this book are mine, and also I could not take on board every piece of advice I received.

Over the years of observing and listening and pondering about Sheng, I have received valuable insights and links to people and places in the *mitaa* of the Eastlands from Martin Wamburu (Matɔɔ), Thomas Wamburu (Tom), Peter Kala, and Frederick Irungu Muriuki, my good friend and teacher of Science and Mathematics at St Teresa's Boys Secondary School in Eastleigh, Nairobi: much appreciation to the vibrant students of this school, and of Ainsworth Primary School and Bahati Primary school and Brucewood Education Centre also in Nairobi, and of Mutuma Secondary school in Kiambu county. To Professor Kimani Njogu for being the steady anchor for many *majuu* (Diaspora) scholars such as myself based outside Kenya at the time of writing. Last but not least, I am very grateful to my wife, Tuesday Njeri, and our two *vijanaa*, Githiora (Gee), and Wambui (Wabs), for persevering while I stole family time in my garage-office at home during the long periods of writing this book.

List of Abbreviations

AAVE   African American Vernacular English

BEV   Black English Vernacular

DHO   Dholuo (Luo) language

ENG   English (Standard or Kenyan)

GKY   Gikuyu (Kikuyu) language and dialects

IPA   International Phonetic Alphabet

KAM   Kamba (Kikamba) language and dialects

KE   Kenyan English, the spoken variety based on 'Standard English'

KS   Kenyan Swahili, the spoken variety in informal and some formal settings

LUY   Luhyia (Oluluyhia), a macrolanguage

MAA   Maasai language and dialects

MT   Mother Tongue

NPE   Nigerian Pidgin English

SE   'Standard' English, official variety based on 'Standard British English'

SES   Socio-economic Status (old SEC – Socio-economic Class)

SOM   Somali language and dialects

SS   'Standard' Swahili, the official variety taught in Kenyan schools

Introduction

African multilingualism is changing the languages and identities of (urban) communities, and indeed entire nations. Sheng, a variety of Kenyan Swahili closely associated with Nairobi's urban youth, is a product of the multilingual dynamics of Nairobi city specifically, but it is also part of a continental and worldwide phenomenon. The speech code exists on a continuum of Kenyan ways of speaking Swahili within a complex and stratified multilingual society in search of a modern identity. 'Sheng talk' has evolved into a 'vernacular' that is a variety of Kenyan Swahili spoken spontaneously in informal, and some formal registers, often in response to the speakers' audience (Bell 1984). The nature and fluidity of Sheng defies a straightforward characterization of it as a separate 'language' from Swahili, thus fitting in well with the concept of 'translanguaging', a recent term in linguistics that challenges earlier ones in the literature such as 'code-mixing' and 'code-switching' (Myers-Scotton 1993). The analytical difference between the terms lies in the discrete boundaries between languages set by the code-switching perspective, while translanguaging pays more respect to the inherent fluidity and creativity of multilingual speech codes such as Sheng or 'Chinglish' – English influenced Chinese (Wei 2018). There is growing recognition that 'language' is a process rather than an accomplished fact or closed system, and of the need to recognize the complexity of language in everyday interaction, by taking into account what have long been considered sociolinguistic factors such as setting, participants, or extra-linguistic ones such as expressions, gestures, movement, etc. Indeed, linguists such as Lüpke (2016:39) argue for the need to pay more attention to 'the dynamic nature of language, and non-static nature of multilinguals' language use'. Furthermore, there are language ideologies at play, or 'beliefs about language or varieties of it, inter-subjectively held by members of the speech community' (Milroy 2004:163). In the context we shall discuss in this book (Kenya, Nairobi) these ideologies index languages or their varieties to socio-economic status and group identities, such as Maasai (language and community), Luo (Dholuo) or Gikuyu and so on. These ideologies can also be used to create and sustain difference and group identity, or to redefine existing situations. For example Sheng can be deployed to exclude those who would themselves exclude the Sheng speakers, such as members of the upper socioeconomic status who speak English and little or basic communicative

Swahili. To others, for example the '*matatu* men' who harbour 'grievances of dreams deferred' (Wa Mũngai 2013:30), it is a symbolic rebellion against the normative sociolinguistic structures that link high achievement to the mastery of Standard English, or Standard Swahili (*Kiswahili Sanifu*). Therefore some Sheng talk has elements of what are known as 'anti-languages', which exist primarily to create group identity and to assert group difference from the dominant group (Halliday 1976). But Sheng does not fit neatly into this description either, because it is no longer restricted to disenfranchised 'inner city' neighbourhoods (*mtaa*) youths, *matatu* men, street families, *jua kali* operators and such: '*Kila msee anabonga Sheng'* – 'everybody speaks Sheng', according to many participants in interviews for this book.

Sheng speakers consist of a huge section of Kenyans, described as the 'fastest growing speech community of Kenya' (Mutiga 2013:14), primarily the 60 per cent aged under 25years, specifically adolescents (9–13 years), teenagers (14–19 years), and young adults (20–25 years). But many mature adults over 25 years also speak Sheng and in total about 75 per cent of Kenya's population of 44 million are under 35 years of age (KPSA 2013, World Factbook 2016). These speakers of Sheng are primary and secondary school students, *matatu* industry operators consisting of drivers, touts, conductors, painters, graphic artists, etc., university students, city workers, street families, radio deejays and journalists, aspiring and elected politicians – practically the whole range of mostly urban based Kenyans (*wananchi wa kawaida*). Our most recent data shows that many parents, and teachers and professionals and business men and women speak Sheng 'sometimes' or 'most of the time' in self-reported data (Nairobi Data Set 2017). It is no wonder that Sheng attracts a lot of attention of Kenyan *wananchi* (citizens), scholars, educationists, and media, both local and international. This is also due to its pervasive influence on language, education, culture, and society of Kenya, and its defiance of the normative *Kiswahili Sanifu*. There also are valid concerns about the effect of Sheng on 'standard' varieties of the two official languages of Kenya, and questions as to why efforts to entrench *Kiswahili Sanifu* among Kenyans have not succeeded well. Sheng also attracts commercial and other interests as businesses, advocacy groups and social activists increasingly turn to Sheng in film, social and broadcast media, in *jua kali* (informal) enterprises and business. Banks and large corporations have jumped on the wave through advertising in Sheng across the Kenyan landscape as has been amply demonstrated by Githiora (2018a), Kariuki et al. (2015), and Mutonya (2008).

Rapid urbanization in post-colonial Africa is a key factor in the language dynamics that have produced somewhat similar speech codes to Sheng. They emerge from a multilingual, multicultural context that brings peoples and languages into contact under similar conditions of great ethnolinguistic diversity, and socio-economic differentiation among internal migrants who have settled in a new urban environment. These include among others, Camfrangalis (Kamtok) spoken in Yaounde, the capital city of Cameroon (Kouega 2004), or 'the collection of urban language phenomena' known as 'Tsostitaals' in South Africa (Hurst and Mesthrie 2013), or 'Urban Wolof' which, like Sheng, has grown to influence significantly the language ecology throughout Senegal (MacLaughlin 2008). In the specific case of Nairobi, it is about 50 years since the decolonization process started a few years before the country's official independence from Britain in 1963. The 1960s oversaw a massive influx of indigenous Kenyan Africans into a previously prohibited life in the capital city in search of employment and other opportunities, or fleeing landlessness and seeking a better life. It was followed by a decade and half of relative stability and economic progress which gave further impetus to rural–urban migration. From 1979 to 1999, Nairobi grew at a sustained and constant rate of about five per cent per year (KPSA 2013:198). Sheng grew along with the city not because of a real communicative necessity, which is typically filled by a pidgin, since the existing lingua franca, Swahili, was and remains available. Sheng is really a natural mutation of Kenyan Swahili and a product of the specific sociolinguistic ecology of the Kenyan nation-state, and more specifically of its capital, Nairobi.

A national education policy that emphasizes Standard English and Swahili and places indigenous languages at the periphery, coupled with ethnic tensions, has produced a situation in which Sheng acts as a 'strategy of neutrality' (Myers-Scotton 1976). In other words, speakers may choose Sheng as the linguistic variety which is most 'neutral', which allows the speaker to refuse to define the interaction in terms of a particular indigenous language or ethnic community or 'tribe', as many Kenyans describe their social identity. The diversity of Kenya's languages is also reflected in Sheng, which has absorbed influences from different languages such as Dholuo, Hindi, and Gikuyu, among others. Sheng, like Swahili is also linked to language ideologies as it is indexed to group solidarity ('language of the masses or ordinary Kenyans') and state identity (of being Kenyan, not Tanzanian), both the result of political and historical factors that have contributed to shaping a distinct form of Kenyan Swahili. These characteristic features make Kenyan Swahili distinct from Congo Swahili or Tanzanian Swahili, in effect creating important markers that are used to project national identities. We shall examine the particularities of Kenya's language history in more detail in the next chapter, after explaining the terminology used in the discussions ahead.

Sheng is a product of the natural changes that emerge from a situation of language contact in a multilingual context. It is also an integral part of Nairobi's social history and a reflection of social stratification in Kenya. In my first publication on the subject, I concluded that Sheng was neither pidgin nor creole but an 'age-marked urban dialect of Swahili' (Githiora 2002).

However, linguistic change is inevitable, and so is the fluidity of Sheng, which now operates in many domains of life in Kenya. Its social status has become enhanced and its acceptabilty in the wider society has grown. Although chiefly spoken in Nairobi, Sheng is now heard in many parts of Kenya, East Africa and even Europe and North America. Sheng is also a generational phenomenon: but who are the 'youth' that allegedly speaks it? Is it an urban youth language or a vernacular speech code of general Kenyan Swahili and what are its likely future directions? These are some of the issues or questions I wish to address or respond to in this book. 'Generation Sheng' is largely made up of millennials under 35 years old who reached adulthood in the early 21st century, i.e. they were born around the mid-1980s. They are making a claim to their rightful place in society using language among other means, and taking great advantage of modern technology, particularly the global interconnected computer network (the internet) and social and broadcast media. The creative arts are also spaces through which Sheng has expanded its domain in Kenya.

The core of this book is based on an analysis of linguistic data comprising of natural, spoken (and some written) speech samples in a variety of settings. These were obtained using standard sociolinguistic methods to obtain (targeted) data through participant-observation, audio-visual recording, field notes, questionnaires and transcriptions of interviews with individuals or groups in Nairobi, in Thika town and in a rural setting located about 60 kilometres from Nairobi. The language data – interviews, collections from media, etc. – draw from longitudinal data collected intermittently for more than a decade and a half. They are complemented by secondary sources such as newspapers, archives, radio and television, and a few *genge* (Kenyan Hip Hop) music lyrics. Participant-observation is essential in drawing up an 'ethnography of communication' (Hymes 1974) in order to understand the sociolinguistic background to a situated study of a multilingual community of practice.

In fieldwork, one must be flexible and expect the unexpected, so it helps very much to have the ability to navigate linguistic and cultural nuances around the topic of research. In this sense, the full command I have of the main languages involved in the construction of Sheng – Swahili, English, and Gikuyu – is a critical asset in the interpretation of language data. Some studies on Sheng or other African language phenomena use limited survey methods which rely necessarily on field assistants for the translation and interpretation of data. I became conscious of Sheng as the code of choice among my urban peers in the 1980s, and I have continued to be regularly immersed and interested in the sociolinguistic reality of Nairobi and Kenya during all this time. Nevertheless, I remain conscious of the limitations I face as a 'lame' (Labov 1972), that is, an outsider to the real vernacular culture of Sheng. Therefore I always tested the linguistic data and my intuitions with other speakers of Sheng, speakers of native Swahili dialects and other Kenyan indigenous languages relevant to the study. About half the questionnaire data were collected in school settings, which may have affected the production of vernacular ('spontaneous') speech. However, through the use of various field methods and triangulation, every attempt was made to overcome this limitation. That myself and most of the students I interviewed were 'lames' was mitigated by the fact that it was not my objective to study the vernacular of a restricted in-group such as criminal gangs, secret societies or *matatu* operators.

In the first survey of 2002, I collected questionnaires and conversational data including personal narratives and semi-structured interviews with many different subjects. In the second instance (January–April 2017) I replicated the fieldwork I first carried out in 2002 and collected similar data by not making radical changes to the questionnaire. This approach helped me obtain a comparative, longitudinal perspective of what has happened to Sheng over the last decade and a half because one of the objectives of this study was to see if Sheng has changed significantly over that period. Additionally, during 2017 fieldwork I administered a 'Test of Bilingualism', and a preliminary, experimental 'Matched Guise Test' whose results and method I shall describe in Chapter 2. The Matched Guise Test aimed to elicit language attitudes towards the discrete language categories (Sheng, Swahili, English, etc.), basing myself on a widely known sociolinguistic experimental technique used to determine the true feelings of an individual or community towards a specific language, dialect, or accent (Lambert et al. 1960). I shall refer to these original data gathered, inputted and organized for use in this book as the 'Nairobi Data Set 2002–2017'. The second test, the Test of Bilingualism, attempted to gauge speakers' 'linguistic competence' or knowledge of an abstracted set of rules or norms – the 'grammar' (Chomsky 1965) of Swahili and English. It was abundantly clear that producing grammatically 'correct' Standard Swahili or English sentences in either language through translation was practically impossible for most respondents. 'Bilingualism' is the result of contact between two communities of practice, but it does not necessarily mean having native-like control of two separate languages: in reality, no one but the idealized, fictional 'native speaker' knows their language absolutely. Also, bilingualism occurs at the individual level, whereas a 'language' or speech variety is a property of the group, i.e. the conventions, rules of interpreting or decoding meaning, and relevant sociocultural norms such as differential terms of addresss or greetings. Like many things about language, bilingualism is a relative concept, more a question of degree: how well does the individual know the two languages, and for what purpose do they use a second language? I shall explore this issue in more detail in Chapter 2.

It was impossible to administer the questionnaire to each individual member of the varied Nairobi speech community. Therefore it was necessary to select participants who would provide data which formed the basis for generalizations about language use in Nairobi, with particular reference to Sheng. The 'stratification' divided the population into broad demographic groups (strata) by relying on a defined population of participants who were representative of the Nairobi population: male and female preadolescents (9–13 years), adolescents and teenagers (14–19), young adults (20–35), and adults (35+). On both occasions, I used a combined strategy of 'stratified random sampling' and 'cluster sampling' by dividing the city into clusters and taking a random sampling of the groups. We mapped the city into four regions or boroughs of Nairobi: Eastlands, Westlands, North and South Nairobi, and their areas of residence. With a team of assistants, we then took random samples within each stratum – 'random' because every Nairobian was equally likely to be selected for the interview. This was especially true among the people we interviewed on the streets and in shopping centres, bus stops and in downtown Nairobi as those respondents could be residents of any part of the city. Even in the school setting, responses to the questionnaire showed a wide distribution of residence radiating from the school. For instance, boys at St Teresa's secondary came not just from Eastleigh where the school is located on Second Avenue, but also from nearby estates of Mathare, Mathare North, Ngara, Pangani, etc. This is a time-consuming method, but it yields a more representative picture of the population strata, which can then be compared with each another to find similarities or differences. But, because there are different proportions of representation for each layer (e.g. more males than females, more youths than adults), it does not give an accurate picture of the population as a whole. However, by keeping data on their proportions, we can weigh these data to make a more representative image. Among other exciting things, the research data helped us to have a better idea of perceptions and ideologies about Sheng, but it was beyond our capabilities to conduct a systematic sampling survey where we would systematically interview or visit every third or fifth home or residence in all the estates of Nairobi. In the first (2002) study I worked with the assistance of a team of ten field assistants, young university students, but during the 2017 research, I worked with six assistants, five of them residents of Ofafa Maringo, who are currently unemployed and possess only secondary school education. They grew up in the Eastlands or moved there at a very young age. The sixth assistant was a college graduate who spent most of his youth in the Eastlands but has recently moved out. With the invaluable assistance of the research assistants, we administered a total of 350 questionnaires to add to the 600 we collected in 2002. These are a sufficient number to even out any interference from errors on my part or views restricted to a small set of individuals.

On both occasions (2002 and 2017), we first conducted a sociolinguistic survey of the city to identify interview locations, participants, and so forth, then followed this with a formal selection of markers for systematic study from a variety of phonological, syntactic and lexical features. I then briefed the team assistants on the aims and objectives of the research, and gave them a brief training session on how to conduct interviews and administer questionnaires, and the basics of linguistic data collection such as how to approach people and how to take field notes. We then collected stratified data samples in teams of two or three, from ordinary Nairobians in many city locations and four compass directions. East(lands) (Dandora, Buru Buru, Bahati, Pumwani); West (Uthiru, Westlands); South (Embakasi, Industrial Area, South C) and North (Parklands, Githurai). We collected additional data at shopping centres and during door-to-door interviews in various Nairobi neighbourhoods such as Buru Buru, South C, Westlands and Adams Arcade. The larger part of the survey consisted of quantitative information collected in a written questionnaire, but we also recorded speech samples of Sheng during open-ended interviews, and as many personal narratives as possible. These data are used here to sketch a description of Sheng by outlining the chief markers of Sheng contrasted with those of Standard Swahili. Beyond establishing Sheng's structural properties (morphology, phonology, and lexical), a comparison of the similarities and differences between the two may also help to pinpoint the areas of reading, speaking or comprehension difficulties experienced by Sheng speakers in the classroom. It was easier to collect data from a group of teenagers sitting together in a class or focus group, with the invaluable assistance of their teachers. It also ensured that I could obtain a large number of responses more quickly than through approaching the same kids on the neighbourhood streets or when they were busy at the video gaming stalls. It was not particularly difficult in Maringo and Jericho estates where the field assistants themselves live, but it was slower since every response had to be captured and noted by the field worker while standing on the street. The drawback of collecting data in schools is that their speech may be monitored in the school setting more than in the natural environment, but various control mechanisms such as reading lists, animated story-telling, etc., helped cancel out the possible effects on the research. In most cases, their teachers left the room after helping my team organize the students. Among the schools we visited, three are owned and managed by Nairobi City Council, one by the Catholic Church, one is a private academy (secondary school), and two others are rural schools run by the local authority. The public schools are attended by children of low-income families, representative of the range of Kenyan languages and ethnic backgrounds. We interviewed pre-adolescents and young adults (10–18 years), adult individuals and groups, during careful speech and in face-to-face interaction with adults, as well as excited, spontaneous speech activity among them.

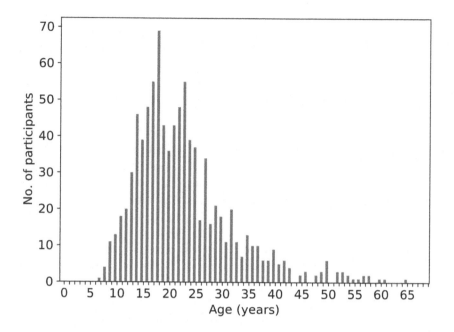

Figure 1a Age distribution of participants (Source: Nairobi Data Set 2017)

The respondents were male and female primary and secondary schools students aged 13–20 years, but many adults also responded to our questionnaires and participated in interviews. These included university students, teachers, lecturers, musicians, famous artists, wananchi on the streets of the various housing estates (*mtaa*) and in downtown Nairobi; in hair salons and barbershops and video arcades. It is axiomatic in the study of human language that 'the native knows best'. To a linguist, a native speaker's intuitive knowledge about their language makes them an expert in their language. An ordinary, native speaker may provide more authentic linguistic data for his or her language than one who, say, is fluent in foreign languages or has a high level of education, travelling experience, high social status, and such. Religion is important to most Kenyans, and it occupies a central place in national discourse: most formal and informal meetings – including political rallies – begin with a prayer, there is a national prayer day each year, and many people place religious denomination at the centre of their personal identity. For these reasons, 'what is your religion?' was included in the questionnaire, but the results did not show significant correlations between religion and language behaviour.

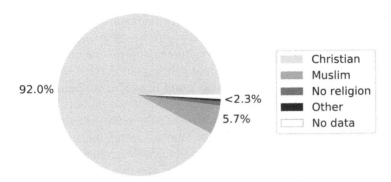

Figure 1b Religion of participants (Source: NDS 2017)

A note on Sheng orthography

There is no 'official' or 'standard' orthography – spelling conventions and symbols – of Sheng, but the writing found in various texts mirrors that of Standard Swahili (SS), with marks of influence by English, Gikuyu and Dholuo. For example, Sheng appears to follow Standard Swahili (*Kiswahili Sanifu*) use of the grapheme <*dh*>, a carry over from Arabic, e.g. *dhambi* 'sin', *tafadhali* 'please', *adhuhuri* 'at noon', etc. The grapheme <dh> is also used in Standard Dholuo, e.g. the personal name *Odhiambo* (Sheng: *Odhis*), or in the words *oridhi?* 'How are you?' *Adhi maber, to in*? 'I am doing well and you?' etc. In both Dholuo and SS, the <**dh**> represents a voiced sound which ought to be distinguished from the unvoiced one <**th**> which is prevalent in Gikuyu and English. In spoken Sheng, the voiced sound <**dh**> predominates, pointing at a result of greater influence from Dholuo. In social media and newspaper texts, and handwritten responses by participants in Nairobi, the same word can be written down in various ways, e.g. *story/stori* or *mathee/madhee* or *mdhama* and *mthama* for 'mother'. Or *mathree, mathrii* or even *ma3* (*matatu* in Kenyan Swahili). A sentence such as 'I am coming' in Sheng is written down variously as *Na-kam*, or *Na-come* or, *buda, budah, mbuda* or *budaa* (father, dad, elder, boss). The common Sheng word for money is spelt *doo*, *doh* or *dough* (also *nganji, ganji, chapaa, etc.*).

Orthography is a reflection of the 'psychological reality of the phoneme' (Chomsky & Halle 1968), an attempt to graphically represent (write) the particular sounds (phonemes) which differ from one language or dialect to another. Linguists use the International Phonetic Alphabet (IPA) to avoid the vagaries of different orthographies (graphemes, symbols, letters) used by different languages to represent the same sounds. For example the same palatalized nasal (IPA: [ɲ]) is written as **ny** in Swahili (e.g. Ke**ny**a), [ñ] is Spanish (e.g. Espa**ñ**ol) and [**gn**] in Italian (e.g. Bolo**gn**a).

Two observations about Sheng vowels are relevant in this respect: first, Sheng vowels tend to be long when in final position as in *vijanaa* (SS: *vijana* – youths) or *chapaa, dɔɔ* (money), *gavaa* (government) etc. Second, the SS mid vowels [e] and [o] are articulated differently, being more 'open' in Sheng (IPA [ɛ]) as in the English word 'ate' or 'ache', and IPA [ɔ] as in 'dough' or 'toe', respectively. Their pronunciation coincides with the two mid-open vowels of Gikuyu, which are written with a tilde <ĩ> and <ũ> in the orthography of that language. The latter also matches that of Dholuo, which makes a distinction between /-o/ and /-ɔ/, according to vowel harmony, for example in alternations of the infinitive suffix -*o* vowels (Ojal 2015). The two Sheng vowels seem to occur mainly but not exclusively in loan words from these two Kenyan languages, therefore they are likely to be the result of contact influence on both phonology and orthography.

Table 1 Examples of phonetic spelling of Sheng

Current Sheng spelling	Phonetic spelling	Source	Gloss
dhuti	dhuti	*thuuti (Gky)*	a suit
githeri	gidhɛri	*gĩtheri (Gky)*	a popular dish of maize and beans
kerende	kɛrɛndɛ	*kĩrĩndĩ (Gky)*	crowd, multitude
keroro	kɛrɔrɔ	*kĩrũrũ (Gky)*	alchocolic drink
madhe	madhɛɛ	*mother (English)*	mother
todhi	todhi	*tosti/tothi(SS/Gky)*	SS (< English 'toast') Gky
rithe	ridhɛ/ ridhɛɛ	*risasi (SS)*	bullet
mukoro	mɔkɔrɔ	*mũkũrũ (Gky)*	parent, elder
shosho	shɔshɔɔ	*cũcũ (Gky)*	grandmother
wera	wɛra	*wĩra (Gky)*	job, work, employment

The current, liberal use of different spelling in Sheng texts reflects the freedom, creativity, and innovation of Sheng, which remains unbound by current SS conventions, or is ready to challenge norms. After all, orthography is a convention – or an imposition – that is accepted (or not) by the community of practice. Yet, as Sheng gains traction in more domains and (formal) registers, the freedom and creativity may become challenged by a need for uniformity in publishing. At the same time, the current freedom and creativty enjoyed by Sheng will be lost or curtailed if a 'standard' orthography for Sheng is implemented. But such an outcome is not my main intention when I use the SS diagraph <*dh*>, and two IPA symbols (ɛ, ɔ) to write Sheng words in the rest of the book.[1] It is meant to draw attention to, and maintain the reader's awareness of the significant phonetic differences between SS and Sheng listed below.

1. <dh> (voiced), e.g. *odhe'nga* or *gidheri,* 'a dish of maize and beans' contrasts with the (unvoiced) <th> of ***themanini*** (Swahili) or *githeri* in Gikuyu).
2. The vowel IPA [ɛ] is different from SS [e] e.g. *mathɛɛ* 'mother' vs SS *mate* 'saliva'.
3. The vowel IPA [ɔ] is different from SS [o] e.g. *Kanjɔɔ* 'city council' vs *kondoo* 'sheep'.

---

[1] These examples are presented as they were written down by respondents but the alternations found in the same texts <nd/d>, <mb/b>, or <ng/g> were considered to be common errors of spelling and ignored e.g. some respondents wrote down ***ngari*** instead of *gari,* or *nyubani* instead of *nyumbani.*

Chapter 1

Sheng as Kenyan Swahili

(1) *Sasa! Fiti!*
(2) *Niaje? Poa!*
(3) *Mambo? Poa!*
(4) *Rada? Radua!*
(5) *Jambo! Jambo!*
(6) *Hujambo? Sijambo!*
(7) *Shikamoo? Marahaba!*

These are probably the most common greetings and responses in Kenyan Swahili today, in descending order of frequency based on personal observation and feedback from a small group of respondents. The Standard Swahili (SS) greeting and response *'Hujambo/sijambo'* (6) is heard mostly in formal registers, addressing a meeting, and such. *'Sasa/fii'* (3) is probably the oldest of Sheng greetings dating back to the 1970s. *'Rada/radua'* (4) is used mainly among the millennials, and is a recent coinage. Greeting (5) is a simplified form of the standard greetings in (6), and is used for marketing tourism, and among some Kenyans who do not mind or are unaware of these two facts about it. The *'Shikamoo/marahaba'* (7) form is heard among native Swahili speakers of the Kenya coast and Tanzanians. Elsewhere in Kenya, it is probably only used in Swahili lessons in a classroom setting where students are taught to greet the teacher in this highly formal way. Generally speaking, greetings (1)–(3) are widely used by Kenyans, cutting across age, gender and social class. They also prevail among the younger, native speakers of Swahili in the coastal cities of Mombasa or further up north in Lamu. Until more recent times, these were restricted to Sheng speaking, urban youth or Eastlanders, and were seen as too informal and even inappropriate in many contexts and registers outside youth groups. Although 'deep' Sheng talk is limited to certain in-groups and registers, its characteristic features that stood out in the past (vocabulary, pronunciations) are now much a part of general Kenyan Swahili (KS). In fact very many Sheng innovations have passed onto general KS such that they are no longer marked as belonging to in-group or youth registers, and are in fact no longer stigmatized by adult speakers. The following are examples, whose alternations with SS take place as 'style shifting' which is tailored to the 'audience' (Bell 1984) consisting of addressee and participants, both direct and peripheral ones (e.g. auditors or eavesdroppers). Even though many Sheng innovations are still regarded as 'slang' they have become so integral to KS that in some cases they completely overshadow some SS words or expressions. Some were previously used only in restricted domains among adolescents and young adult speakers, or by *matatu* men and *jua kali* workers. The following are a few examples of Sheng words that have made their way into general KS.

Sheng	Standard Swahili	English
mtɔii	*mtoto*	child
ishia	*ondoka/enda*	go; leave
sonko/mdosi	*tajiri*	wealthy, powerful person
noma	*tatizo/shida*	problem, trouble; tough (adjective)
finjɛ	*hamsini*	fifty (shillings)
sɔɔ	*mia moja*	one hundred (shillings)
mathɛɛ	*mama*	mother; elderly woman
buda	*baba*	father; older man
dinga	*gari/motokaa*	car
chanuka	*erevuka*	be smart/savvy
ng'ang'ana	*pambana*	deal with, confront

'Folk' theories of Sheng

Popular ('folk') beliefs about language are theories, explanations, ideologies about language by non-specialists (Preston 1993). They are beliefs people have about language variety such as 'correct/incorrect,' 'good/bad', 'grammatical/ungrammatical' etc., or about its structure (e.g. 'it's a mixture of languages'). They are also beliefs and stereotypes about language: its acquisition (e.g. 'children learn to speak by imitating their parents'), and about its distribution (e.g. 'Sheng is mainly spoken by inner city youths') and such like. Although folk theories are unscientific and sometimes wrong, they can help us understand more about attitudes towards different languages or varieties including Sheng. Such theories were littered throughout our interviews, reflective of language ideologies defined along parameters of age, domain, character and attitudes.

Parameter	Verbatim quotes from questionnaire responses (Nairobi Data Set)
Age	1. *Ni lugha ya vijanaa* – It is a youth language.
	2. Sheng is used by most young people.

Domain:	3.	*Sisi hapa huongea Sheng* – Here [in these estates] we speak Sheng.
	4.	*Ni lugha ya mtaa* – It's the hood/street language.
Character	5.	Sheng is a language.
	6.	*Sheng ni mchanganyiko wa lugha* – Sheng is a mixture of different languages.
	7.	It is a combination of languages from all tribes of Kenya.
	8.	It is a mixture of Kiswahili and English.
	9.	Words are twisted but spoken in Kiswahili.
	10.	Sheng is the shortening of words.
	11.	It's a mix of English, Swahili and mother tongue (*lugha ya mama*).
Attitudes	12.	Sheng is a cool language – *Sheng ni lugha poa*.
	13.	Sheng is a dirty [bad] language – *Sheng ni lugha chafu*.

Notably, the gender parameter is missing from folk theories about Sheng, and scholarly literature on the subject is also marked by its masculinist focus, with a few exceptions such as Githinji's (2008) study of sexism inherent in Sheng talk. A typical example is the brilliant *Matatu Men* (Wa Mũngai 2013), the very title of which already indicates a certain investment in and reflection of a male-centred world. I am aware of the difference any analysis that factors in gender makes, and the theme runs through the material in this book as gender comes up in a number of the interviews, and in descriptions of our data surveys (Nairobi Data Set). For example, there were significant variations between the self-reported number of languages spoken by male and female participants consisting of roughly equal numbers. Males also reported more positive responses towards Sheng than females. This is clearly a very productive area of future research, and part of what my work aims to do is to identify these emergent trends in the newer scholarship. We shall return to look at the language attitudes in more detail in Chapter 4, but first let us hear, in the following interview, a Nairobian describing Sheng and linking it to those ideologies of solidarity and difference.

Interview with Jemedari (musician and radio host, 23 September 2017)

CG: *Kwanza, Sheng ni nini?*

CG: First, what is Sheng?

Jemedari: *Sheng ni <u>kitu mbili</u>, Sheng ni <u>language yenye</u> **vijanaa** wanatumia ku*-communicate. *Halafu kitu cha pili Sheng ni* culture. *Sheng ni* culture *ju language **haiezi** kuwa language bila* culture...*ina*-come from *kitu watu wana*-practise. So *Sheng ni* language *na* culture.

Jemedari: Sheng is two things. Sheng is a language that young people use to communicate. Then the second thing [is] Sheng is a culture. Sheng is

a culture because a language can't come about without culture. It comes
from something people practise. So Sheng is a language and a culture.

CG: *Vizuri, nani huongea Sheng?*

CG: Good, who speaks Sheng?

Jemedari: *Kila **mse**, KILA **mse**...**mi** nimesikia Sheng mpaka na **mabudaa**,
watɔi wengine waDOGO halafu ukienda kila mtaa kila **msee** anapika sh...
kila mzee <u>anapiga tu</u> language yake.*

Jemedari: Everyone, EVERYone. I've heard Sheng even with older people,
others are SMALL kids then if you go to any estate everyone speaks
Sheng... Everyone is just speaking their language.

CG: *Sasa... unafikiri Sheng inaathiri vibaya lugha ya kisanifu ya Kiswahili na
Kiingereza katika mashule?*

CG: Do you think Sheng negatively affects standard Swahili and English in
schools?

Jemedari: *eeh... chuo inawezekana, chuo inawezekana juu **watɔii** <u>sana sana</u>
wakiongea sana Sheng inafika mahali wanaanza kuuandika Sheng. Lakini
<u>I think</u> mtu **akishakula** kitabu **freshi** ama <u>ukishakuwakuwa</u> brain <u>yako</u>
inaeza eh inaeeza gawanya, unaweza jua hapa <u>enyewe ni</u> place official
wacha niongee **Swa sanifu**, place ya Sheng niko na **maboi wa** mine wacha
sasa **nianguke** Sheng.*

Jemedari: eeh...in school possibly, it is possible in school because if kids
speak Sheng a lot it'll get to a point where they start writing [in] Sheng.
But I think if someone has studied properly, when you grow older your
brain would be able to separate and you'll know here's official [formal], so
I'll speak standard [Swahili], the place of Sheng is with my boys, so now
let me speak Sheng.

CG: *Na ni akina nani huongea Sheng sana sana?*

CG: And who speaks Sheng the most?

Jemedari: *sana sana ni **vijanaa**.*

CG: Mostly its young people.

CG: *Rika gani?*

CG: What age?

Jemedari: *<u>Sana sana</u> ni Vijanaa, **naeza** sema Sheng <u>inatoka</u>... **<u>Sheng inatoka</u>
<u>ten years old</u>**, mpaka group ya <u>**wasee wako**</u> 40.*

Jemedari: Mostly its young people, let's say Sheng starts at ten years old, up
to the [age] group of people aged 40.

CG: *Na huko nje Nairobi inasikika?*

CG: And outside of Nairobi is it heard?

Jemedari: *Nje Nairobi kuna Sheng, lakini tuseme... **juu**... wasee <u>wengi wako</u>
nje Nairobi pia wanaongea lugha za mama. So Sheng iko...Sheng.. iko
kila mahali, Sheng inasikika mpaka **majuu**, Sheng utaipata mpaka kwenye
<u>countries zingine</u>, unaweza ongea hivi tu Mkenya atajua wewe ni Mkenya.*

Jemedari: Outside Nairobi there's Sheng, but let's say, outside of Nairobi many people also speak mother tongues. So, Sheng is there... Sheng...it's everywhere, it's spoken even abroad, you'll find Sheng even in other countries, you can just speak like that and a[nother] Kenyan will know you're Kenyan.

CG: *Basi, kwa hivyo Sheng ni poa au si poa?*

CG: So then, is Sheng cool or not cool?

Jemedari: *Sheng ni **FITI**, ni fiti, ni expression. Hauwezi **katia** expression.*

Jemedari: Sheng's COOL, Sheng is cool, it is a [form] of expression. You can't stop expression…

CG: *Unafikiri inaweza kuwa- kufikia kiwango kuwa Sheng itakuwa lugha ya watu wote?*

CG: Do you think it can get to be- to the point where Sheng will be the language of everyone?

Jemedari: ***Inaeza** fika. **Juu venye** nchi inaendelea saa hii, mtu [**ambaye**] ametoka Nairobi anaenda **ku-settle** Kisumu, **msee** wa Kisumu anaenda Isiolo, itafika time hizi lugha zitachanganyika, itabaki lugha ndiyo- watu wameelewana na lugha moja.*

Jemedari: It can get there, the way the country is developing at the moment, one guy moves from Nairobi to Kisumu, someone from Kisumu goes to Isiolo, there'll come a time where all these languages will have mixed, and there will remain that one language with which people understand one another.

CG: *Vizuri sana nashukuru sana. Mwishowe, kama naweza kukuuliza umri wako?*

CG: Very well, thanks very much. Finally, if I can ask your age?

Jemedari: *Mimi na miaka **salasa** na mbili.*

Jemedari: I'm thirty two.

CG: *Kazi yako ni?*

CG: And your occupation?

Jemedari: ***Mi** ni mwanamziki.*

Jemedari: I am a musician.

CG: Ah...asante!

CG: Ah...thank you!

The parts highlighted in bold italics are examples of 'Sheng talk', which consists of words and phrases (and their meanings), or pronunciations that are distinct from general KS, e.g. *watɔii* for *watoto* (children), or *vijanaa* for *vijana* (youths), *salasa* (thirty) instead of SS *thelathini* or *mse/msee* to mean 'person' [1] (not the same as SS *mzee* – 'elder'). The underlined parts are in ordinary spoken KS, which has non-standard features we shall explore in more detail in the next chapter, e.g. **kitu mbili** for SS *vitu viwili* (two things) or the omission of the relative pronoun *amba-*, e.g. **mtu ametoka Nairobi** for SS *mtu [ambaye] ametoka Nairobi* (someone [who] comes from Nairobi). In cases of overlap between the two ways of speaking (KS and Sheng), the word or phrase is both underlined and in bold, for example <u>**saa hii**</u> (SS: *sasa hivi*, 'right now') or <u>***juu venye***</u> for SS: *kwa sababu vile*. CAPS represent speaker's emphasis on certain words or phrases during the interview. Of course there is plenty of code-switching (e.g. ***Sheng inatoka* ten years *old*** – lit. 'Sheng starts at 10 years of age', i.e. the group of people who speak Sheng starts at ten years of age, and code-switching where English words are inserted into KS grammar, e.g. **ina-come** from *kitu watu wana-***practise** 'it comes from something that people do/practise,' etc. We shall turn to more details of these features of KS in the next chapter.

Dialects and vernaculars

Dialects are natural (linguistic) phenomena, but misconceptions about dialects and 'vernaculars' persist. We found during this study, for example, that for many Nairobians (and Kenyans in general), 'dialect' is equated to 'indigenous' African languages. Many respondents reported that they did not speak the 'dialect' of their parents, when they really meant that they did not speak their parents' first language or mother tongue. Others think of 'dialect' as a (minority) African indigenous language only. There are key intersections between 'language', 'dialect' and 'vernacular' which are relevant to our understanding of Sheng.

Everyone speaks a dialect because a dialect is simply a variety of any language differentiated by region,[2] that is, the geographical area where it is spoken ('regiolect'), or by social factors such as socio-economic status (SES), age or gender ('sociolect'). Swahili has many native regiolects, e.g. Kiamu, Kimvita, Kimtang'ata, etc. In theory, all these varieties are '*linguistically equivalent* because no variety of the language is linguistically superior [my emphasis] to another' (Trudgill 1994). With the exception of varieties of Swahili spoken in Congo, which have received significant scholarly attention,

---

[1] There is a definite masculine bias in it use, but I gloss it as 'person'. It is often used in a gender neutral sense e.g. *kila msee* can mean 'everybody'.

[2] In British usage, the term dialect includes only features of grammar and vocabulary, while features of pronunciation are treated under a separate rubric of 'accent' (Trudgill 1994). In American usage an 'accent' is considered just part of the dialect, as we treat it in this book.

Swahili sociolects have not been described or studied as much as geographical (regional) varieties. Others which have been described as social 'dialects' of Swahili are too simplified and restricted in my view, to be truly 'equal' to native regional dialects, for example the pidginized varieties spoken by European or Asian communities in East Africa (Whitely 1969, Vitale 1980).

> **Native (Regional) Dialects of Swahili**
>
> Chiimwini is spoken in Somalia. Kisiu, Kipate, Kiamu, Kimvita, Chichifundi, Kivumba are spoken in Kenya. Kimtang'ata, Kipemba, Kitumbatu, Kihadimu, Kiunguja, Kimakunduchi in Tanzania. Kimgao and Kimwani in Mozambique. Kingazija, Kimwali, Shinziwani and Kimaote in the Comoros Islands.
> (Mazrui and Shariff 1994:77.

In western societies, e.g. USA (Labov 1972, Preston 1998) or the UK (Trudgill 1974), dialects are short of prestige; they are thought to be unsuccessful attempts to speak the standard, that they are deviant (hence illogical) forms of the standard spoken by disfavoured groups, that they only have negative connotations (Labov 1972). Sheng talk may be spoken by socio-economically disadvantaged Nairobians, but it is not a failure to speak Swahili because speakers can switch between Sheng talk and speech forms closer to SS at will, depending of course on interactional factors (participants, register, etc). Additionally, Sheng enjoys 'covert prestige' (Labov 1966) among the younger (mostly male) Kenyans with its associations of local solidarity, toughness, and stereotyped masculinity. This important social motivation for maintaining stigmatized language forms (e.g. pronunciation, word choice) has been studied elsewhere in great detail: Trudgill (1979) in Norwich, England; Labov (1966) in New York City, and Milroy (1980) in Belfast, North Ireland. Sheng is also an expression of solidarity among the masses at the lower end of the SES hierarchy of Kenya, the urban proletariat known in Sheng as '*masafara*' (< 'sufferers'), a coinage that captures many things discussed in Chapter 6. As a strategy of neutrality, many believe that Sheng helps to downplay 'negative ethnicity' (Wamwere 2003) by its inclusiveness, which is demonstrated by its easy acceptance of influences from indigenous Kenyan languages, and English.

A significant population of Kenya speaks Sheng as their 'vernacular', that is, the variety of language used for spontaneous, natural expression by members of a speech community (Hymes 1974). The alternative term 'community of practice' (Wenger 2000) claims to eliminate the assumption of homogeneity of a 'speech community', however, both in essence refer to a community of speakers (Kenyans in this case) that shares common rules of decoding meaning of their linguistic interactions and speech codes specific to their language ecology. It is the type of language one speaks when least monitored, that is, when they are least conscious of their speech behaviour. It is usually the language of informal talk such as when one is chatting with peers and friends or family, telling stories or jokes, singing and laughing. It is also the speech variety that is most likely to be the first learned by a child from his or her local environment. Therefore it is highly unlikely anyone but native Zanzibaris acquire or speak what we know as SS (*Kiswahili Sanifu*), and only a select group of native English speakers speak 'Standard English' as their vernacular, because it is an idealized form of language that exists in published grammar books and dictionaries. One only attempts to speak them in formal situations, for example during a job interview, in the school debating club or when writing an examination *insha* (Swahili composition), or in a corporate board meeting (English), and so forth. But people speak Sheng because it is the language in which they find it easiest to express their feelings and emotions, and to narrate personal experiences; it is their vernacular.

This understanding of 'vernacular' is very different from its ordinary usage – at least in Kenyan English where it is used to refer to indigenous African languages. This is in fact a statement of their restricted role as 'home' languages, in contradistinction with 'official' or 'book' languages, English and Swahili. But such an understanding of 'vernacular' does not capture important nuances, for example, that a native speaker of Kimeru (Meru), an indigenous language ('vernacular') of the Mt Kenya area might speak a different vernacular based on a regional dialect, if they are from Igembe, Tigania, Imenti, Miutini or Igoji. Similarly, Kamba children will speak different vernaculars of Kikamba (Kamba) language if they are from North or South Kitui, Mumoni or Masaku. The vernacular speech of Gikuyu speakers is different if they are from Kirinyaga, Nyeri or Kiambu, and even within specific localities in these regions (e.g. Kimathira in Nyeri). Likewise, the vernacular of most Nairobians is Kenyan Swahili, Sheng or a variety (dialect) of the 60-odd Kenyan indigenous languages.

'Urban youth languages'

Sheng si lugha ya vijanaa tu. My uncle is 50 years old and speaks only Sheng. *Ako* 50 years old, *jamaa ni wa* panel beating Industrial Area. *Anafanya na* garage *[ambapo] kuna* everybody, *kwa hiyo lugha yao ni Sheng.*

Octopizzo, and award winning *genge* (Kenyan hip-hop) artist,
Interview, 23 March 2017.

[Sheng] Language is not just for the youth. My uncle is 50 years old and speaks only Sheng. He is 50 years old; he is a panel beating guy in Industrial Area. He works in a garage [where] there's everybody [i.e. all ethnicities]; therefore their language is Sheng.

The contemporary scholarship of Africa is brimming with studies on 'youth cultures' and 'urban youth' languages, e.g. Abdulaziz & Osinde (1997), Kießling & Mous (2004), Kouega (2004), MacLaughlin (2008), Hurst and Mesthrie (2013), Barasa & Mous (2017), among many But this widely used term is insufficient to describe Sheng or its speakers, especially if 'youth' is understood purely as numerical age. What about those middle-aged men and women in their forties and even fifties who speak, advise, joke or admonish their children and those of their neighbours in Sheng? Many older Kenyans over 35 years of age speak Sheng because it is the vernacular speech of their daily environment. It fills the practical need for communication with the younger, more numerous age group of under 35s who make up about 75 per cent of the country's population in their daily occupations as workers, labourers, mechanics, *matatu* men and women, operators of the *jua kali* (informal) industry. Therefore in terms of their linguistic behaviour and language ideologies, these mature adults must be considered 'youth' because they share with the younger millennials a common 'cultural system of ideas about social and linguistic relationships' (Irvine 2009:255). There is further reason to avoid the term 'urban' whose definition varies widely across diffrent parts of the world and even within Africa, according to the UN Demographic Yearbook (2016): for example, '2000 or more' inhabitants in Ethiopia, Mexico, and Argentina; '10,000 or more' in Senegal; '16 gazetted townships' in Tanzania, and in Zambia, '5000 or more inhabitants, the majority of whom all depend on non-agricultural activities'. In USA and Canada, 'urban' is defined in terms of population density – 'having a population density of more than 400 or more per square kilometre and 1000 per square mile, respectively. In China, 'urban centres' are designated by the state and among other criteria, have at least 1,500 people per square kilometre, while in Peru (South America) an urban centre includes all urban centres with 100 or more dwellings.

Many such urban settlements in Africa and around the world do not possess the linguistic ecology required for the evolution of a speech code such as Sheng: sharply defined socio-economic class (SEC) divisions, and a multilingual population, coupled with limited exposure to Standard English or Swahili. Similar conditions are only found in Kenya's big towns and cities such as Nairobi, Nakuru, Mombasa, Thika or Kisumu where indeed, Sheng thrives. Furthermore, our research indicates that Sheng is no longer a purely 'urban' phenomenon as it is already embedded in rural areas of Kenya in no small part due to (social) media, and the boarding school system of education in Kenya (see Chapter 5).[3]

The whole notion of 'youth language' must be contested anyway, if it is based on no more than the fact that they develop in urban, and multilingual contexts, and that the 'youth' are the main speakers. Such codes do not merit the tag 'language' if they do not demonstrate a system apart from the languages upon which they are based, e.g. French for Camfranglais (Kouega 2004), or Wolof for 'urban Wolof' (McLaughlin 2009), or English for 'Engsh' (Barasa & Mous 2017) and Swahili for Sheng (Githiora 2002). All these speech codes are characterized by extensive language mixing and innovations (loan words, coinages), a few pidgin-like features such as reduced morphology, metonymy, and clipping of words. But there are also important structural differences between them. The 'matrix language' (Myers-Scotton 1993) for Sheng is Swahili – an African language, upon whose grammar base English or indigenous Kenyan languages are grafted. The same can be said of 'Urban Wolof' which is based on Wolof, an African language of Senegal. But the matrix language for Camfranglais is French, one of the two official languages of Cameroon (English in another part of the country), as it 'integrates non-French lexical items into a French morphosyntactic frame' (Nchare 2010). In other words, 'a Camfranglais utterance is a French sentence in which one or two keywords are replaced by items drawn from Cameroonian French, English, Pidgin or other Cameroonian language'. A similar description applies for Engsh, which is 'mostly based on English grammar, but with vocabulary from Standard English, urban English slang, Sheng, and Swahili' (Kaviti et al 2016). This difference is significant because it relates to language ideologies which index the speech codes with socio-economic status.

Although I was very interested in Engsh – Sheng's supposed 'alter ego' (Abdulaziz & Osinde 1997) – none of the hundreds of subjects we interviewed were able to identify the name even after much prompting. Finally, one respondent concluded that '...that [Engsh] is just BAD Sheng...it is by the boys of Westii [Westlands] who want to sound bad, like tough' (Octopizzo, personal interview, March 2017). In a scholarly publication by Kaviti et al (2016) Engsh is described as a 'hybrid' language and compared with Nigerian Pidgin English (NPE), which they identify inaccurately and tautologically as a 'pidgin with no native speakers' (ibid:51). The name mirrors Sheng (Engsh in reverse), which may indicate that perhaps it was coined as a direct reaction to Sheng, an 'anti-Sheng slang' (Kießling & Mous 2004) which developed as a form of protest by speakers who were against Sheng. According to these researchers, Engsh developed in the richer suburbs of Nairobi Westlands,

[3] Barasa and Mous (2017) also noted that the opening of many satellite university campuses around the country has contributed to the wider spread of Engsh.

mostly based on English grammar, but with vocabulary from Standard English, urban English slang, Sheng, and Swahili. More recently, Barasa and Mous (2017) set out to confirm the existence of Engsh through a description of its features, observing that 'Engsh borrows extensively from Sheng but not the other way around... in fact, Engsh speakers prefer Sheng lexicon over Swahili' (ibid:4). Previously, Ferrari (2009) had observed that 'Engsh developed in the richer suburbs of Nairobi Westlands, mostly based on English grammar, but with vocabulary from Standard English, urban English slang, Sheng, and Swahili'. It is quite interesting how, unlike Sheng, alleged speakers of Engsh remain so elusive that there seems to be no symbolic awareness of its existence as is enjoyed by Sheng. The label Engsh is a creation of African 'urban/ youth language' scholarship, however it is true as the literature suggests that Engsh is another Kenyan 'way of speaking' English by younger speakers of the upper SES, not a 'youth' restricted speech code. In my own analysis, Engsh and Sheng are both intergral to the spectrum of speech codes I describe as 'Kenyanese' in the next chapter.

Is Sheng a pidgin or a creole?

Sheng is neither a pidgin nor a creole, and it is important to clear up this point at this early stage of the discussion about Sheng because authoritative voices such as judges, politicians, teachers, government ministers, journalists, commentators, and some academics propagate the idea of Sheng as a 'pidgin'. For example, Chimerah (1998:13) briefly described a 'new form of Kiswahili that seems poised to conquer the entire population of the city's youths...the language is a *pidgin* Swahili [my emphasis] popularly known by its users as Sheng'. He then went on to describe Sheng as having Kiswahili's grammatical structure, 'although its vocabulary consists of almost equal numbers of Kiswahili and English words, with the former having a slight edge over the latter' (ibid:14). He also noted that Sheng consisted of 'items' from Kenyan languages notably Gikuyu, Luo, Kamba, Luhyia, Hindi/Gujarati, and Arabic. Although he was correct in predicting the rise and spread of Sheng in Nairobi, he offered no justification for calling it a pidgin, nor an objective measure of the 'equal numbers' of English and Swahili words that make up Sheng.

Sheng is different from 'pidgins and creoles' in fundamental ways, although it shows a few pidgin-like features (Githiora 2002). The grammar of Sheng is straightforwardly that of Swahili, and it shows minimal and often no evidence of a 'highly reduced grammar' such as simple, strict word order, or invariant tense marking and negation (Mufwene 2001). Pidgins around the world emerge under similar conditions to serve a restricted need for communication, 'a marginal language which arises to fulfil certain restricted communication needs among people who have no common language' (Todd 1990).

Pidgins have no native speakers, they are temporary and may disappear once the sociolinguistic conditions that made them arise, have changed. Such was the fate of the reduced or simplified varieties of Swahilis of British settlers in Kenya 'Kisetla' (Whitely 1969) or 'KiKAR' (Mutonya & Parsons 2004). Down in South Africa is the case of Fanakalo, a Zulu-based 'Pidgin Nguni' (Mesthrie 2009), used as lingua franca in mines, plantations, kitchens (hence also, 'Kitchen Kaffir') and other labour intensive industries of South Africa. These characteristics of a pidgin or creole do not fit Sheng: it has many 'clippings' but no extensive reduction of grammar; fundamentally, Sheng did not arise to fulfil a communication need among Nairobians since Swahili (and English and indigenous languages to an extent) have always been available to play the function of a language of wider communication (LWC). As for any possible loss of its functions, Sheng does not exhibit any signs of disappearing at this time or soon.

There are a few pidgin-like varieties of Swahili for use in limited and specific registers. Some of these are coined between tourists and locals (e.g. *'Jambo Bwana*! *Hakuna Matata*!'). 'Asian Swahili' is used to communicate with non-English speaking Africans and Asians who do not share a common language, such as Gujarati speakers who came from Zanzibar to mainland Tanzania (Maho & Sands 2003). There is another pidgin dubbed as 'KiHindi' (Vitale 1980) but it is just a non-standard Swahili sociolect spoken by Asian traders in Tanzania. Similarly, an earlier generation of European settler farmers in Kenya used 'Shamba Swahili' or Kisetla (Whitely 1969) with African workers and employees. Both sociolects used by Asians and Europeans were based on the asymmetrical social relationships which characterize many pidgins. The examples provided in Vitale's study, for instance, are overwhelmingly commands, orders, warning and so on, typical of a colonial interaction with the colonized. In fact, it was noted in the same paper that 'Kisetla thrives in its purest form where coffee and wheat flourish (plantations) in preference to coconuts, sweet potatoes and *wimbe* [sic]' (millet) (Whitely 1969:52). Some long-term residents of Kenya such as expatriates may also use a restricted pidgin variety of Swahili for exclusive use among their in-group, which also serves as an exclusionary marker of in-group identity. Those Swahili pidgins died away when conditions changed to disfavour pidgin as a means of communication following independence and nationalism projected through language (slogans, focus on the unifiying role of SS etc), and the emancipation of Africans from European (and to a lesser extent, Asian) dominance. In our view, these so-called 'Pidgin Swahilis' fall broadly under 'Kenyan Vernacular Swahilis', which are characterized by significant variation from the standard, and the strong influence upon them by a variety of first languages.

Kinubi: a creole language of Kenya

Kinubi is the only real (Arabic based) creole language of Kenya, and it is worth a bit of discussion because it shares the same sociolinguistic space as Sheng. It is spoken by a minority group of 6000–8000 Wanubi ('Nubians') (Ethnologue 2016) chiefly in Kibera (Kibra), a densely populated settlement located just 8 kilometres from downtown Nairobi. Kinubi is not the same as the Nubian language of the ancient Kingdom of Kush formerly used in sacred religious texts, whose descendant languages are Nilo-Saharan. Smaller communities of Kinubi speakers are resident in several parts of Uganda, while groups of speakers who settled in Tanzania have been assimilated into the Swahiliphone landscape they live in and no longer speak Kinubi (Parsons 1997). Unsurprisingly, modern Kinubi is strongly influenced by Swahili not just in the lexicon, but also in the phonology, morphology and even syntax, as the two languages have been in contact with each other for more than one century (Xavier 2014). The *mtaa* of Kibera is fondly referred to as 'motherland' in Sheng because many rural–urban migrants settle there when they first come to the city because of cheap housing and proximity to the city centre or industrial areas where jobs may be obtained. Thus many immigrants into Nairobi fondly think of it as their point of origin or 'motherland' upon arriving in Nairobi, a starting point in their life in the big city even after relocating elsewhere in the city.

Historically, Kinubi was spoken by African soldiers from southern Sudan and the Nuba mountains who joined the British army in the 1880s, fighting in the King's African Rifles (KAR). Due to the high linguistic diversity in southern Sudan and the newly formed armies, a pidginized form of Juba Arabic came to be used as lingua franca, and the original languages were forgotten by the descendants of those KAR who settled in Kenya, where the community continues to thrive to this day. Over the years, parts of the reserve where the Nubians were settled by the colonial government were taken up by public utilities, including Nairobi National Park, the Lang'ata Cemetery, Lang'ata Women's Prison, Jamhuri Park showground and residential estates. Echoes of the past resonate in the names of some 13 'villages' within Nairobi's Kibera today, patterned around the original 'pre-Nubian' identities with the names of places of origin of those Sudanese soldiers, prefixed by the word Kambi (Swahili for 'camp'). A Nubi elder enumerated the following settlements within Kibera during an interview: Kambi Aluru, Kambi Kirwa, Kambi Bakwaa, Kambi Kakwaa, Kambi Lendu and Kambi Muru. Newer names of parts of Kibera reflect a changing reality, and possibly competition or response to a challenge of territoriality. For example, Kambi Kirwa to Wanubi is Kisumu Ndogo (Little Kisumu) for some Luo residents of Kibera while another area is known as 'Raila', after a prominent politician who commands a large following in Kibera. An area known as Salama by Wanubi is at the same time known as Karanja, a Gikuyu personal name; it also the name of the main road that cuts through Kibera from Kibera Drive to the end of the estate. Another area of Kibera is called Kianda, which means 'valley' in Gikuyu, while *Laini Saba* comes from *Laini Shabaha* (shooting range), the area formerly occupied by a shooting practice range. Katwikira apparently has the origin in the phrase 'Kwa Roho Safi' (lit. 'with a clean heart' or 'in good faith'). Toyi is the site of a large, open-air market specializing in used clothes (*mitumba*), which is also known as Fort Jesus after the fort built by the Portuguese in Mombasa in the 16th century. The Nairobi Dam area is known as Shilanga to the Nubians, and Anyany Estate is known to the community as Lomle, according to informants.

According to personal observation in Kibera, it is clear that while the language is alive across generations, greatest proficiency was among the elders, while many teenagers and pre-adolescents, who navigate their world mainly in Sheng, appeared to have difficulties with simple tasks such as counting numbers in Kinubi. It is indeed the household language of the Wanubi families visited, the language of intimacy among family members and friends. Proficiency in Swahili and Sheng is very high among Kinubi speakers, who wield both as essential to their belonging and identification as Kenyans, which has in the past been cast in in doubt. Swahili and Sheng are the speech codes of Kibera, of the street, local business and daily interaction in the broader, non-Nubi community. Kinubi is not used in any of the schools as a medium of instruction during the first years of school, and there is no known radio programming or any publication in the language. Kinubi is typical of Kenya's minority languages as it may be endangered due to the relatively small number of its fluent speakers living in one of the most densely populated neighbourhoods, within a strongly assimilating context of Swahili and Sheng, especially among the young generation.

Other African creoles: Sango, Lingala, and Nigerian Pidgin English (NPE)

Some creole languages have a bearing on Sheng in terms of their emergence as contact languages and lingua francae, and their subsequent development. For example, Sango, a creole language and lingua franca in the Central African Republic has since 1994 become one of the two official languages of that country, the other being French (Karan 2001). Another creole language relevant to Sheng is Lingala, which is quite familiar to Kenyans because it is the main language of Congolese music, which has been very popular in Kenya for many decades. Like Sheng in Kenya, Lingala in DRC is considered the language of fashion and entertainment and it is indeed the language of fashionable role models and musicians. Lingala conveys much more 'worldliness' to young people, connecting them to a global world, but Swahili is used by speakers consciously to project positive prestige, much like SS (Kiswahili Sanifu) in Kenya. Regional Swahilis of the DRC such as Bunia Swahili, Lumbumbashi Swahili, Kivu Swahili, or Kisangani Swahili are seen as polite, well mannered, of a respectful tone (Nassenstein 2015). In Chapter 3 we shall see similar attitudes towards SS among those who participated in the Nairobi study.

NPE is an English based creole which is confusingly known as a 'Pidgin', and it is the lingua franca for many more millions outside Nigeria. It is in fact, a variety of English, with influences from Nigerian indigenous languages. It is one of several related languages known collectively as 'West African Pidgin Englishes' (WAPEs) spoken in several West African nations including Cameroonian Pidgin (or, Cameroon Creole English, Kamtok, Wes Cos), Krio of Sierra Leone, Gambian Krio, Ghanaian Creole, and Liberian Pidgin. Further afield, they are linked to Southern and Western Atlantic English-based creoles such as Jamaican Creole. Indeed, some speakers of WAPEs are descendants of Africans repatriated from Jamaica and US; many are also voluntary returnees from North and South America (Brazil). It is probably the best-known creole of the African continent, and most prominent in terms of number of speakers (30 million), and as the principal language of 'Naija films' (Nigerian –'Nollywood' – made films) and 'Naija music' (Nigerian popular music), which have a big presence in Kenyan popular culture. Nigerian evangelical preachers are also popular, reaching out to millions of Kenyans every day through radio, television and the internet. There is a considerable number of Nigerians in Nairobi living ordinary lives in the same estates where Sheng is the vernacular: some of them work alongside Kenyan artists, others are in the *jua kali* (informal) trade as barbers, deejays and vendors of new and used clothes and such. Nigerian students are enrolled in Kenyan universities and tertiary institutions, and a few participated in some of our interviews. The impact of NPE on Kenyan language can only increase as it is already used in some comedy shows whose dialogues are based on imitations of 'Naija Talk', for example when a Kenyan takes on the guise of a Nigerian pastor to deliver a sermon, or to advertise a product. A trendy phrase these days in Kenyanese is '*dobo dobo*' (<'double-double') meaning 'bountiful' or 'rich blessings,' as promised by the evangelical pastors who have made it so popular as to appear in a headline of Kenya's only Standard Swahili newspaper ('*Mambo ni Dabo Dabo*', *Taifa Leo*, 24 Februray 2017). Some similarities with Kenyanese are structural rather than a result of cross-linguistic influences. For example, Kaviti et al. (2016) note that in both NPE and Kenyan varieties of English (Engsh) reduplication (e.g. '*small small*' = *kidogo kidogo* in Swahili/Sheng) can add an augmentative or diminutive sense to a word. It can also express an adverbial sense to words in KS and Sheng, (e.g. <u>*sana sana*</u> *ni vijanaa huongea Sheng* 'it is *mostly* youths who speak Sheng'). It is not impossible to imagine that recognition of Sheng as part and parcel of Kenyan language and culture may see it take up other roles, as Lingala and Sango have done in central Africa. With a change of attitude, NPE too should one day become an official language of Nigeria alongside Nigerian English, like Filipino (Tagalog) and English in the Philippines, or Haitian French and Kreyol (Haitian Creole) in Haiti.

Swahili as a macrolanguage

Kiswahili ni kingi ('There are many Swahilis')
Prof. Tom Hinnebusch, ASA conference presentation, 1993.

The concept of 'macrolanguage' is useful to analyse 'language' in terms of 'waves or bundles of features that extend across time, geography, and social space' (Weinreich et al. 1968). This view of language takes away the need for placing it in discrete, idealized categories such as 'Swahili' or 'Chinese' or 'Arabic', which are in fact, multifaceted and fluid constructs. Spoken varieties of any language can deviate significantly from the 'book standard,' therefore 'standard' languages are best treated as constructs (idealizations) that emerge from the particulars of a nation's history and social structure (Milroy 2004). Therefore an understanding of Swahili as a macrolanguage also emphasizes the dynamic processes of language use, variation and change. Macrolanguages are different from a simple list or collection of closely related languages, and are different from dialects because the degree of mutual intelligibility is too low, or language ideologies may prevent speakers from understanding each other. Swahili speakers from Lubumbashi (DRC), Tanga (Tanzania) or Lamu (Kenya) and those who speak it as a second language or LWC all mutually recognize their diverse ways of speaking as 'Swahili', although the degree of mutual intelligibility may be very low.

The Swahili speaking community now extends far beyond the East African coast and the Indian Ocean islands, or the 'interior' (*bara*), into nearly all the urban centres of east and central Africa, and in the diaspora among immigrants living in North America, Europe and elsewhere in Africa. These communities are further linked by the internet, radio, television, YouTube and many websites with Sheng content. Social media platforms such as WhatsApp and Twitter are also spaces in which Sheng is widely used. At a national holiday gathering in London, or New York, or Cologne, Germany, Kenyans mingling with Congolese, Comoriens, Tanzanians and Ugandans are likely to be listening to *genge* music or *Bongo Fleva*, or watching YouTube, or music videos of the latest music and film, interspersed with (live) news and advertisements produced in various forms of Swahili including Sheng, Congolese, 'Tanzanian', native regional dialects, and 'vernacularized' varieties of Swahili.

In a macrolanguage environment, one variety is more developed, and there must be some domain (written, official, formal) in which only a single language identity is recognized: *Kiunguja* (Zanzibar dialect) in the case of Swahili. A common 'standard' Swahili is widely used in Kenya and Tanzania as the formal language of education and government; therefore official documents and school textbooks are published in a similar code known as *Kiswahili Sanifu* (Standard Swahili) in both countries. In similar ways in North Africa and the Middle East, 'Standard Arabic' is used in business and media across communities although they speak different languages known as Moroccan or Egyptian or Sudanese 'Arabic'. The individual languages that comprise a macrolanguage must be closely related, and there must be some context in which they are commonly viewed as comprising a single language (Ethnologue 2016). This rules out 'Romance' as a macrolanguage since although Spanish, Portuguese, Italian, French, and Romanian are closely related, they are separate individual languages in all domains. It also rules out 'Mijikenda' to describe Chidigo (Digo), Chiduruma (Duruma), Chichonyi (Chonyi), Kipfokomo (Pokomo), and Chigiriama (Giriama), which are linguistically and culturally very close. Because although one of those languages may be selected as a common 'language' within a region or town where it dominates numerically or for other reasons, speakers of these other languages do not recognize and accept it as their own. Separate orthographies for each of these languages can be another marker of difference, for example where the grapheme <pf> is used in Kipfokomo spelling, but not in that of Chidigo (ibid).

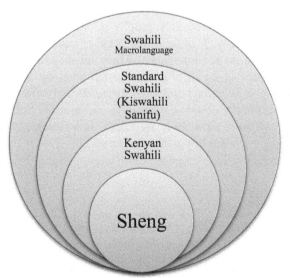

Fig 2 Sheng in the Swahili macrolanguage

Swahili enjoys positive (overt) prestige as a well-known, international African language that is used in government and education, and different Swahilis are perceived as integral members of one multifaceted macrolanguage. At the same time, those Swahilis project different identities based on local, regional or national aggrupations which take shape as 'Tanzanian' or 'Kenyan' or 'Congolese' Swahili, etc. Of course, these names only mark 'state' thinking since there is further internal differentiation within those 'national Swahilis', e.g. Bunia, Kisangani, Lubumbashi Swahili varieties are subsumed under the overarching designation of 'Congo Swahili'. 'Kenyan Swahili' is indexed to a 'state identity', but Sheng projects a particular Kenyan identity that is modern (urban), youthful, and with global connections.

Over an extended period of its history, from the 9th century to the 19th century, Swahili adopted many words of Arabic and Persian – 'oriental influences' (Lodhi 2000), and a few ones from Portuguse, and even one or two from German. Throughout the 20th century up to the present, it has expanded immensely in demographic and geographic terms, and gained fresh – and to some degree mutual – influences from English and some indigenous languages of east and central Africa. The observable, historical admixture led to some early descriptions of Swahili as 'a mixed' or 'hybrid' language' of Arabic and African languages (e.g. Johnson 1930 and Broomfield 1931, in Mazrui 1993). These were generally premised on old notions of language 'purity' but surprisingly the tradition of analysing language solely as discrete entities in multilingual contexts or as deviants from the norm, continues. Speech codes with extensive innovations are viewed with unease during their initial stages of development as is the case of Swahili in the past, and Sheng in the present where it is variously described as a 'pidgin' (Chimerah 1990), 'mixed code' (Abdulaziz & Osinde 1997), 'hybrid language' (Samper 2002), or 'bilingual mixed language' (Barasa & Mous 2017). Those labels with their implied hierarchies and ignorance of the difference between language and speech, or the true nature of language contact and change, are strongly critiqued by, among others, Mazrui & Shariff (2004) for Swahili, and more broadly by Milroy & Milroy (1985) and more stringently by Lüpke and Storch (2013) when they discuss the need for greater complexity of analysing speech codes of African multilingual repertoires by using a set of different parameters.

So, what is Sheng?

'[watu] wote wanabonga Sheng hadi ma-punks wale wametoka Westlands. Ile attitude ya zamani ime-fade, tena ni lazima unabonga Sheng.'

'Everyone speaks Sheng, even the punks – those who come from Westlands. That old attitude [against Sheng] has faded. Also one must speak Sheng.'

Adam, 25 yrs, Ofafa, Nairobi.

The name Sheng is known throughout Kenya, around East Africa and overseas, what is known as *majuu* in Sheng. Kenyan *wananchi* readily identify Sheng as a distinctive way of speaking Swahili, and there is general agreement about its origins in the Eastlands estates of Nairobi city. The word Sheng appears in the earliest studies on the subject by Spyropulous (1987) and Mazrui (1995), and more recently in numerous scholarly publications, and in news and opinion articles published in the national and international press, such as the UK *Guardian* newspaper, and the BBC. The word Sheng has no known antecedents in a pre-existing social or regional dialect of Swahili, therefore it is an innovation created by two typical rules of Sheng word coinage: (1) transposition (re-arrangement) of syllables - '*eng*' and '*lish*' of the word 'English' in this case, and (2) clipping (shortening) of the syllable (-*lish* > *sh*). The coinage also reflects language ideologies behind the symbolic appropriation and transformation of the name of the high status language, English. Born in the margins and nurtured in the 'ghetto' by low SES speakers, Sheng is the new 'posh' in terms of 'covert prestige' that plays an equal or greater role than English in Kenya's vibrant creative industry of *genge* (Kenyan hip hop) music, film, radio, television, creative writing, live entertainment and in urban conversations. It is not a surprise that another section of upper SES speakers wish to imitate Sheng, by creating a parallel 'youth' code based on English – Engsh (Barasa & Mous 2017).

'Sheng talk' is a good term to describe this distinctive way of speaking Swahili, which is indexed to social identity and language ideologies of Kenya. Furthermore, Sheng is linked to a myriad of native dialects or macrolanguages, the 'Swahilis' ('*Viswahili*') spoken around east and central Africa. An analysis of Sheng must, therefore, extend beyond a description of its age-marked roles, and its novel loans and coinages (neologisms). And rather than look at Sheng and Engsh as 'parasitic codes' (Barasa & Mous 2017), it is better to explain these two as Kenyan speech codes on a continuum which is indexed to 'style', which is in turn dependent on participants in a conversation, and the relationship between those participants and the audience (Bell 1994). This perspective of Sheng enables us to remove the tags 'youth' and 'urban', without discarding their importance in the dynamics of Sheng's development within the broader ecology of the Swahili language.

There are competing claims about Sheng's specific local origins among its users depending on their local identities within the Eastlands. Although Abdulaziz & Osinde (1997) claimed that it emerged from one particular estate in the Eastlands – Kaloleni – it is difficult to pinpoint a specific point of diffusion of Sheng. There is no contention however that it emerged from the complex, multilingual and multi-ethnic situation of Nairobi, specifically the low-income residential section of the city known as the Eastlands. Sheng is founded on the coexistence of speakers of many different languages, further differentiated by age and SES. Therefore on one level, Sheng is a 'sociolect' of KS, a product specific to the ecology of Nairobi's Eastlands. Which is to say that it is not separate from general KS, although in its extreme registers ('deep Sheng') such as among some *matatu* operators (*makanga*), or criminal gangs, or indeed among groups of close friends (*ma-bestε*) it can take on the character of a secret language (argot), unintelligible to outsiders, non-members of the ingroup. Such codes must be learned as part of re-socialization (induction) into a group as in the case of 'Kibalele, a secret language' of Bukavu, DRC (Goyvaerts 1996).

Table 2 Sheng and Kibalele: similarities and differences

Parameter	Sheng	Kibalele
Age group	under 35s	irrelevant, only by initiation into group
Functions	solidarity, identity	secrecy
Gender	males and females	males only
Community of practice	mostly but not restricted to *mitaa* (low income neighbourhoods)	shanty towns
Languages involved	Swahili, English, Dholuo, Gikuyu, Kamba, and others	Swahili, Lingala
Mechanisms	transpositions, code-mixing, clipping, etc.	syllable permutations
Attitudes	mixed (negative and positive)	negative

Nairobi's '*matatu* subculture' is vividly described as 'the totality of interactive acts between crews, designers, passengers and other motorists, based on practices that have evolved around traveling and commuting' (Wa Mungai 2013:23). Some Sheng talk – words and expression – do emerge from argot (secret language) among criminal gangs that thrive in parts of Nairobi, but more likely from the *matatu* men who Kenyans love to hate, yet their influence upon young Kenyans is enormous. Most of them 'fall under the age bracket of 24–50 years, although some hang on to their jobs until their sixties' (ibid: 27). They are flashy, loud, rude, and often fashionably dressed in a rugged way. Their Sheng talk is colourful and irreverent – 'uncouth' to the 50 per cent haters – and they come from low-income estates and SES. Their Sheng talk is loaded with symbolic expressions of manliness and speed, all very appealing to youths of both sexes. A majority of ordinary Kenyans travel to work by *matatu*, and many Nairobi school children of all ages travel to and from school by *matatu;* the *makanga* argot is taken up by the youth and becomes Sheng talk, which may eventually join mainstream vernacular KS.

For example words like *karao/makarao* and *makanga* are now acceptable in ordinary KS, while others such as *ngati/mngati* (mean, cruel person) and *kaba* (take cover, lie low) still remain at the periphery of mainstream KS, i.e. they are Sheng talk.

Karin Barber (2018) makes an apt observation that 'every expression of popular culture in Africa today has a past', that is, the popular culture practices we observe and study in various parts of Africa today have precursors: West African street theatre, the South African 'gum-boot dance', and so on. Sheng started to develop in the late 1950s 'from among the "parking boys" (street children and families) of Nairobi, migrant labourers, Kikuyu ex-mau-mau and their relations, school dropouts and the like,' (Spyropoulos 1987:130). Those Nairobians coined a new code from linguistic resources available to them in the new multilingual urban context that was also at the heart of anticolonial activity during the late 1940s, culminating in an armed struggle led by Mau Mau that lasted throughout the 1950s. Its nerve centre was Nairobi, the source of arms and intelligence that were indispensable to the forest fighters. Such a context was likely to create the need for an 'argot' or secret language to facilitate activities of the underground movement. Indeed, some Sheng words of today can be traced to those origins, with the same or modified meanings: *makanga* (old 'tribal police', now *matatu* conductor in Sheng); *ngati/mngati* ('homeguard', African colonial police, now 'a mean, hard person' in Sheng). The verb *kaba* means 'take cover, or fall in line' then and now, and the same with *karao/makarao* (police) which comes from *karai*, a type of metal helmet worn by colonial police and KAR soldiers. In such ways Sheng demonstrates a clear link to Kenya's turbulent colonial past, and places it squarely in the social history of Nairobi.

'Kenyanese': a continuum of speech codes

Linguistic, regional and historical factors, as well as political ideologies, have helped shape an identifiable KS with distinctive characteristics, a definable speech community or community of practice. KS is the spontaneous variety of Swahili spoken in ordinary situations by individuals to express themselves in a variety of informal registers: at home, with friends, on the street, at the market, shops, in *matatus*, and so on. It is spontaneous language, least stylistically monitored, i.e. the speaker is not being careful. However, it can also be heard in formal contexts, e.g. at work, in a journalistic interview, in giving a church testimony and so on because it is the vernacular speech of most Kenyans. It has been enriched by loan words and expressions which reflect the cultural history of Kenya, social stratification, and the influence of indigenous languages. KS is also marked by unique features of morphosyntax (grammar), constructs that are perfectly understood by Kenyans, but 'wrong' or 'incorrect' when held against the 'standard'. Those 'deviations' from the 'standard' are lexical and grammatical, noun class agreement, tense marking, and lots of 'restructuring'. We shall see many more examples such as the following:

> Mama mboga: *niko na deni yako*
> SS: *nina deni lako*
> I owe you money [lit. I have your debt]

> Politician: *Chama yetu itapigania viti mbili.*
> SS: *Chama chetu kitapigania viti viwili.*
> Our party will fight for two seats.

The highlighted prefix [in bold] should be *ch-* on the possessve (*chetu*) and *ki-* on the verb clause, *kitapigania*. The subject (*chama*) is marked on the verb clause, with an NC9 marker i-, instead of NC7 (*ki-/ch-*). Similarly, the second noun *viti* is not marked on the following adjective in the prescribed way (*vi-*); a NC9 prefix *mb-* is used instead.

The extensive language mixing that takes place in Kenyan speech reflects the social dynamics embodied by speakers who are, on average, trilingual to varying degrees of competence. The language shifting and code-mixing is determined by audience design (those who the speaker thinks are paying attention to him or her) as suggested in previous sections, as well as the setting (time, place), register (appropriateness of speech), and speech roles (speaker, addressee) or participatory framework (Goffman 1981). In its fluid forms, KS is chiefly marked by lots of code-mixing and shifting with English and indigenous languages. Kenyan English is deployed in high-status domains of higher education and professional activities, government and policy making, high status journalism. It can be used to project power, such as between a customer and shopkeeper, in which the former wishes to exercise some authority over the latter, or between a well-dressed man and a police officer where the former deploys English to express power and privilege over the latter. SS, also jocularly known as '*Kisanifu*',[4] is the 'good' Swahili which is indexed to 'coastal' or 'Tanzanian' speakers, and is considered 'difficult'. Vernacular influenced Swahili (KS) is associated with uneducated speakers, and rural or urban poor. Despite the lesser prestige afforded KS, it is high ranking on the affective filter because it projects speakers as 'ordinary *mwananchi*' or 'salt of the earth' Kenyan, and Sheng too identifies the speaker as one of 'us' – *masafara* (sufferers, proletariat). These attitudes towards Kenyan languages (English,

---

[4] The coinage is a deliberate violation of SS norms, because an adjective of Arabic origin such as *sanifu* (clean, pure), should not take an agreement marker (the ki-prefix). *Kiswahili Sanifu* is the correct from.

Swahili, and all others) are neutralized through switching between languages and code-mixing as a strategy to reduce social distance during interaction, e.g. between low and high SES speakers, or between speakers of different indigenous languages. By using all these language resources, combined with the language ideologies discussed earlier, Kenyans produce what I refer to as 'Kenyanese,' or the range of localized varieties of Swahili and English in both formal and informal settings. Sheng and Engsh are products on that spectrum of mixed codes, favoured by younger speakers because they enjoy positive attributes of upward mobility and global interconnectedness, each one leaning towards a different SES. These ways of speaking are deployed to neutralize ethnic tags within their community of practice – Sheng and Engsh among millennials, and KS in the general population. The speech codes are also symbolic of broader social structures of differentiation regarding SES, and a rejection of normative standard languages which are seen as removed from the true Kenyan identity.

(SS) Kiswahili Sanifu   (KS) Kenyan Swahili   Sheng/Engsh   Educated Kenyan English

Figure 3a 'Kenyanese': continuum of speech codes.

Figure 3a shows on the extreme left, SS or 'text book Swahili', which is taught in Kenyan schools and based on the Zanzibar dialect. It is known as *Kiswahili Sanifu* 'Standard Swahili' or the somewhat derisive, '*Kisanifu*'. It is different from Kenya's native Swahili dialects, which existed before the spread of the language in the interior (*bara*) and before the implementation of SS in the 1930s onwards. The variation among them is significant, especially at either end of the dialect continuum that stretches all along the east African coast from Somalia to Mozambique, and occurs at all levels – lexical (vocabulary), grammar, and especially phonology (pronounciation and sound changes, etc.). On the extreme right lies 'educated Kenyan English' (KE) described by Buregeya (2006) as the type of English spoken by those Kenyans with approximately 14 years of exposure to it, that is English as the medium of instruction up to and including secondary level. Space in between, but leaning to the left, is occupied by 'Kenyan Swahili', the variety of Swahili spoken spontaneously by a majority of Kenyans, as a second language and with varying degrees of competence. Sheng and Engsh lie in between but next to each other, drawing on the two matrix languages as well. Kenyan indigenous languages interfere with each code to varying degrees, but of course, most individual speakers naturally navigate between the varieties of Kenyanese

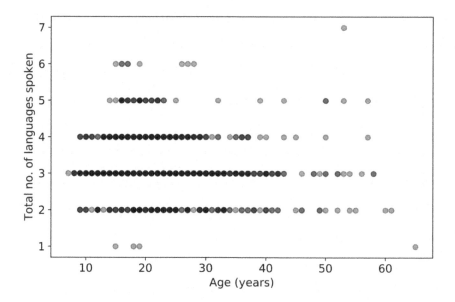

Figure 3b Number of languages spoken by age (Source: NDS 2017)

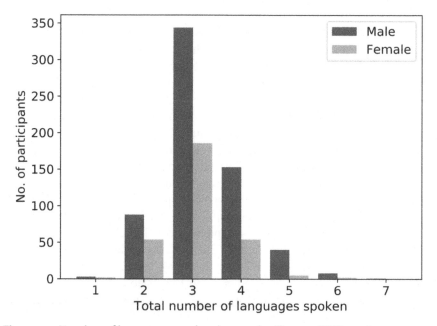

Figure 3c Number of languages spoken by gender (Source: NDS 2017)

depending on social context, domain or register. Most Kenyans navigate in the shaded section of the continuum, with KE and SS being spoken in very formal registers within educational and government institutions.

It is almost absurd to attempt to establish speakers' 'multilingual competence' if we look at speech habits of the majority of Kenyans, who speak at least one other second language in addition to their first (an average of three in the Nairobi Data Set). They speak Swahili or a Kenyan indigenous language at home, but a significant minority speak English at home. The three codes alternate in a fluid manner – translanguaging – as conversations move from taking place among youthful siblings (English, Swahili and Sheng), to an interaction with parents (Swahili, English and indigenous language), or with the house help (Swahili, Sheng and indigenous language). In this scenario, it is not hard to sympathize with the position taken by some modern linguists, that 'while languages are differentiated at a metadiscursive level, their actual separability is called into question by the fluid nature of actual speech, even if misleadingly equipped with a language label' (Lüpke 2016:39).

Chapter 2

An overview of language in Kenya: power vs solidarity

Sheng is embedded in a multilingual, multi-ethnic state where tens of languages and dialects are spoken. Therefore it is essential to understand the broader linguistic ecology in some detail as it relates to how Sheng is grafted upon the Swahili language. This short chapter will highlight some historical facts, with comments about Kenya's weak language policy, which has contributed to the existing stratification of language. While acknowledging the difficulties of providing an exact figure, scholars such as Webb & Kembo-Sure (2000) and Ogechi (2003) use the working figure of 42, which is also the de facto 'official' number of Kenyan languages. But in its catalogue of the languages of Kenya, Ethnologue's 19th edition (2016) lists 68 languages (Figure 4 Linguistic map of Kenya), of which seven are 'non-indigenous' (e.g. English, Hindi, etc), and about four 'dying' ones. These widely differing figures are a reflection of insufficient ethnographic research by state functionaries or trained scholars, and differences in counting methods and criteria of determining what is 'language' or 'dialect'. There may also be an administrative need to 'fix' the number of languages at whichever figure, for policy planning, political or other reasons, as well as competing interests. For example, a commission established to revamp the nation's constitution declared 70 to be the number of Kenyan languages (CKRC 2002), and more recently, Ethnologue rejected a proposal to list Sheng as a 'language' in its catalogue of Kenyan languages (GoSheng, personal communication, December 2017). Clearly, no one should state categorically the exact number of languages spoken in Kenya, but through extrapolation from our own research, and from these published sources and older ones such as Whitely (1974) and Heine and Möhlig (1980), the more realistic number of languages of Kenya is 60.

The languages of Kenya reflect a diversity of families and subfamilies, and some mutual, cross-linguistic influences which naturally take place wherever different languages are in contact with each other. For example, some dialects of two major Western Bantu languages, Luhyia and Ekegusii (Kisii), have borrowed words from the regionally dominant Dholuo (Luo), a Nilotic language. Gikuyu, Kamba, and Ekegusii (Niger-Congo, Bantu) have also adopted extensively from neighboring Maa (Nilo-Saharan, Nilotic) dialects.

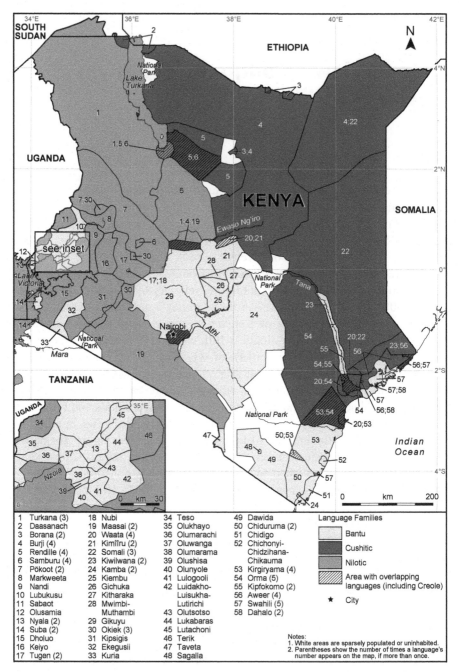

Figure 4 Linguistic map of Kenya (Source: adapted from colour original © Ethnologue 2016)

These mutual influences across very different languages as a result of contact extend to all parts of Kenya where they co-exist, and we shall see that Sheng is no exception. Non-indigenous Indo-European languages were introduced to Kenya by immigrants from Europe (English) and the Indian sub-continent (Punjabi, Gujarati, Hindi, and Goan). They too have contributed to Swahili and Sheng, adding to their richness and enhancing their pluralist character. Some words entered Sheng in more recent times, for example, *buda* or *budaa*, the Sheng word for 'father' (also *mbuyu*) borrowed from Gujarati (and Hindi) *buda* 'old man'. But other words such as *chokora* from Hindi *chokkra* 'little boy' entered Standard Swahili (SS) with the modified meaning of 'street child' long before the emergence of Sheng, which merely lengthened the final vowel to *chokoraa*.

The current population of Kenya which is estimated at 47 million (KNBS 2012) is distributed thickly in the coastal, central and western regions of the country, and sparsely in the northeast. Areal distribution of languages in Kenya makes a striking contrast; the majority Bantu (Niger-Congo) languages (in terms of numbers of speakers) are spoken in only about 20 per cent of the national territory, while Nilotic (Nilosaharan) language speakers occupy about 35 per cent, and the Cushitic (Afroasiatic) languages more than 40 per cent of the country's territory. Of course, this distribution only reflects a static view of African communities because it is modified by the movement and settlement of Kenyans of different ethnolinguistic backgrounds in different parts of the country, far from their original precolonial territories. The impact of this is most evident in towns and cities, but also in rural areas of the Rift Valley and coast region where farming and business communities have established themselves in areas which are not within their precolonial boundaries. Today there are probably more non-coastal people living in Mombasa or Lamu than native Swahili or Mijikenda people, and there are as many Gikuyu speakers in Uasin Gishu in Western Kenya, as there are Luhyas in Kiambu county, central Kenya. This increased circulation and movement by Kenyans around the country is a factor in the spread of Swahili and Sheng.

Kenyan Swahili (KS) is the universal 'lingua franca' of the nation and the primary language of its media. It is still closely connected with urban life, and with certain occupations such as market and small-scale trade in general, industrial workers, and informal artisans and traders (*jua kali*). Its capability to adapt to changing contexts is only one of the reasons that have contributed to its unique position among the languages of East and Central Africa; the other more powerful reason is its status as an administrative, evangelical and official language. Swahili is taught as a mandatory subject in all levels of primary and secondary education in Kenya, and public universities offer degree courses on the language and its linguistics, producing many graduate teachers, tourism industry workers, journalism and mass media practitioners

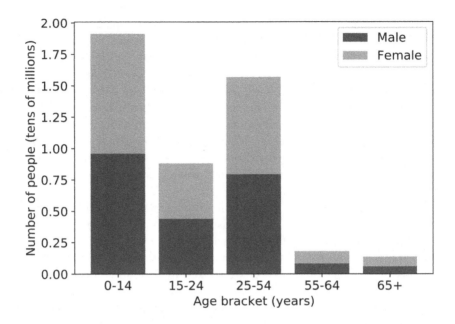

Figure 5 Kenya population by age and gender (Source: Kenya Population Situation Analysis 2013)

each year from the three leading national universities and tertiary colleges. In rural schools, children are taught in their local language up to Standard 4. They learn Swahili and English as a second, examinable language. Swahili is a medium of instruction in urban areas, but in practice, English is emphasized much more in all schools not only because it is examinable at every level but also because the entire curriculum for all subjects is in English.

Kenya's inception by European powers dates back to the Berlin Conference of 1884 and its subsequent appropriation by Britain as its 'protectorate' in 1895, and a proper 'colony' in 1910 (UNESCO 2000). The symmetric boundaries of an entity named 'Kenya' brought together diverse peoples, but they also tore apart existing settlements, and population movements were frozen within the newly established 'state' boundaries. For example, large portions of some Kenya communities such as the Somali, Borana, Luo, Luhyia, and Maasai communities are split up between the neighbouring countries of Somalia, Ethiopia, Sudan, Uganda, and Tanzania. The English language was stamped on the new colony, and it fast gained currency as the language of power within the new order in which a tiny settler minority backed by colonial administrative machinery spoke in English. Colonial institutions were represented by settlers (both British and Asian) and military officers who facilitated the growth of simplified, pidgin varieties of Swahili such as Kisetla, Kihindi, and KiKAR 'because they considered [Standard] Swahili to be a low prestige language necessary only for facilitating basic communication with their African subordinates' (Mutonya & Parsons 2004:115).[1] However, a pragmatism was born from missionaries' urgent need to use African languages for spreading Christianity. Swahili's potentiality in aiding the colonial agenda of building a labour force of Africans with basic literacy made it the most suitable language of administration. Those practices of the colonial state had the practical effect of solidifying the role of Swahili as a pan-ethnic language of solidarity that would later threaten the colonial regime by its role in the political unification of African subjects of British East Africa (Kenya Uganda, Tanzania). Swahili was the language of the Maji Maji rebellion against German colonialism in Tanganyika in 1905, and subsequent agitation by the East African Federation Workers' Union (Thuku 1970).

Pre-colonial Swahili has throughout the generations been intimately connected with urban life and with certain occupations, a 'mercantile society' (Middleton 1994). Its functional roles in Kenya remain strongly linked to the rural–urban divide, economic activity (small trading in shops and markets), and to socio-economic class (unskilled labour, domestic or industrial workers, etc.). In post-independent Kenya, Swahili is respected and valued as an official language of the nation, one that unites citizens, and which expresses nationalism and ethnic neutrality. However, language in Kenya is also indexed to socio-economic status (SES) (stratification) through differentiated use of language: higher status groups are more dominant in English than in Swahili; the lower ones are more dominant in KS or other indigenous languages, and only basic communication is in English. Negative, colonial attitudes against Swahili linger among Kenyans of the higher SES, a minority but economically and politically powerful group of English speakers – native and assimilated. They disdain Swahili as the language that was used by colonialists to their servants, and elevate English for its role in higher level civil service positions. They find no anomaly in being nationalistic while having limited competence in the national language; they still believe they can be English (and 'Engsh') speaking only, without necessarily failing to be 'good Kenyans'. Therefore the relationship between language, power, and ideology is central to Kenya's sociolinguistic situation.

The English language remains a core element of Kenya's colonial legacy. It is the language of prestige and high SES occupations in areas of education,

---

[1] The imperial military machinery (the King's African Rifles – KAR) used a simplified version of Swahili dubbed 'KiKAR' with its KAR east African battalion soldiers in a deliberate attempt to 'construct a distinct identity in the colony...out of the diverse ethnolinguistic backgrounds of the African soldiers' (Parsons & Mutonya 2003).

science, big business and laws, parliament, well-paid jobs, and so forth. English is, therefore, the language of power, whose deployment often serves to establish formality and social distance between interlocutors. In independent Kenya, English was conceptualized as the access to the world's technical and scientific information and knowledge, necessary for modernization and economic development. Across the border, in Tanzania, some attempt to achieve these objectives through Swahili was made, but English remains the de facto official language of big business and preferred medium of instruction in secondary and higher education (Mohr & Ochieng 2017). In Kenya, there are constant calls from intellectuals and cultural activists for a more elevated use of Swahili in national curricula (e.g. Mbaabu 1991, Chimerah 1998, Thiong'o 1981, etc.) but English continues practically unchallenged in all levels of education. It still dominates in the workplace, but Sheng is challenging this situation by 'intruding' into some of those high status domains. Many cite inadequate knowledge of Swahili, the lack of books, journals and other literature on science and technology in Kenyan languages as a necessity for the use of English in the workplace and in education, by scientists, engineers, technocrats, and researchers. Among the best educated, individuals soon become dominant in English rather than in Swahili (if its not already their mother tongue) although a minority attains excellent skills in both languages and an indigenous Kenyan language. Thus English in Kenya is not only used in written communication, board-level discussions, and such but also in everyday communication among educated Kenyans and professionals. KS and Sheng are the real speech codes in the streets, inside households, in shared, close-knit tenements known as 'plots' (*ploti* in Swahili or *tiplo* in Sheng), in mass politics and popular culture.

Swahili and nationalism

As early as 1922, an East African Workers Union had been formed to fight for African and Asians' rights, and against compulsory labour, increased tax, and against land alienation (Singh 1969). This early political organization comprised people from all regions of Kenya whose main common language, and the language of their mutual political solidarity, was Swahili. Throughout the late forties and fifties, intense political activity ('agitation') defined Kenya; the anti-colonial message was delivered to Kenyans principally in the Swahili language as political leaders sought to unite all Kenya Africans in their demand for independence. The very success of Swahili in giving a single voice to African political dissent led to intervention by the colonial state that feared the consequences of Swahili's expanded role. By 1952, the anti-colonial movement was breaking into violence and a state of emergency was declared over the entire colony. In a classic divide and rule tactic, the colonial government recommended that Swahili be eliminated from the school and administrative system except where it was mother tongue; selected 'tribal vernaculars' would be preserved. Within a few years, yet another commission ushered in the 'English Medium Approach' to primary instruction by endorsing English as the only language of instruction (Chimerah 1998). The nascent linguistic nationalism was nipped in the bud, a move that also stunted the spread of Swahili by emphasizing the use of Kenyan indigenous languages, or English. Nationalism would then have to be expressed in specific native languages understood by smaller numbers, thus drastically limiting the reach of the message. Many political pamphlets in Gikuyu, Kamba, Luo and other languages were issued, but their impact would be severely curtailed outside these communities in the rest of Kenya.

Kenyan nationalists soon understood the antagonism behind the British colonial administration's policy that promoted English and actively worked against Swahili. In the immediate post-independence period, Swahili was quickly adopted as the language of expressing national ideals, political aspirations and optimism about the future independent Kenya. As was the case in the newly independent states of Latin America in the early 19th century (Anderson 1991), the new leadership rallied the people of Kenya around new icons of *Uhuru*, freedom, such as the new flag of an independent Commonwealth republic, a national anthem, and patriotic songs. The most suitable language that would express the nationalist, solidarity message of the new Kenya in political speeches at mass rallies or in public broadcasting, was Swahili. The very first post independent commission of 1964 saw national unity as the primary aim of the new state while taking care to preserve the cultures and languages of different ethnic groups. It called for Swahili to be recognized as the language of national unity while retaining English as the chief medium of instruction; indigenous languages were relegated to a few teaching hours per week and only in the first three years of school. In a 1969 speech in parliament, the founding president, Jomo Kenyatta, who was eloquent in *Kisanifu*, declared it a 'national language' and English an 'imperialist' language from which new Kenya must now free itself. He went on to urge parliament to institute Swahili as the nation's language of pride and identification, and in 1974 declared Swahili as the de jure national language of Kenya (Chimerah 1998). In the same year, the Department of African Languages and Linguistics, which focused on Swahili studies, was opened at the University of Nairobi.

Fifty years since the early appeals to return to 'authenticity' through an African language, the tension between a desire for 'authenticity' and the reality of Kenya's ideological approach to modernity has not been resolved. But there has been progress: the Swahili language is now formally enshrined in a clause in the new Constitution of 2010 as the 'national' as well as second official language of Kenya:

Article 8.1. The national language of the Republic of Kenya is Kiswahili

Article 8.2. The official languages of Kenya are Kiswahili and English, and all official documents shall be made available in those languages.

But parliamentary debates overwhelmingly take place in English, with far fewer members contributing in Swahili. But it is undeniable that one can navigate the Kenya government bureaucracy in Kenyan Swahili, which co-exists with English in a diglossic manner. The choice of language depends on the function of the interaction: while seeking services at the tax office, bank or hospital, a citizen may be served in Swahili interspersed with a few key English words and fixed expressions (e.g. clerk to a customer at Huduma Services: 'Deadline *ya hiyo* application *ni tarehe kumi.*' ('The deadline for that application is on the tenth'). But during a high-level consultation between cabinet secretaries, English will serve as the matrix language, which may be interspersed with Swahili idiom and expressions such as, 'The government is fully committed to serving all *wananchi.*' There is continued the debate in parliament, in the popular press, in universities, in media, etc., about whether Swahili can replace English as the language of power in higher education, international business, etc. Some argue that Swahili is not sufficiently developed in scientific or higher education terminology, nor are there enough books and other teaching materials available in this language; that students need to train in an international language to compete in the world of business and international job markets. The same school of thought argues that former colonial languages such as English remain the most 'neutral' since they come in as 'outsiders' to a politically charged context of ethnic competition and rivalries with each group wishing to promote their language. But the most powerful and widely accepted argument for Swahili is that it is the best unifier because it is an African language that is widely accepted by Kenyans of all ethnic and regional backgrounds. It is viewed as a 'neutral' language, devoid of connotations of power as its native speakers constitute an ethnic minority that is neither politically nor economically powerful. The results of our research demonstrate that Swahili and Sheng are the preferred means of expressing national solidarity or that sense of shared fate as one nation.

In mass politics and popular culture Swahili speaks for itself; it is by far the language used to articulate or illustrate Kenya's popular history and politics, to communicate pan-ethnic messages and evoke nationalist images. The state leadership uses vernacular Swahili to reach out to the people, in countrywide political campaigns, to immortalize episodes in the national memory, to create a nationalist ethos and cultivate similar sentiments through Swahili words, coined phrases, and slogans. A few prime examples of slogans known to every Kenyan serve to demonstrate how Swahili is used to engrave politics into popular culture: *Uhuru na Kazi* (Freedom and Work), a rallying call of the

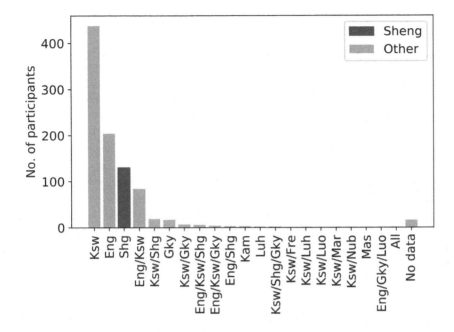

Figure 6 Solidarity languages of Nairobi (Source: NDS 2017)

first post-independent government exhorting the people to work hard in the spirit of *Harambee* or 'pulling/working together' – self-help – to build schools and hospitals and improve their general welfare. *Fuata Nyayo* (Follow the Footsteps), a government slogan of the eighties, a promise by his successor not to change the course of the nation after the demise of the founding president. An optimistic political climate that saw the demise of one-party rule and ushered in an optimistic period of multipartyism was heralded by a refrain, *yote yawezekana* – 'everything is possible', i.e. without a corrupt government. This victory was followed by another also popularized through the song, *Unbwogable*, popular Kenyan hip hop (*genge*) song meaning 'unbeatable/unconquerable' in Sheng. The political party that won the general elections of 2002 very successfully adopted the phrase as a campaign slogan. In all, there is little doubt that Swahili is 'the language of the nation' and is favoured as such by the most considerable majority of citizens as the results of surveys in Nairobi city have demonstrated (NDS 2002 and 2017).

A national plan for the institutionalization of Swahili laid out in the early days of independence has been hampered by bureaucratic resistance against a background of a strongly pro-Western, elitist political ideology. Successive governments have continued to give English a primary role in conducting its business, tendering processes, administering justice, etc., while reserving

Swahili to lower status functions such as basic citizen services, addressing the masses during political campaign rallies, or at the end of official speeches delivered in English. The laissez-faire attitude towards language in Kenya has prevailed since independence, a paralysis based on the fear of contradicting the desire for authenticity with the pro-capitalist, pro-western reality of Kenyan economics. It has resulted in unregulated development of languages with little conscious or focused planning, unimplemented decisions, and informal pursuance of existing policies in uneven ways. For example, in a few regions of the country, the policy of mother tongue instruction in early primary school education is implemented, but it is not followed in most others.

The indisputable increase in the use and spread of Swahili has not been a result of consistent planning and implementation. One consequence is that ways of speaking Swahili in Kenya vary from one region of the country to another, from one social group of speakers (SES) to another according to local and regional language influences. These ways of speaking Swahili are recognized by interlocutors, who go on to make judgments about speakers (see Chapter 3 on language attitudes in Nairobi). Language indexing becomes even more marked, and the rural–urban and ethnic divide is more starkly demarcated because of the apparent correspondence between language and economic and regional imbalances. Speaking Swahili in Kenya (vernacularized Swahilis) defines rather than obscures ethnic identity, as discussed in Chapter 3. For the majority of Kenyans, primacy is accorded to English for prestigious purposes and vernacular for local solidarity. Swahili retains its ancient role as a vehicular language, which is at the same time recognized as the language of a particular ethnic group of people known as Waswahili. As such, it may be resisted as a home language or vernacular in many non-ethnic Swahili households, a position that is consistent with the Kenyan tensions between local and broader forms of nationalism. It also reflects an acceptance of language and ethnicity as two faces of the same citizen.

In the intellectual arena, linguists, educators, and cultural activists advocate for the use of an African language (i.e. Swahili) to express national identity and promote integration and to preserve the cultures through languages. They wish to avoid alienating the vast majority from the minority elite of those educated to high levels in English (about 20 per cent) by failing to provide a meaningful education in an alien language which is far removed from its context. They also argue that it is in fact pedagogically more comfortable and better to impart knowledge in a language that is well understood by the student (Thiong'o 1981; Chimerah 1998; Mutiga 2013, etc.). Some academic organizations such as CHAKITA (National Council for Swahili), CHAKAMA (East African Council for Swahili) and most recently CHADUNI (World Council for Swahili) advocate for Swahili policy in education and also for its having more space in formal government and politics. The role of such groups and individuals in Kenya has been important in persuading the state to fully embrace and formalize Swahili as the language of government and public policy. Swahili's position in the country's constitution as an official and national language was made possible by lobbying exercised by such groups

Language and state identity: Kenya vs Tanzania

The different ideological paths taken by the two main Swahili speaking countries (i.e. where it is widely spoken and the official language), Kenya and Tanzania, also influenced state and identity formation. The political philosophy of Ujamaa promoted by Tanzania's first President Mwalimu Nyerere placed language at the centre of development and nation building while Kenya's 'African socialism', a conservative political and economic model, placed English at the centre. It is worth making a brief comparison between the only two African states that use Swahili as an official language; at least 100 million people in east and central Africa also speak it on a daily basis as vernacular or regional lingua franca.

Swahili is the universal lingua franca of Kenya today in small-scale trade (*jua kali*) and media, but its development and unifying role remains elusive especially when contrasted with neighbouring Tanzania. Ironically, it is not formalized in the Tanzanian constitution although it is the de facto official language. In discussing the language situation in Italy, Ruzza (2000:174) describes how 'with fascism, primary education became universal, diffusing the knowledge of standard Italian among peasants and the urban poor'. In addition to the fascist emphasis on the nation, its history and power suggested a pride in standard Italian or Italiano, the prestigious, literary dialect of Tuscany. New attention on the language emerged, requiring that the language should reflect the revolutionary zeal of the fascists; things were renamed, and migration from other parts of the country was encouraged, etc. Certain features of this model of social engineering adopted by post-independent Tanzania echo the Italian case described above. It was anti-imperialism rather than a fascist ideology that inspired the founding president of Tanzania, Julius Nyerere, to take a 'socialist' path of social and economic development popularly known by its Swahili form, Ujamaa. One of the tenets of this model was the complete institutionalization of (Swahili) language at every level of the new nation's workings: in the free and universal education programme, in politics, government and administration. A vocal anti-imperialist stance and a people-centred leadership fostered strong nationalist and pan Africanist sentiments among citizens of the new state, resulting in a widely acknowledged sense of cohesion and national identity that is the envy of all African states up to the present. Nyerere was an ardent proponent of a philosophy that required the Swahili language to reflect a revolutionary, anti-colonial, anti-imperialist zeal; streets were renamed, migration within the country's borders was highly encouraged and undertaken, youth brigades comprising of university graduates were dispatched across the nation to teach a nationalist curriculum in Swahili. Among other effects of such earnest planning and implementation was a linguistically unified nation. Swahili truly became the 'national language' of Tanzania with two important consequences. One, it appropriated the Swahili language for the larger nation while dissociating it from the localized ethnic identity of the original native speakers; the 'new Tanzanian' was projected by his use of standard, rather than a localized dialect of Swahili. Two, fast and widespread adoption of a single language eventually led to a massive loss of minority languages of Tanzania (Batibo 2005).

Comparatively, post independent Kenya's path of national development has been devoid of ideological positioning despite early, vague assertions to pursue a national economic policy based on 'African socialism'. However, in fact, Kenya's statehood did not waver from the colonial project built around a focus on ethnic and regional interests and control. This position was concretized by a leadership that exercised a 'cautious, conservative nationalism' (Maloba 1989), one that merely sought political independence without changing in any fundamental way colonial structures or Kenya's position within the declining British empire. The government was top down just like the colonial one, the new elite was trained in it, and they found it most convenient to perpetuate such elitism which, regarding language, depended on English. Recent constitutional changes to government structure – devolution (*ung'atuzi*) – have relaxed that rigid structure but it remains to be seen what direction the question of language will take since the devolved governments are structured in similar ways to the national one. The role of language, for example, mirrors that of the national government in that while services can be delivered in Swahili or the local indigenous language, higher functions – even local, county assembly debates and statutes – are conducted in Kenyan English.

The policy of language in education

The language question has dogged Kenya's education policy since colonial times. In 1922, the Phelps Stokes commission recommended the use of the indigenous language of the catchment area as a medium of instruction in lower primary (Mbaabu 1991). Swahili was recommended as the medium of instruction in all primary education across the country. The Phelps-Stokes Commission was set up, among other efforts, by an eponymous American philanthropist in 1920 to 'investigate the educational needs of the African people with special reference to the religious, social, hygienic and economic conditions'. It made several visits through countries in West Africa, South Africa, and East and Central Africa from 1920 to1921, and produced a report in 1922 titled 'Education in Africa'. It made similar visits to East Africa between 1923 and 1924 and produced its second report, 'Education in East Africa', in 1926. The East African report had important repercussions as, among other things, it recommended the use of African languages as medium of instruction in lower primary, and Swahili as the medium for all primary education across the country. This sensible policy was reversed in 1952 by the Binn Report, which removed Swahili as the medium of instruction in favour of regional languages of wider communication, a move that corresponded with the apex of anti-colonial protest in Kenya (Githiora 2008). In 1964, the first educational com-mission of independent Kenya led by an African produced the Ominde Report, which recommended the use of English in both primary and secondary school as the medium of instruction, and the relegation of African languages, includ-ing Swahili, to lower primary, as taught subjects only. A decade later, another commission issued the Gachathi Report of 1976, which recommended English medium of instruction in urban primary and secondary schools. But the most significant curriculum reform regarding the Swahili language was the 1981 McKay Commission, which introduced a new national curriculum popularly known as '8-4-4' – eight years of primary school education, four years of sec-ondary schooling, and four of university undergraduate training. It replaced the previous O- and A-level system inherited from British colonialism, which was seen as too narrow and lacking creativity by focusing on non-practical education and too few subjects. The 8-4-4 system also emphasized 'practical education' such as handcraft, agriculture, design and technology, and sports, but it too is associated with poor teaching, and learning methods which rely heavily on rote-learning and memory tasks rather than problem-solving and imparting useful skills. Heavily criticized over the years as an extra heavy load for children, the decision was made to abandon the 8-4-4 curriculum and replace it with a new one; the phasing out programme starts in 2018. Although English would continue to be the medium of instruction, Kiswahili was made a compulsory and examinable subject in both primary and second-ary levels of education in the 8-4-4 model. Indigenous languages retained their position, playing a minimal role in the early grades of primary school, but over the years, the pressure to master English for economic advancement and Swahili for its educational value has undermined vernacular languages enough to make their teaching or use in the classroom virtually inexistent, according to personal observation and interviews with teachers. Ironically, some teachers argue that they prefer to invest the time assigned to vernacu-lar language instruction to improve students' skills in English, the language needed to perform well in national examinations. In opposing Sessional Paper 14 of 2012, for example, the Kenyan National Union of Teachers (KNUT) leadership described the move to implement government policy on the use of indigenous languages in the classroom as 'retrogressive and difficult to implement' and that there are dangers of adopting such kind of a policy which 'will not promote national cohesion'. The union leaders pointed out that most teachers have no training in how to teach Kenyan indigenous languages.

'Of what purpose is the policy paper that has made it a requirement that teachers in public primary schools teach in the vernacular? What studies have been conducted to conclude that teaching in mother tongue will add value to the learning process for children below Class Four?' (*Daily Nation*, 28 January 2014)

In effect the 8-4-4 system which is currently being phased out has shaped the millennials, the Sheng generation of Kenyan students by making the formal learning of Swahili compulsory throughout the early years of primary and secondary school education. But this also raises the question of why Sheng has emerged to counter the expected outcome of higher proficiency in Swahili, national cohesion, etc., as a result of 12 years of study of the language. Did the compulsory imposition of Swahili result in the emergence of a counter-language, Sheng?

A new Basic Education Curriculum Framework (2017) model correctly places emphasis on the formative years of learning where learners will spend a total of eight years – two in pre-primary and six in primary school (lower and upper). They will then move on to six years in lower secondary and upper secondary school (senior school), and three years in tertiary (college or university). In upper primary (year 3) and junior secondary (years 7, 8 and 9) students will continue to study Swahili and English, with an option of one of four foreign languages – French, German, Mandarin and Arabic. The new curriculum envisages study of an African language (but only English and Swahili literature) at higher levels, in senior school under the Social Science or Arts and Sports pathway. There is a fresh opportunity to bring back language to the centre of learning and formal education in this new competency based curriculum which emphasizes the complex outcomes of a learning process, i.e knowledge, skills and attitudes to be applied by learners, 'rather than focussing on what learners are expected to learn about in in terms of traditionally defined subject content... a learner centred curriculum adaptive to the changing needs of students, teachers and society' (KICD 2017:23).

Chapter 3

Nairobi: a linguistic mosaic and crucible of Sheng

Nairobi – '*Naii*' – is the crucible and birthplace of Sheng, the capital city of Kenya from where – including the metropolitan area – about 60 per cent of the country's economic output is produced (KNBS, 2015), and from where many influences (fashion, style, language) radiate to other parts of the country. It is one of the fastest growing cities in Africa of about 4 million, a complex, multi-ethnic population with vast economic disparities. Nairobi is typical of cities, with problems, crime and insecurity, but it is also a place of opportunity for achievement in life, a complex, multilingual 'linguistic ecology' (Bokamba 1989). Nairobi is one of the 47 counties of Kenya, consisting of Starehe, Dagoretti, Lang'ata, Kamukunji, Makadara, Kasarani, Embakasi, Njiru, and Westlands sub-counties. Nairobi River and its tributaries run through the city under severe threat from over-construction, which encroaches their banks, and garbage pollution. These rivers have names: Ruaraka (Rũĩ Rwa Aka or 'women's river' in Gikuyu), Kasarani (Gathaarainĩ) and Kitisuru (Gitathurũ), Mathare and Karura.

These rivers also mark natural boundaries between Nairobi and its neigh-bouring counties: River Kasarani marks the boundary between Nairobi and Kiambu, while River Mbagathi (< Maasai, *Em-bagas* – Mol 1996) runs through the boundaries with Kajiado county to the south, and with Machakos county to the east. These are large and densely populated counties, whose indigenous populations mainly speak Gikuyu, Kamba, and Maasai languages. Therefore they have a greater influence on the language, culture and society of Nairobi. For example, the name of both the river and the city is in Maasai language, and the original names of the five tributaries of Nairobi River are Gikuyu (in parenthesis above), adapted to Swahili except the last two whose pronunciation presents no issues to the Swahili speaker.

The colonial city

'Nairobi' is a Maasai language place name meaning '[that] which is cold', or in its full version, *-are-na-irobi* or 'the stream which is cold, the Nairobi river' (Mol 1996). The town of Nairobi started in 1899 as a railway depot on the

Figure 7 View of the city from Uhuru Park (Photo © Chege Githiora)

Kenya–Uganda Railway where British contractors decided to establish a base before heading west towards the escarpment. It was a convenient stopping place 300 miles from the Indian Ocean before Uganda to the west, at Mile 317 of the Mombasa to Lake Victoria railway line. By 1907, the town had grown to replace Machakos as the capital of British East Africa Protectorate. During the colonial period, the town became the colony's centre for coffee, tea, and sisal industries. It also grew into a financial (banking) centre and many British subjects settled in its suburbs. The town became a municipality in 1919, and Nairobi Municipality formally became a city by Royal Charter in 1950, with a population of 150,000 (KNBS 2015). After independence in 1963, the city became the capital of the newly born Republic of Kenya, and today it is one of the most prominent cities in Africa, both politically and financially, with over 100 international organizations operating in the city. It is the headquarters of the United Nations Environment Program (UNEP) and the main coordinating headquarters for the United Nations (UN) affairs for Africa and the Middle East. According to the Kenyan Bureau of National Statistics (KNBS 2015), a population of 4 million in 2014 makes Nairobi the second largest city in the region after Dar-es-Salaam (Tanzania), and the 14th largest city in Africa. It is an established commercial and cultural city with the tag line, catchphrase or slogan, 'The Green City in the Sun'.

The city grew into four distinctive areas: a large area in the west and north-west of the city with substantial homes or 'leafy suburbs' such as Westlands, Lavington, Muthaiga and a smaller zone for Asians in the north and northeast – the wealthier Asians in suburbs near or equal in status to European ones such as Parklands, and less affluent ones living above their shops in areas

Figure 8 Eastlands housing Estate (Ofafa), with *mabati* extension in foreground (Photo © Chege Githiora)

such as Ngara. In the late 1950s, a series of basic, block housing estates with social amenities were built for Africans on the east side of the city. They are all located near the industrial area of Nairobi where many residents work or were meant to work. However, many workers also commuted from the nearby villages such as Kabete and Kiambu to work in the city. It was in the housing estates of the Eastlands where Sheng was eventually born in the streets and backyards and community centres of Jericho, Kaloleni, Makongeni, Mbotela, Bahati, Shauri Moyo, and later Starehe, Kariokor, and Ziwani. The affordability of the council rents has meant a high population density that continues to grow, but there are on-going plans to demolish and renovate the aged housing estates. These have been overgrown by unauthorized *mabati* (corrugated iron sheets) 'extensions' which have worsened the overcrowding. The 'extensions' are built by council tenants who rent them out to others for an affordable cost of between 3000 and 7000 shillings ($30-$70) per month.

Nairobi grew in size (150,000) and importance by the mid-20th century, becoming a city by Royal Charter by 1950. At the time of Kenya's independence and for about a decade thereafter, it was an orderly, dry colonial city, 'a lovely city, well designed, with gorgeous bougainvillea flowers lining many sidewalks; the slums are being cleared as the city expands its limits…there are no beggars on the streets and the City Council is busy trying to find ways of getting rid of prostitutes as well (Ng'weno 1968). Cultural activity was unimpressive then, and a far cry from what it is today: a city awash with entertainment spots, cinemas, bars and restaurants. Nairobi's alienness as a European city in the middle of Africa was evident, as another observer remarked:

Nairobi is not Kenya...there is nothing African about these wide avenues with their smart shops and handsome multi-storied buildings, and their islands and traffic circles of flowery bushes and waving palms trees. Nor is there anything African about the large Asian business section, with its incredibly cluttered little shops on congested narrow streets, permeated with the aroma of exotic foods. (Werlin 1963)

Fifty years later, the face of Nairobi has changed dramatically, with Africans as the overwhelming majority to be seen about in the streets of the city, and popular theatre (held in real theatres and in bars) in indigenous languages as well as Sheng, Swahili and English. A legacy of the colonial past remains strong, not only in the architectural designs of many buildings (and their names) but also the sectioning of the city's neighbourhoods along socio-economic status with its intersections with race and ethnicity. Downtown Nairobi remains strictly a business, administrative and entertainment centre following a 1948 (colonial era) Master Plan of Nairobi which heralded the provision of a Royal City Charter two years later. A colonial administrator campaigning for the charter during a turbulent time as Kenyans began to take up an armed anti-colonial struggle, described the 'African Social Welfare in Nairobi' using data that gives us insights of African life in Nairobi in 1950 (Werlin 1974). It was a life apart for the European and Asian, with relatively menial facilities for a population that was meant to remain on the margins of the city while providing the necessary domestic and industrial labour needed to run the city.

Many social structures that were initiated then continue in slightly different forms today: the housing estates built for African labour still stand, housing the large mass of the city's urban proletariat, hastening the rise of slums. Most of the social halls built in the workers' estates no longer function as they did for recreation, child and adult education classes, and as beer halls. However, they are iconic in the Sheng landscape, since they were built in the estates of the Eastlands where Sheng had its beginnings in the streets and in those social halls where Nairobians of diverse ethnic and language backgrounds enjoyed their recreation together. Many Nairobians, including millennials, remember with nostalgia when such public spaces for the urban masses functioned well for the designed purposes. These include Starehe Hall, Kaloleni Hall, Railway African Club, Shauri Moyo, Kariokor and Pumwani.

The formerly European-only estates in the west end of the city (e.g. some parts of Westlands, Muthaiga, Lavington) remain low-density zones for high-income residents, expatriates, UN employees, diplomatic staff and suchlike. The best known of these neighborhoods are Westlands, Lavington, Muthaiga, and Karen. Newer establishments are found in Runda, Kitisuru and parts of Lang'ata where rents are high and population density low. The former 'Asian quarter' in the north and northeast estate of Parklands remains predominantly

Asian. The former civil servant quarters in Kileleshwa, Kilimani, and Runda that used to be low population density now have large populations of the new middle-class Nairobians living in a jungle of flats and apartments. Some older houses in these areas close to the city centre have been converted into offices and restaurants. Other high-density parts of Nairobi were built in the 70s and 80s including Ngara, Pangani, Dandora, Buruburu, Umoja, Kariobangi South, Harambee, Donholm and Outer Ring.

The majority of the city's low-income population lives in the eastern part of the city, and in former rural villages beyond the city's periphery in the adjacent counties of Kiambu, Kajiado and Machakos – 'Nairobi's bedroom'– including settlements such as Kangemi, Dagoretti, Ong'ata Rongai and Githurai. A lot of housing development has taken place, and is on-going at speed, along with the newly built highways towards Thika town and Mombasa city, and along the recently completed eastern, southern and northern bypasses which skirt the city. Along these major arteries, new market centres are being established.

The precursors of *jua kali* industry were born when the council set aside plots in housing estates on which Africans were permitted 'to build workshops and stores to carry out their trades in carpentry, metal working, shoe making, tailoring and the like, to manufacture such goods as beds, furniture, charcoal stoves, mugs, shoes and clothing for sale'. African residents' 'guilds' similar to modern day *chamas* (self-help groups) and SACCOs (savings and loans cooperatives) were encouraged to take up some of these plots to put up their businesses on a cooperative basis, provide themselves with offices, machines or small forges. Suppliers of charcoal, the main type of fuel used by Africans in Nairobi then, were also permitted to build sites. Today's slums of Nairobi can also be traced back to that 'master plan' which proposed that villages be laid out for Africans to build houses in local materials as an answer to the housing problem that was already present in 1950s Nairobi. Africans were also granted permits to operate butcheries and dairies to serve those unable to get meat and milk from hawkers. Markets were established to offer affordable stalls (15 cents per day in 1948) for African traders who found it impossible to afford shops in permanent buildings (King 1996).

The rapid pace of change has continued amidst the coexistence of old and traditional Africa and colonial and westernized Kenya, and is still evident as Maasai men and women dressed in bright red *shukas*, beaded necklaces and belts stroll the streets of downtown Nairobi alongside men in woollen business suits and youths clad in hip-hop gear, jeans and tees shirts. Nairobi is where one generation later, former rural folk have become urbanites, and their children even more rooted in urban ways, where two generations speak different languages: indigenous mother tongue, English, Swahili, 'Engsh' and Sheng.

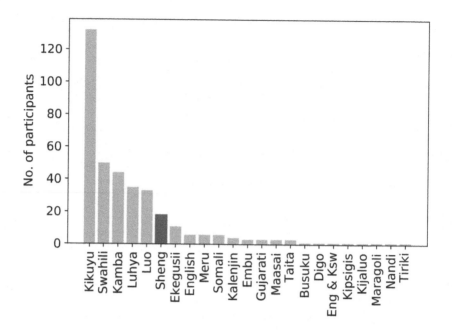

Figure 9a Mother tongues of Nairobi in descending order of frequency (Source: NDS, 2017)

The sociolinguistic context

The Nairobi Data Set shows that on average Nairobians speak three languages, but about 20 per cent of the 935 respondents speak four languages, and Sheng is the sixth most cited as 'home language' (see Figures 9a and 9b). Therefore it is not possible to analyse Sheng without fully understanding the sociolinguistic environment in which it is immersed by exploring the state of multilingualism and language use in the city of Nairobi with a population of about 4 million, representing 25.6 per cent of the total urban population of Kenya (KNBS 2015). The eastern section of the city (the Eastlands), where Sheng is most prominent, is also the most densely populated with housing estates and several 'slums'. The western side of the city is wealthy and suburban, most residents are higher socioeconomic class, and accordingly, they go about speaking mostly in Kenyan English (KE).

Nairobi's population is primarily accounted for by rural–urban migration (KPSA 2013), therefore the capital city is characterized by a multi-ethnic population and vast economic disparities. These are clearly reflected in the disparities between housing conditions in various sections of the city, which range from slums to elaborate mansions in gated communities. In total, the following 41 languages were reported as 'mother tongue' by the sample set of Nairobians who participated in this study, reflecting the great variety of languages spoken in Nairobi and the country's linguistic diversity.

> Amharic, Arabic, Boran, Busuku, Chaga, Dholuo ('Kijaluo', **'Kijaka'**), Digo, Duruma, English (Kingoso), Ekegusii (Kisii), Embu, Gikuyu (Kikuyu, **'Kisapere'**), Giriama, Gujarati, Kalenjin (**Kikalɛɛ**), Kamba, Kiborana, Kiganda, Kimeru, Kinubi, Kidigo, Kipsigis, Kisuhka, Kitaveta, Lugisu, Maragoli, Maasai, Mbeere, Nandi, Nubian (Kinubi), **Sheng**, Somali, Suba, 'Sudanese', Swahili, Taita, Tiriki, Turkana, Waya, 'Zairean'

The alternate language names (in brackets) are retained in the form they were transcribed from questionnaires, and ones in bold letters are Sheng names of the same. For example, some respondents wrote down 'Kijaluo' or 'Dholuo' or 'Kijaka,' while Gikuyu was reported as 'Kikuyu,' 'Kikikuyu' and 'Kisapere'. It was not possible to clarify with the individual respondents at the time, what language of dialect 'Zairean' and 'Sudanese' represented, but we understood them to mean that the respondents were of Congolese and (South) Sudanese origin, respectively. The self-reporting is important as it demonstrates the awareness of 'names' of languages, including 'Sheng' which is cited by 12 per cent as 'the first language'. According to our data, in about 26 per cent of households of Nairobi, the 'vernacular' ('household language') is Swahili, Sheng or English. Older members of the household only use the mother tongue of either parent. In Kenyanese, 'vernacular' refers to Kenyan indigenous languages, but in this book, I use it in the standard way to mean any language or mixed code used in the most fluent and relaxed manner such as at the dinner table with family at home, or when relaxing and telling jokes with friends, etc. Therefore, a young Nairobian's vernacular does not necessarily correspond to the 'mother tongue' (MT), that is the first language of one or both parents.

Sheng is listed as the sixth most common homestead vernacular by the participants in the 2017 Nairobi Data Set. Many of those interviewed insisted that they know people, relatives or friends who were parents themselves and in the thirties, forties, and fifties, who speak Sheng in their daily lives at home, or work, or in trade. The Sheng speaking former 'street children' first reported in Spyropolous (1987) would be among those middle-aged adults who now speak Sheng as their first language or mother tongue. The youths we interviewed in 2002 are now parents themselves, raising children and plainly speaking

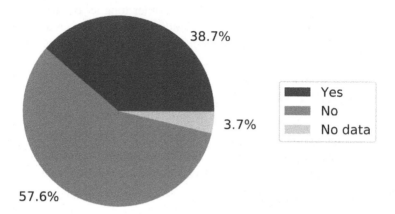

Figure 9b Is mother tongue also homestead language? (Source: NDS 2017)

Sheng, especially if they continued to live in Nairobi. Unsurprisingly, nearly 40% of the youths reported that the 'first' language or mother tongue of one or both parents is not their homestead language or vernacular.

A few demographic facts about Nairobi city are relevant to this discussion in terms of how they have contributed to the expansion of Sheng's domains, and its acceptance as a code of wider communication. The capital city's estimated population represents about 10 per cent of the country's total population, and approximately 34 per cent of the total urban population of Kenya lives in Nairobi. The most unfortunate 60 per cent of Nairobi residents live on only 8.7 per cent of the city's land base, mostly in informal settlements (UNEP 2009). This means that a significant portion of the city's multilingual population live in crowded low-income neighbourhoods ('estates') where Sheng has its origins, or in informal settlements ('slums') where it now thrives. The housing shortage combined with improved infrastructure has caused Nairobi's population to spread into adjacent counties. The densely populated low- and medium-income suburbs such as Githurai, Kawangware, Ongata Rongai, and the nearby towns of Ngong, Machakos, Ruiru, Thika, and Limuru are now part of the city's larger metropolitan region. Many people now come into Nairobi daily to work or bring in goods and supplies, and commuters are estimated to contribute an additional half-million people to the city's population (KPSA 2013).

Urban–rural linkages persist as migrants maintain close relations with their rural homes even from a distance; they visit, invest in economic and social activities, education and health amenities; migrants unable to find jobs in the city are often forced to 'return home' (Owour 2007). Others return to rural homes out of fear or threat of living in hostile, ethnically dominated towns of Kenya, or sections of Nairobi. These demographic changes and movements have contributed to the growth and spread of Sheng linked to the city's on-going expansion from its original boundaries into the larger metropolitan region. Such demographic shifts have extended Sheng's reach to beyond the city enclaves. The origin and spread of Sheng are therefore embedded in the complex, multilingual situation of Nairobi, compounded by language asymmetry created by age and socioeconomic disparities. The coexistence of speakers of many different languages, further differentiated by age and socioeconomic class, provide ideal conditions for the development of a code which reflects that asymmetric reality.

One important and often neglected area of managing societal multilingualism, is to understand the degree of competence in those languages. One can fruitlessly address a group of people who claim to be bi- or multilingual, yet have limited competence in those languages, because these may be linked to specific registers in which they, as individuals, do not participate. For example, a *mama mboga*, Nairobi's small scale version of the greengrocer, may lay claim to speaking X or Y Indigenous language of Kenya whereas, in fact, they are fluent only in a few short phrases or words which may suffice to conduct a brief transaction when dealing with a customer. Of course this is not sufficient for such a person to lay claim to being bilingual in X or Y language. Furthermore, there is a difference between production and synthesis of language: one may understand a certain language but find it hard to express themselves in it.

So how well do Nairobians know Sheng, Swahili, and English? To answer this question, I asked respondents to translate ten sentences from Sheng into *Kiswahili Sanifu* (Standard Swahili – SS), and English to test degrees of bilingualism in English and Swahili and bi-dialecticism in Sheng and SS. The idea was to test the linguistic competence of the respondents in three speech codes that lie on the continuum of Kenyan ways of speaking ('Kenyanese'), by testing the ability of subjects – all students – to switch between the three ways of speaking which predominate in Nairobi's sociolinguistic environment. The sentences were isolated from a short text obtained from a weekly newspaper column which is published in Sheng in *The Nairobian*, authored by a prominent radio DJ who goes by the name 'Mbusii', and who writes a regular commentary on topics that affect the lives of Nairobians; it is in familiar, even emotive language, with substantial code-mixing and Sheng words and idiom titled, *Stori za Mtaa: Landlord Anakunyima Hao* ('Stories from the Hood: Landlord refuses you a house', see Appendix 1).

All respondents (14–18 years of age) understood the Sheng sentences without any problem. They were able with ease, to orally explain the meanings and nuances behind the words or statements. However, describing the same meaning in SS or English proved quite challenging for most respondents, who are all in full-time secondary school or university. Most struggled to translate Sheng into English or SS, and when they did, meanings would be distorted by differences of sentence interpretation, word choice, and inappropriate word order in both English and Swahili, such as in the following example (Nairobi Data Set 2017).

Sheng: *Huyo mtɔii ako kwa mgongo ni wa nani?*
KS: *Huyo mtoto **ako** <u>kwa mgongo</u> ni wa nani?*
KE: The baby whose [sic.]on your back is for who?

Clearly, the grammar of Sheng is that of KS, since the only difference between the two questions is the word *mtɔii* in Sheng (SS: *mtoto* 'child'). The Standard Swahili (SS) and Standard English (SE) forms are different and more complex as shown below for comparison. The key differences are underlined.

Table 3 Translation of the word 'landlords'

Translation of 'landlords'	Frequency			
	University UGs (19–25 years)		Secondary School (13–19 years)	
Wenye nyumba	16	36.4%	21	19.1%
No translation (blank)	12	27.3%	31	28.1%
Wakodeshaji/wakodishaji	1	2.3%	15	13.7%
Landlords	1	2.3%	10	9.1%
Wakomboleshaji	0	n/a	5	4.5%
*Wapangaji**	0	n/a	12	10.9%
Wenye ploti	0	n/a	4	3.6%
Don't know	1	2.3%	0	n/a
Wapangishaji	6	13.6%	0	n/a
*Wakodisha**	5	n/a	0	n/a
Wamiliki nyumba	1	2.3%	0	n/a
Walipwa kodi, wenye kukodisha, warentishaji, wawekaji, wachungaji*, wakodinyumba, waajiri*, watoza kodi, wenyeji wa nyumba*, walipishaji kodi*	0	n/a	11	10%
Total	44	100%	110	100%

Note: Items marked with an asterisk are mistranslations of 'landlords': *wapangaji* ('renters'); *wakodisha* (lacks a complement, *nyumba*); *wawekaji* (possibly confused with *wawekezaji* 'investors'); *wachungaji* ('shepherds'); *waajiri* ('employers'); and *wenyeji wa nyumba* (possibly confused with *wenye nyumba* 'home owners').

SS: *Huyo mtoto **aliye** mgongoni ni wa nani?*
SE: Whose baby is that you're carrying on the back?

Over 65 per cent (see Table 3), were unable to retrieve the Swahili equivalents of the words 'landlord' and 'tenant' suggesting that low proficiency in Swahili may also be one of the motivations for Sheng which is characterized by code-switching. A modest 36.9 per cent of undergraduate university students got the right equivalent (*wenye nyumba*), but only 19 per cent of secondary school students got it right. However, an equal number of young adults and adolescents were unable to find an equivalent, leaving the word blank, or leaving the entire sentence untranslated; some honestly responded, 'I do not know.' Slightly more than 10 per cent of the younger respondents (13–17 years) code-switched by leaving the word 'landlord' un-translated in the sentence. Moreover, 10 per cent of secondary school students used the wrong word *wapangaji* (tenant), which means the opposite, while another 10 per cent used non-standard coinages that were unacceptable or outright wrong translations, marked with an asterisk in the table above. At least one coinage, '*warentishaji*' (< *wa (NC2)-rent-sha(causative)-ji* (nominalizing suffix)) can be considered a Sheng innovation, very creative.

The second item I tested was the word *noma*, with the same set of respondents which included 50 university students (ages 21–40) and 110 secondary school students (13–17 years). The word is ubiquitous in Sheng talk, and nearly all respondents to the exercise were unaware that *noma* exists in SS as synonym of *kipingamizi* (or *pingamizi*), which means 'obstacle'. In Kenyan Swahili (KS), *noma* is rarely heard outside Sheng talk. Respondents variously described *noma* as 'problem,' 'trouble,' 'difficult' but in many other instances it was translated or used in contexts to mean 'good', 'great', 'fantastic', for example:

Sheng: *Hiyo stori ni **noma.***
SS: *Hicho ni kisa cha kushangaza.*
          That's an *amazing/great story.*
Sheng: *Hizo mahewa ni **noma**, jo!*
SS: *Huo mziki ni mzuri [sana] bwana!*
          That music is great, man!'

Generally, *noma* seems to function mostly as an nominal adjective but it can also take another 'true' nominal form such as *mnoma* (plural: *wanoma*) to describe an individual (NC1/NC2 (*m-/wa-*) class only), in which case the meaning narrows to human qualities such as 'hard', 'tough,' 'dangerous,' and so on, for example,

Sheng: *He! huyo jamaa ni **mnoma** sana!*
SS: *He! Huyo mtu ni mkali sana!*
          That guy is very tough!

We then located the word *noma* in the following sentence obtained from the research data, and following discussions with the team of research assistants and Sheng practitioners, it was agreed that the best SS equivalent of *noma* in this particular sentence is *-gumu*: 'hard' or 'difficult' [-animate]. This was supported by the range of meanings listed in the monolingual SS dictionary (Kamusi 2004) that is widely used in Kenyan school system, and formally approved 'for use in primary and secondary schools, and Teacher training Colleges' by Tanzania's Ministry of Culture and Education in 2005.

My translation of *-gumu*: (1) hard, dry – synonyms: *kavu, kavukavu*, e.g. *Chuma ni kigumu* (The iron is hard); (2) difficult to understand, e.g. *hesabu hizi ni ngumu* (These sums are difficult); (3) hard hearted, merciless, e.g. *ana moyo mgumu* (s/he has a hard heart); (4) mean – synonym: *kakamizi*. However, *noma* cannot be used to mean 'hard' in the sense of 'dry' which in Sheng and KS is ordinarily expressed by *-kavu*, e.g. *mkate mkavu* (dry bread). Therefore, the following is a well formed Sheng sentence which I asked participants to translate into SS and English:

Sheng: *Maisha hapa Nairobi ni **noma** ile mbaya.*
SS: *Maisha hapa Nairobi ni **magumu** sana.*
English: Life here in Nairobi is very **difficult**.'

Table 4 Translation of the word 'noma'

	Translation of '*noma*'	Frequency			
		University UGs (19–25 years)		Secondary School (13–19 years)	
a	*ngumu/ghumu/gumu*	21	42%	47	42.7%
b	*magumu/mangumu*	16	32%	26	23.6%
c	*mabaya, mbaya*	4	8%	5	4.5%
d	*shida*	0	n/a	7	6.4%
e	*si rahisi* (x3); *ina taabu nyingi, si nzuri*	2	4%	5	4.5%
f	*blank (no translation provided)*	1	2%	7	6.4%
g	*very bad; very tough*	0	n/a	2	1.8%
h	*nzuri, vizuri*	1	2%	3	2.7%
i	*changamoto, hatari, pagumu, balaa, imezoroteka, kali, makali, hatari, ya kubabaisha, ghali* (x2); *gharama; 'ni ngumu soo!'*	5	10%	13	11.8%
	Total	**50**	**100%**	**110**	**100%**

A total of 12 per cent of translations of the word *noma* among adults were incorrect or unacceptable (rows g–i). A further three respondents (2 per cent) did not provide a translation (blank), so it was assumed that they did not know the correct answer, and three responses (2 per cent) were outright wrong, while another 10 per cent provided inadequate translation/equivalents with related meanings. Secondary school students (13–19 years) performed worse since a total of 22.7 per cent were unable to provide an acceptable *Kiswahili Sanifu* equivalent for the Sheng word *noma*. Adult university students scored higher (32 per cent) than secondary school students (23.6 per cent) in selecting the correct adjective (*-gumu*) and appropriate NC6 agreement marker (*ma-*). However, the similarities between the two groups were greater than the differences. Almost the same percentage of each group used a form of periphrasis such as *si nzuri* (not good), indicating lexical deficiency as they clearly could not retrieve the appropriate or most accurate SS equivalent for Sheng's *noma*. Similarly, nearly the same proportion of adult undergraduates as secondary school students searched broadly to find creative equivalents for *noma* including: *changamoto* (challenging), *hatari* (dangerous), *balaa* (disaster), *kali* (fierce), *ghali* (expensive), *ya kubabaisha* (amazing), and in typical Sheng creativity: '*ni ngumu soo!*' (it's hard bigly!) complete with an exclamation mark. There was parity between the percentage of adult and teenage respondents who used the right word *-gumu*, but with non-standard agreement or spelling (*ngumu* and *ghumu*). All these words and expressions generally belong to the same semantic field, but they are not accurate equivalents of *noma* as understood by consensus of Sheng speakers. This may be a demonstration of gaps of meaning between some key words such as *noma* in Sheng and *-gumu* or *shida* in Kenyan Swahili. In summary, the results of this test demonstrated some of the differences of word meaning between SS on the one hand, and KS and Sheng on the other. It shows that secondary school students may be more familiar with Sheng vocabulary than that of SS. It also raises the question of whether some of these KS/Sheng meanings should have a place in dictionaries and other formal texts.

Attitudes towards Sheng and other languages

Language attitudes are culturally informed, and they can congeal into stereotypes (Lambert et al. 1960). People develop the ability to identify a language and make associations which are derived from the surrounding environment, culture, and society. In order to test this hypothesis in Nairobi, we conducted a 'Matched Guise Test' which is a widely known sociolinguistic experimental technique first applied by Lambert et al. (1960) in Canada. There have been numerous variations to this test for application in many other contexts since then (e.g. Papapavlou 2004, for Greek Cypriot dialect), to determine the true feelings of an individual or community towards a specific language, dialect, or accent. It is used to identify language or dialect attitudes (see also Shuy and Fasold 1973). For example, some researchers have used different speakers for their recordings. This takes the 'matched' aspect out of the test and introduces other variables. However, it does make each recording more natural. For the Nairobi Matched Guise Test, I recorded the voice of a 29-year-old, male professional voice artist and musician reading a short passage in different Kenyan ways of speaking Swahili or English, and carefully explained the aims of the exercise to him. After some rehearsal, he ably read out a short text I had prepared, in ten different Kenyan ways or 'Kenyanese' (Githiora 2018a). I then made participants in the test listen to each of the ten voices, and asked them to rate the voices along the following 12-point criteria: age, looks, intelligence, honesty, sociability, religiousness, level of education, leadership, self-confidence, character and finally, the likely occupation of the person behind the voice. While I got to know what a sample of people thinks about a recorded voice, these views in themselves are not language attitudes; rather, I extrapolated language attitudes from these verbal reactions and written responses, while paying attention to paralinguistic features such as gestures, facial movements, etc. Each voice was recorded in the following Kenyan ways of speaking, without the participants being told of the labels attached to them:

Table 5 Matched Guises

Guise	Code	
Sheng (SHG)	SHG	Swahili variety and vernacular of most teenagers and millennials (14-35 years) of Nairobi and other urban areas of Kenya. It is characterized by extensive code-mixing with English, and some Indigenous Kenyan languages.
Kenyan Swahili (KS):	KS	Swahili as spoken spontaneously in informal settings by Kenyan *wananchi*, as a second or additional language of probably 95% of Kenyans. It is the vernacular speech in a majority of Nairobi households, and in other urban communities of Kenya.
Kiswahili Sanifu (Standard Swahili)	SS	Standard Swahili such as is taught and examined in schools, used in academic publishing, official documents (including the Kenya Constitution of 2010), or in news broadcast on radio and television. It is spoken only in very formal settings.
Kenyan English	KE	Defined by Buregeya (2006), as the type of English spoken by those Kenyans with approximately 14 years of exposure to it, that is, have used English as medium of instruction up to secondary level. Although it is based on 'Standard British English' it has non-standard features, 'at least fourteen which are definitely characteristic of the grammar of Kenyan English'. (p. 213).

Vernacular Swahilis

The same voice artist then recorded the following vernacular marked ways of speaking KS, that is KS with the marked and easily recognizable 'accent' of the following six Kenyan languages. Two of the languages are selected for practical reasons, not necessarily for being among the 'big five' languages of Kenya, which one would expect to predominate in the city of Nairobi in proportion to the size of their population.

'Vernacular Swahili'	Code	Description
Gikuyu	GKY	Bantu, approximately 6.7 million speakers
Dholuo	DHO	Nilotic, approximately 4.2 million speakers. Also 'Luo'.
Luhyia	LUY	Bantu. A 'macrolanguage' with approximately 5.1 million speakers and many dialects and microlanguages
Kamba	KAM	Bantu, spoken by approximately 4 million Kenyans
Somali	SOM	Cushitic, approximately 2.5 million speakers in Kenya, and many more in Somalia, Ethiopia, Yemen, Djibouti, and among large immigrant communities in Europe and North America, totaling about 15 million.
Maasai	MAA	Nilotic, spoken by approximately half a million Kenyans, and smaller numbers in Tanzania.

Although Maasai and Somali are not among the 'big five' languages of Kenya, they were included in the study because of their importance. Nairobi is located in traditional Maasai country (*Enkare Nyairobi*) as we have already seen, and Maasai people have a visible presence in the city partly because of their distinctive traditional dress and continued pastoral lifestyle even within the city limits. The people can be seen sauntering around the city in this distinctive clothing, at times grazing cows and sheep along the streets of the city during dry spells. Maasai culture resonates in the national psyche due to their steadfast retention of many aspects of their culture and traditions, such as the type of dress (red *shukas*, beadwork adornments, etc). Some of these have been co-opted as national dress icons, and Maasai culture is 'sold' on tourist circuits all over Kenya. The relatively larger community of Somali speakers lives in different parts of Nairobi, but with a higher concentration in Eastleigh (also in the Eastlands), for which reason it is also known as 'little Mogadishu'. Ethnic Somalis add to the large community of Muslims of Nairobi, which is home to many mosques and Islamic community schools and cultural centres. Somali people are known for their entrepreneurship, and have deep historical roots in Nairobi. They are a visible as well as 'audible' presence in all parts of Nairobi where they engage in small trade or large enterprises. In contrast, although Kalenjin is one of the 'Big Five' and a macrolanguage with many dialects in the Rift Valley region of the country, spoken by about 5 million Kenyans, it is not much represented in Nairobi. Very few of our 950 randomly selected respondents on the streets and estates and schools of Nairobi self-identified as 'Kalenjin'. For example out of 95 questionnaires collected in downtown Nairobi (Central Business District or CBD) in one day, only two participants reported their first language as 'Kalenjin', and one respondent 'Nandi', which is one of its dialects. At the Brucewood Academy in Kayole Eastlands, not a single student of the 84 interviewed reported Kalenjin as a first language. Therefore Kalenjin was not included in the attitudinal survey.

Such ways of speaking are readily recognized by all Nairobians who participated in the test, in fact, there never was a doubt about what the voices represented, even when a few respondents asked or revealed that they thought the texts were guises done by the same person. Impersonating voices speaking Swahili or English with identifiable ethnic or regional accents is far from unusual: Kenyan television shows, such as the hugely popular *Churchill Show* or soaps such as *Real Housegirls of Kawangware* thrive on humour based on ethnic language stereotypes. While taking the test sometimes, members of the group would get animated when a particular vernacular marked Swahili was played for them on a speaker. In one instance, a group of five girls broke into spontaneous smiles while looking meaningfully at one of their partners immediately I played a particular voice. When I asked what the matter was, the girl in question quickly offered that it was because 'I am Luhyia' – and the particular voice playing was of 'Luhyia Swahili'. In another instance, a Somali boy was evidently delighted when the Somali Swahili voice was played: participants seemed to take pleasure in hearing 'their' voices played during the test. We did not record any adverse reactions during any of the video recorded interviews and testing.

The experiment

Ideally, each subject is given the test, by randomly playing for him/her one of the readings while listening on earphones (e.g. Lambert et al. 1960). He or she is then asked to respond to prepared questions, or fill out a questionnaire, with the tester doing as little as possible to affect the subject as he or she answers the questions. The responses are recorded, and the process is repeated for all subjects. Such a repetitive process is best done in laboratory conditions where each respondent fills out their questionnaire while working an individual workstation with earphones, with perhaps the ability to shuffle and replay as required. However, a language lab was unavailable at the time of this research, and in any case, it would have been difficult to obtain permission for teenagers to leave home or school, and for me to transport them to wherever the laboratory would have been available. Working with teenagers, I therefore improvised by playing a short audio clip to a group of five respondents at a time, using a reasonably powerful external speaker attached to my laptop. I worked with four groups, making up a total of 20 teenage responses (11 males, nine females). I played each voice just once and then stopped to ask for their most immediate reactions, which I noted down on the prepared list of attitudes towards each variety. The original text of 222 words in Sheng was redacted from a newspaper column in Sheng (see Appendix 1).

Each recorded clip was on average 1.05 minutes long, but there were slight variations in length of the same text in translation: Sheng and KE texts were the shortest at .57 and .58 seconds respectively, while Maasai and Somali were the longest at 1.16 and 1.20 respectively. Each interview session, therefore, took about one-and-a-quarter hours (50 mins + discussion/ response). The participants were encouraged to give the shortest descriptions possible of each voice, using single words or adjectives or phrases (e.g. 'tall', '*roho safi*' (lit. clean heart, 'good, sincere person' etc.). Just a simple 'yes/ no' was required to many of the questions. However, in most of the cases, reactions were unanimous among the group of four or five respondents, but they were also encouraged to voice their thoughts and independent answers. Nonetheless, it is impossible to completely rule out the effects of group talk where some respondents were more passive and would let others respond to most questions, or simply nod in agreement. In some cases, I would ask respondents to clarify an answer (e.g. 'Did you mean he sounds "tough"?'), and also engaged in brief discussions about a particular point or response. I also paid attention to non-verbal language including hand gestures and facial expressions. These were important corollaries to the responses during the interviews, and afterward, since all interviews were video recorded. Where applicable, I noted two or even three different responses separated by a semi-colon in the same box, indicating different or even contradicting opinions about some responses, which were very few. In effect, this first test was based on focus groups in that it involved discussions and summary of opinions. But in the second test, respondents made their answers individually by filling out the provided worksheets. The methodological difference introduced through my improvisation appeared to have little effect on the views and attitudes; it therefore enhanced the results of the triangulation.

Sheng original text

Maisha hapa Nairobi ni <u>noma</u> ile mbaya. *I think 90%* ya <u>raiyah</u> za Kenya ni wale <u>wamerent keja</u>. *Landlord* wengine <u>joh</u> hata kama <u>keja</u> ni zenu, msisahau mnahitaji *tenant* ndio mambo ikue [sic] <u>irie</u> kwenu. Kumbuka *no man is an Island*, and *no man stands alone*. Sana wale *landlords* wanaishi <u>tiplo</u> moja na *tenants* wake wanakuanga <u>mangati</u> ile *serious*. Wale hunishikisha moto ni wale *landlord* wanajifanyanga eti ploti zao ni *special* hawataki <u>wamama</u> wazee na mtoto. Akiuliza kama kuna *keja*, *landlord* anaanza maswali za ujinga: 'Kwanza we umeolewa? Huyo mtoi <u>ako kwa mgongo</u> ni wa nani? Na mzae wako <u>ako works wapi</u>?' Mwingine anamwambia keja iko lakini mtoi amemharibia <u>juu</u> hiyo ploti <u>hawarentishangi</u> <u>watu wako</u> na mtoi ama watoi. Ma landlord wengine <u>sareni za ovyo.</u>

Standard Swahili (SS – Kiswahili Sanifu) translation

Maisha hapa Nairobi ni <u>magumu sana.</u> Nafikiri 90% (asilimia tisini) ya wakenya ni wale ambao <u>wamepanga nyumba.</u> *Wenye nyumba* wengine <u>aisee</u> hata kama <u>nyumba</u> ni zenu, msisahau mnahitaji *wapangaji* ndio mambo iwe <u>sawa</u> kwenu. Kumbuka *no man is an Island*, and *no man stands alone*. Hasa wale *wenye nyumba ambao* wanaishi <u>ploti</u> pamoja na *wapangaji* wake huwa wakali sana na sio kwa ubaya. Wale ambao <u>hunikasirisha sana</u> ni wale *ambao* huchukulia kwamba ploti zao ni *za pekee sana ili kwamba* hawataki <u>akina mama</u> wazee na watoto. Akiuliza kama kuna *chumba wazi, mwenye nyumba* anaanza maswali ya ujinga: 'Kwanza umeolewa wewe? Huyo mtoto <u>aliye mgongoni</u> ni wa nani? Na je bwanako <u>anafanya</u> kazi gani?' Mwingine anamwam-bia nyumba iko lakini mtoto <u>amemharibia kwa sababu hawapang-ishi</u> hiyo ploti <u>kwa watu ambao wana</u> mtoto ama watoto. Wenye nyumba wengine acheni kupenda kunyanyasa.'

English

Life here in Nairobi is really tough. I think 90% of people in Kenya are those who rent their homes. Some of you landlords should not forget that you need tenants so you can be happy. Remember, no man is an island, and no man stands alone. In particular, those who live on the same plots as their tenants are the worst/meanest. Those who make me mad are those who think their plots are so special that they do not want women or those with children. When she asks if a room is vacant, the landlord starts to ask stupid questions like: 'First of all, are you married? That child on your back who's is it: And your husband what does he do?' Another one says there is a vacant room, but having a child spoils it for her because he does not rent to people with children. Some of you landlords better stop being so greedy.

Table 6 Female attitudes towards Sheng, Kenyan Swahili, English and Standard Swahili (Group A, Age 14–17) n=25

Parameter	Sheng	Kenyan Swahili (KS)	English	Standard Swahili (Sanifu)
Age	19–20	20–25	21–28	20–25
Looks	Young	*'hajui Kiswahili sana'*	Modest	*'lugha tamu'* (eloquent)
Education	Form 4 (Sec)	Form 4 (sec)	University	College
Height	Tall	Tall	Short	Medium
Honesty	No	Yes	Yes	Yes
Intelligence	No	No	Yes	Yes
Leadership	No	Yes	Yes	Yes, a little *'kidogo'*
Sociability	Yes	Yes	Yes	Yes
Religiosity	No	No	Yes	No; maybe
Self-confidence	Yes	Yes	Yes. *sana* (*'very'*)	A bit
Character	Courageous; *'haezi ogopa'* (is fearless)	*Mtu wa kawaida* (ordinary person)	Serious	Creative
Occupation	Hustler, *makanga*. *'anauzanga scrap metal'* (sells scrap metal)	Footballer; businessman	Student; business; accountant	Student; university; college

According to these results, Sheng speakers are understood to be young, on average 19–20 years old. They are sociable and self-confident but are not religiously inclined. They are not seen as honest or intelligent and have only secondary school level of education. Sheng speaking man is courageous ('has no fear') and he is a 'hustler' in the Kenyan sense described earlier, or a *makanga* (matatu tout) or 'scrap metal dealer'. KS and SS speakers are evaluated as of the same age, slightly higher than the Sheng speaker (20–25). They are both honest, but the KS speaker is not as intelligent as the SS speakers, who are likely to be in college (e.g. mid-level, diploma). Perhaps the most interesting observation is that teenagers find the SS speaker very eloquent for having a 'sweet language' but the KS speaker is considered 'not fluent in the language'. Participants in the experiment made a clear demarcation between native/fluent coastal, grammatically correct Swahili, and the 'broken' one that typifies the Kenyan Swahili. Nonetheless, the KS speaker has 'good leadership' abilities which the SS speaker does not possess. The average Kenyan politician or government representative is best known for their relatively weak skills in SS.

Teenage attitudes towards languages

Teenage girls judged the Sheng speaker to be about 19–20 years old, and the English speaker 25–28 years of age. Ethnically marked Swahili speakers were also generally perceived as older (for Gikuyu, 25–30 yrs.). Ethnic division of labour is also evident in the language attitudes. English, the high-status language, is rated highly and positively evaluated in all categories: a modest person, a university graduate with confidence and leadership ability. He or she

Figure 10a Students listening to Matched Guises (girls) (© Chege Githiora)

Figure 10b Students listening to Matched Guises (boys) (© Chege Githiora)

is perceived as religious (a valued character in Kenyan society), and if not a
student, runs a business or is a professional such as an accountant, or office
manager. SS speakers are also positively evaluated by female respondents who
judged them college or university graduates, creative, 'talk sweetly' and are of
good character. However, male teenagers thought differently of SS speakers:
educated only up to secondary school, they may be a hawker or just another
'guy in the hood'. They are not sociable nor do they possess leadership skills.
They may have a job or a business or are in school. Finally, teenage boys
regarded Swahili (SS and KS) speakers as 'untrustworthy'. The gender differences may reflect girls' awareness of prestige markers in a language, which
are to be found in Standard (Coastal) Swahili and English. Males, on the other
hand, are more sympathetic towards covert prestige markers such as those
found in Sheng. Furthermore, female respondents (14–19) rated all vernacular
Swahili speakers as 'unsophisticated', and of low education (primary and secondary only). What is interesting are the occupations assigned to vernacularized Swahili speakers, which correspond to stereotypes about the communities
who speak that language. The Maasai Swahili speaker is without hesitation
assigned occupations such as 'watchman' (security guard), herdsman, or herbs
and charcoal vendor. The Somali Swahili speaker is thought to own a clothes
shop or café/restaurant and sells camels. The Luhyia Swahili speaker is a
'comedian' or water vendor, while the Kamba Swahili speaker is likely to be
a shoemaker. The Dholuo speaker 'sells fish' or operates a *boda-boda* taxi,
while the Gikuyu speaker is judged as likely to be unemployed, or a butcher, a
mkokoteni driver, or sells water. All speakers with a marked vernacular Swahili
were assigned low-status occupations, revealing teenagers' views that reflect

Table 7 Teenage attitudes towards 'vernacular Swahilis' (age 13–18 years)

	Gikuyu	Dholuo	Kamba	Luhyia	Maasai	Somali
Age	25–30	22–25	20–24	21–24	25+	25+
Looks	*mshamba* (un-sophisticated)	*mshamba* (un-sophisticated)	*mshamba* (un-sophisticated)	*mshamba* (un-sophisticated)	*mshamba* (un-sophisticated)	*kawaida* (ordinary)
Education level	Class 8 (primary)	Form 4 (secondary)	Form 4 (secondary)	Class 8 (primary)	Class 8 (primary)	Class 4
Height	Short	Tall	Short, thin	Tall	Tall (emphatic)	Tall (emphatic)
Honesty	Maybe	No, not much	Yes	Yes	Yes; no	Yes
Intelligence	No	No; yes	No	Yes; no	No	Yes
Leadership	No (Emphatic)	Yes	Yes	Yes	Yes	Yes
Sociability	Yes	Yes	Yes	Yes	Yes; no	Yes
Religiosity	No; yes, maybe	No	Yes	Maybe	No; yes	Yes
Self-confidence	Yes	Yes	Yes	Yes	Yes (Emphatic)	Yes
Character	Good; funny	*Anapenda vita* (likes to fight)	*	*		
Occupation	Unemployed; *mkokoteni; kuuza maji na punda* (water vendor)	*boda-boda* (motorbike taxi); *kuuza samaki* (selling fish)	Shoemaker; *kuuza chapɔɔ* (selling chapati)	'Comedian' or water- vendor	(1) sells charcoal, herbs and sandals; (2) watchman; (3) cattle herder.	(1) selling clothes in a shop; (2) owns a hotel (café/restaurant); (3) sells camels or miraa.

Kenyan stereotypes that are nonetheless grounded in the reality of a division of labour and skills and small trade along ethnic lines. (See Table 7).

The first striking observation is that young female teenagers evaluated all vernacularized Swahili speech samples negatively as unsophisticated 'mshamba' in Sheng/SS or 'country bumpkin' in UK English. None of the vernacularized Swahili speakers is attributed with more than a secondary school level of education, and most are imagined to be primary school leavers, that is, no secondary or higher education. The Maasai, Dholuo, and Somali are imagined as 'tall' and Gikuyu and Kamba Swahili speakers 'short'. Kamba, Luhyia and Somali speakers were evaluated as 'honest' but there was hesitation and divided opinion about Gikuyu and Dholuo speakers on this parameter. Overall, none of the speakers are seen as 'very intelligent', but they are 'sociable' and 'self-confident'. There were peculiar statements by individual participants: one thought that the character behind the Dholuo speaker 'likes to fight', and another one that the Gikuyu speaker sounded 'funny'. In their description of the people they see and interact with daily, they revealed an awareness of the division of labour roles and trades which are rooted in cultural practices or the social history of different Kenyan ethnolinguistic communities. The type of occupations assigned to these language guises were illuminating about Nairobi teenagers' reality in an ethnically stratified socio-economic environment. The Gikuyu speaker, for example, is likely to 'sell water' on a *mkokoteni* around the estates on a donkey (a common occupation in the dry estates of Nairobi), while the Dholuo speaker 'probably' runs a *boda-boda* motorcycle taxi, or 'sells fish'. The person behind the Kamba guise is understood to be a 'shoemaker' or 'sells *chapoo (chapati)*' while the Luhyia speaker either 'sells water', or is a 'comedian' on a TV or radio show. The Maasai man behind the voice probably 'sells charcoal, sandals or traditional herbs' and he may also own cattle or be employed as a watchman (night guard). The Somali man is straightforwardly imagined to be a merchant of clothes in a shop, or 'sells camels or miraa'. He may also own a 'hotel', which in KE refers to a café or restaurant in Standard English. Whether or not this perceived ethnic distribution of *jua kali* trades is real or not, traditional low-status *jua kali* trades (carpentry, masons, older mechanics, etc.) are certainly carried out mainly by speakers of vernacularized Swahili. Modern *jua kali* trades (some mechanics, matatus, hawkers, etc.) are generally carried out in Sheng.

Adult attitudes towards Sheng and Kenyan Swahili

A further 20 adults were subjected to the Matched Guise Test – 10 females and five males – aged between 25 and 40 years, all postgraduate students at Kenyatta University. There are several important differences between the teenage groups and adults. First, they filled in an individual questionnaire response, so there was no group activity or discussions over responses. They all listened to the clips once, after which they were allowed a few minutes to fill out their responses, one voice recording after another. Therefore, we obtained a more personalized profile of responses. Second, their residence cannot be assumed to be Nairobi since many students come to live in the city or suburbs when they first come to the university. In fact, two respondents in this group were international students, one a speaker of Hausa (Nigeria) and the other of Bemba (Zambia) language. Nevertheless, their views were equally important as they revealed an interesting internalization of the same language attitudes that prevail among Nairobians and Kenyans at large: both for example, labelled the Sheng voice as belonging to a '*makanga*' (bus or matatu tout) or 'matatu driver' respectively, referring to the notorious occupation associated with Sheng by many native Kenyans during the test. The Hausa speaking respondent indexed vernacular varieties of Swahili to specific, common types of small trade and such occupations such as 'farmer' for the Dholuo speaker, 'poultry farmer' for the Luhyia voice, 'tout' for the Gikuyu Swahili voice, and 'shop-keeper' for the Somali voice. The results of this Guise Test are summarized into negative (-) and positive (+) or neutral attitudes.

Table 8 Adult male attitudes towards Sheng, KS, English and SS (age 25–44)

	Sheng	Kenyan Swahili (KS)	English	Standard Swahili (SS)
Age	20,25,26	25,25,25	25,26,27	27,26,29
Looks	Young, bad guy from Eastlands; rough	Presentable; smart	Smart; presentable	Smart; presentable
Education level	Form 4 (secondary); Grade 8	Form 4; in college; Form 4	University; degree	College; university
Height	Tall; short	Tall; tall; tall	Short; short; tall	Medium; short; short
Honesty	No; not reliable; frank	Yes;	Yes; yes; yes	Yes; yes; yes

Intelligence	No; average; low	No; moderate	Yes; yes; eloquent; presentable; yes	Yes; no
Leadership	No; bad leader; no	No	Yes	Yes; yes
Sociability	Yes; yes; gang	Yes; yes; yes	Yes	Yes; yes; yes
Religiosity	No; not; pagan	No	Yes	No; maybe; no
Self-confidence	Yes; high self esteem	Yes	Yes; yes; highly	A bit; yes
Character	Outgoing; arrogant	Sociable; nice	Confident; nice	Creative; reserved
Occupation	Casual jobs; driver	Sells *mitumba*; jua kali	Office job; cyber(café) guy	Student; university; *jua kali*; college; businessperson

Observations

Sheng is associated with some negative social markers among this group of male adult respondents: 'a bad guy from the Eastlands'. 'Sheng lacks respect' or is used by 'gang' members. Other descriptors included 'arrogant', 'unreliable' and of low or average intelligence. The Sheng speaker does not make a good leader and on average is aged 25 years, a higher figure than that elicited from teenage respondents. However, he is perceived as 'outgoing', enjoys high self-esteem. He is irreligious ('pagan like'), but frank (opinionated), is of average intelligence, and probably works as a driver or casual worker. KS speakers, on the other hand, are positively evaluated on most scores except leadership, and low-status occupations in petty/informal trade (*mitumba* and *jua kali*). One significant difference between the KS and SS speaker is that the former (KS) is thought to have a lower education level (secondary school), and work in an office or cyber café. However, the SS speaker projects higher social prestige as he is thought to be creative and occupies higher status occupations as a university student or business person. The English speaker is confident, pleasant, has high self-esteem, is presentable and eloquent, studies in university or has an office (white collar) job.

Table 9 Adult female attitudes towards Sheng, KS, English and SS (age 24–43)

	Sheng	Kenyan Swahili (KS)	English	Standard Swahili (Sanifu)
Age	Av. 23	Av. 27	Av. 27	Av. 28
Looks	Young; strong; rugged; wears jeans + t-shirt; shaggy; unkempt; 'dark-skinned'	Young; smart formal	(Very) smart; presentable; tidy; 'thin.'	Smart; presentable; 'stout'
Education level	Form 4 (leaver or dropout) college; undergraduate; graduate; not well-educated	Form 4; in college; Form 4; educated	University; degree; high	College; University; Form 4
Height	Tall; medium	Tall; medium; tall	Short; short; tall; medium;	Medium; short; short
Honesty	Very; yes; 'straight'	Yes; no; yes	Yes; yes; yes	Yes; yes; yes
Intelligence	Yes; intelligent; average; fair	No; yes; quite	Yes;	Yes; yes; no
Leadership	No; bad leader; no; youth leader; average	Yes; no; no	Yes; yes; yes; eloquent;	Yes; yes
Sociability	Yes; yes; very.	Yes; yes; yes	Yes; yes; yes	Yes; yes; yes; not sure
Religiosity	No; not; pagan; no	No; no; no	Yes; not very;	Yes;
Self-confidence	Yes; high self-esteem; courageous; very confident	Yes; yes; yes	Yes; yes; highly	Yes; high
Character	Outgoing; arrogant; questionable; outgoing but a crook; intelligent; free spirit; charming	Sociable; nice; good respectful	Confident; nice; good; social; can be rude; bad; wise; sociable; intelligent	Creative; nice reserved; moral; polite; well mannered; respectful.

Occupation	Casual jobs; driver; *mitumba*; university student; hawker; sells wines and spirits; *makanga*; hustler.	Sells *mitumba*; *jua kali*; civil servant; teacher; sells (pirate) movies; student; office clerk; employed	office job; cyber guy; auditor; bank employee; small business owner; business man; teacher	Student; *jua kali* university; college; business-person; teacher; white collar job; civil servant; business man.

The responses of adult (university) females were very expressive, using an array of descriptors and a more extensive repertoire of vocabulary than their male counterparts. They showed greater independence of expression than the younger respondents. Sheng speakers are described as 'rugged', 'shaggy', 'arrogant', 'free spirit', or of 'questionable character'. The SS speaker is said to be 'creative', 'reserved', 'moral', 'well-mannered' and 'respectful'. The educational level of a Sheng speaker appears to be a mixed bag of Form 4 (secondary school) leaver or dropout, and it could also be an undergraduate university student. In other words, the speaker could have been of any level. Interestingly, at least one respondent opined that the Sheng voice on tape belonged to a 'dark-skinned' man.

Summary

The test of language attitudes in Nairobi demonstrates that they are indeed culturally and socially informed, built around stereotypical views about speakers' language. They are illuminating about a number of things: how people react to language and draw conclusions about the speakers, based on evaluations of the imaginary community behind the speaker, rather than the individual who is talking. The results in general show that indigenous African languages are poorly evaluated even when couched behind a Swahili façade; they are backward (*mshamba*) and unsuitable for high status activities. Their speakers are not attractive to young people, and the occupations linked to them are of low status, undesirable to the young people. The results reflect the general social status assigned to different languages, and that of its speakers including that of non-standard 'Kenyan Swahili' vs H-variety *Kiswahili Sanifu* (SS). They also reveal some of the attitudes of minority groups about their own non-standard dialects or language self-esteem; most Nairobians for example, have positive attitudes towards SS, but the same cannot be said about any other language spoken in Kenya. Many believe that the best or even only way of expressing nationalism is through Swahili, and that the best language for upward mobility is English. In sum, Nairobians have interesting attitudes and feelings, even beliefs about their own languages, and about the languages spoken by others. One interesting feature of the linguistic ecology of Kenya which emerges from this experiment is the fluidity and some tension within the Swahili macrolanguage: on the one hand, Kenyans want to demonstrate a national identity through KS, formal education through SS, and a modern, urban identity through Sheng. At the same time they seem to cling to their ethnic community identities by speaking 'vernacularized Swahilis' which are spoken varieties of Swahili that are noticeably influenced by speakers' vernacular or mother tongue.

Chapter 4:
'Kenyan Swahili': complex and multifaceted

A sketch of more unique features of 'Kenyan Swahili' (KS) will help the reader to better understand Sheng or 'Sheng talk' as integral to ways of speaking Swahili in Kenya. KS is markedly different from the 'official' Standard Swahili (SS – *Kiswahili Sanifu*) which is the 'textbook Swahili' taught in Kenyan (and Tanzanian) schools. Since its creation, 'standard Swahili' was grudgingly accepted by East Africans because some saw the standardization of Swahili by European scholars, missionaries and colonial administrators as a transformation of Swahili into, 'something lifeless at best, unintelligible at worst...it was pejoratively called *Kizungu* ("European language") or *Kiserikali* ("Government language")' (Whitely 1969:87). In Kenya today, some call it '*Kisanifu*' instead of *Kiswahili Sanifu,* in a deliberate tongue-in-cheek violation of SS's own rule that an adjective of Arabic origin such as '*sanifu*' should not bear a concord agreement marker (i.e. the prefix *ki-*). Notwithstanding, SS based on *Kiunguja* (Zanzibar) dialect was successfully implemented by a series of coordinated actions of the East African Language Committee, which was established in 1930 to succeed the Interterritorial Language (Swahili) Committee of 1925. The standard orthography of Swahili quickly took hold in the British ruled east Africa where it was promoted through textbooks, a new dictionary edited by Frederick Johnson (1939), 'correcting' texts before their publication, translations, and training of teachers and authors (ibid:90).

Different political ideologies and state practices produced versions of Swahili, each with a distinctive character and flavour, 'ways of speaking' that make one or the other nation identifiable as a very large 'community of practice' (Wenger 2000). The variations in what is essentially the same language is a literal marking of boundaries of 'us' and 'them' that in itself mirrors national identity. The phrase '*Sisi Wakenya…*' is commonly heard to preface commentary about linguistic (and social or cultural) peculiarities that are shared by members of the speech community of Kenyans who, for example, are famously known for using imperatives rather than polite forms, when making requests. Some literally 'order' for food or services at a 'hotel' – which means a cafe, restaurant or kiosk in Kenyanese – thus it is normal to hear without necessarily being seen as rude, *Nipe chai*! (Give me [a cup of] tea) or *Leta chai mbili hapo*! (Bring two [cups of] tea). Such tendencies may be related to the common association between Swahili language in Kenya, and colonial hierarchies, perhaps even a continuation of 'Kisetla' Swahili discussed in Chapter 1. In contrast, the hypothetical Tanzanian speaker is more likely to say, *Naomba chai mbili, tafadhali* (I [respectfully] request me two [cups of] tea, please). Kenyan Swahili is distinguishable from 'Tanzanian' Swahili, which is characterized by a higher degree of uniformity of speech behaviour in the formal variety, and near-universal use of it in its national territory. 'Congo' Swahili, in its various regiolects (Bunia, Kisangani, Lubumbashi, etc.) has borrowed words from regional languages such as Lingala or Kikongo, and French, the colonial language of that central African region (see, for example, Bokamba 1989 and Nassenstein 2015). Kenyans too speak a form of Swahili that is strongly marked by substrate influences, in pronunciation and grammar, by indigenous languages as well by regional, native dialects of Swahili, vernaculars of the coast communities: words such as *regea* (return) in place of SS *rejea* or *rudi*; 'government' is pronounced by many as '*sirikali*' in the Kimvita (Mombasa) way, rather than '*serikali*' as in Standard (Zanzibari) Swahili, and *runinga* (television) which was coined from the Kiamu dialect, is used more in formal (TV news) Kenyan Swahili than '*televisheni*'. A few more examples of expressions that are typically Kenyan Swahili include: KS: *tupa mbao* (SS: *enda wazimu)* 'lose one's mind'; KS: *matatu* (SS: *gari la abiria* – also *daladala* in Tanzania 'public service vehicle'); KS: *Wanjiku*[1] (SS: *mwananchi wa kawaida – kabwela* or *yahe*, in Tanzania) 'poor, ordinary citizen'; KS: *mdosi/sonko* (SS: *tajiri*) 'wealthy person'; KS: *mpango wa kando* (SS: *hawara*) 'illicit love affair'[lit. 'side arrangement']; and many more.

Consider the following exchange at a *mama mboga* kiosk (Dagoretti Corner, 24 January 2017). *Mama mboga* is KS for small trader in fruits and vegetables (*mboga*) mainly, but also cheap, cooked food. They are strategically located in street corners or neighbourhoods where they sell fruits and vegetables in the evening. Sometimes *mama mbogas* make it easier for tired office workers arriving home to make dinner for their families by selling cut up vegetables; customers can also chat with Mama Mboga as she cuts up the vegetables for them, while she also busily looks after the cooking pots. Traders, *matatu* men, craftsmen and women from nearby *jua kali* workshops making metal windows and doors, wooden furniture and coffins come to eat lunch of *ndengu* (lentils), *chapɔɔ* (chapati), rice and beans (*mandodo*). On this occasion, a young lady waits for Mama Mboga to chop up her order of green collards/kales (*sukuma wiki*) to take away home to prepare dinner. Mama

---

[1] 'Wanjiku' is a common Gikuyu female personal name. It was adopted in national discourse to represent the hardworking (female), exploited proletariat who bears the burden of working to feed the nation.

Mboga goes about busily talking to customers while serving them, sometimes speaking on her mobile phone at the same time.

> [Mama Mboga speaking on a mobile phone]: *Haiya! Umeenda? Kuna mwenye alikuwa anataka mtu wa pikipiki lakini sasa nafikiri ashaapata... Sasa nimepiga lakini hashiki simu...kaa hauko? Unagongwa!*

> *Haiya*! [surprise, indignation] Have you left/gone? There was someone who wanted a motorbike person [*boda-boda* taxi] but now I think s/he has got one already...I've just called but s/he's not picking up [lit. not holding] the phone...if you're not there? You get hit hard [cheated]!

Haiya! is a common interjection to express surprise in Kenyan Swahili, likely to have entered KS from Gikuyu where it is prevalent. It is different but similar to Standard Swahili *Haya/heya* which is more of an expression of encouragement: 'Well done! Come on!' In SS, the verb *ondoka* (leave) would be preferred to *enda* (go), so Mama Mboga's *umeenda?* would be rendered *umeshaondoka? or umeondoka?* using the completive (perfective) aspect of the present tense *-me-* or its variant *-mesha-*. The SS 'completive tense' marker, *-mesha-* (or *-me-*) is regularly simplified in KS, to *-shaa-* seen in the second line of the conversation: *ashaapata.* (SS: *ameshapata).* *Kushika simu* and *kugongwa* are also typical coinages of KS: the former in the place of SS *kupokea simu* (accept/receive a phone [call]), and *kudanganywa*, respectively; the phrases *kaa hauko* (ought) to be *kama huko* in SS. Mama Mboga would not pass a test of proficiency in Standard Swahili although she spoke in a Swahili vernacular that is easily understood by any other Kenyan, young or old. Conversely, a non-Kenyan Swahili speaker may have problems correctly interpreting the short conversation above.

Grammatical features of Kenyan Swahili

A comprehensive grammar of KS is imminent because there are a number of grammatical features that are peculiar to KS, that is, they stand out because they 'deviate' from prescribed norms of SS. Some of them demonstrate aspects of 'analogical change' or 'restructuring' of SS grammar, while others may be as a result of KS contact and mutual influences with other indigenous Kenyan languages. Some of those features of KS that are considered non-standard include the invariable use of NC9 (*Ngeli ya n-/n-*, in Swahili) agreement marker; use of *-enye* instead of *amba-* in relative clauses; peculiar uses of locative suffixes *–ni* and *-ko*; non-standard inflection of negative phrases with monosyllabic verbs; the use on non-standard 'habitual' tense marker *-anga-*; and non-standard uses of diminutive marker (*ka-*) and amplicative (*ki-*).

Analogical change

One of the key areas of study in historical linguistics is 'analogical change', which seeks to eliminate exceptions in the rules of the grammar of a language. Historical linguists traditionally distinguished between 'extension' and 'levelling' as two important subtypes of analogical change. An extension is said to take place when an alternating pattern is introduced to a previously non-alternating paradigm: for example, the irregular *drive/drove* alternation is extended in some (American) English dialects to produce *dive/dove*. In Early Modern English, the past tense of *catch* was the regular *catched*, but this has been replaced by *caught*, apparently in analogy with *taught* (Trask 1996:105). 'Levelling' is the elimination of paradigmatic alternations ('restructuring') whereby exceptional behaviour is regularized, i.e. made to conform to the rest of the paradigm. In SS, for example, the imperative mode is formed by using the verb stem only in the singular, e.g. *Soma*! 'Read!', or by replacing the final vowel with the suffix *-eni* for plural addresse, e.g. *Someni*! 'You (pl) read!' However, the irregular SS imperative forms *njoo/njooni* ('come' (sg/pl) are very rarely heard in KS, instead the restructured forms *kuja/kujeni* are heard everywhere in all KS speech situations. From the point of view of the speaker, levelling and extension may not seem different, since the speaker is in both cases making different patterns more like the patterns that exists in that language.

There is systematic occurrence of analogical change in KS/Sheng such as in the above example. In SS the marker of an infinitive verb is invariably **ku-** and is dropped when the verb is conjugated in any tense or aspect –present, past or future or perfective, etc. This also occurs in the <u>negative</u> or <u>subjunctive</u> modes, whether or not the verb is monosyllabic (one syllable, not counting the invariable infinitive marker, *ku-*, e.g. *ku-la* 'eat' or *ku-fa* 'die') or polysyllabic (more than one syllable, e.g. *ku-so-ma*), as in the following examples where it can be seen that in KS/Sheng the *ku-* prefix is not dropped in monosyllabic verbs in present and past negative tense, nor in both subjunctive and negative imperative forms. The affected verb phrases are underlined to show the contrast between SS and KS forms.

KS/Sheng: Maina <u>*hakuli*</u> *nyama.* (habitual/present tense negative)
SS: Maina <u>*hali*</u> *nyama.*
                    Maina does not eat/is not eating meat.
KS/Sheng: <u>*Hakuji*</u> *leo.* (present tense negative)
SS: <u>*Haji*</u> *leo.*
                    S/he is not coming/won't come today.
KS/Sheng: <u>*Hakukufa*</u> *mara moja.* (past tense negative)
SS: <u>Hakufa</u> mara moja.
                    S/he did not die at once.

KS/Sheng: *Nataka <u>ukule</u> kwanza.* (subjunctive affirmative)
SS: *Nataka <u>ule</u> kwanza.*
           I want <u>you to eat</u> first.
KS/Sheng: *<u>Usikule</u> nyama/Msikule nyama.* (negative imperative, singular
           addressee)
SS: *<u>Usile</u> nyama/Msile nyama.* (negative imperative, plural
           addressees)
           Do not eat meat/ Do not (y'all) eat meat.

In KS, the paradigm of negative subject markers (*ha*+subject marker) is also 'rectified' such that the second person singular is marked by insertion of the subject marker *–u-*, instead of the merging of vowels that takes place across the morpheme boundary in SS: *ha+u > hu-*. The result in KS is *haujui* 'you do not know' instead of SS *hujui* or *<u>haukujangi</u>* instead of SS *<u>huji</u>*. This is comparable to the regularization of the English third-person singular in certain non-standard dialects of English which prefer 'S/he <u>don't</u> know' rather than the irregular 'S/he <u>doesn't</u> know.'

KS*:*   *Wewe <u>haujui</u> kitu!*
SS: *Wewe <u>hujui</u> kitu!*
        You don't know anything!
KS: *Kwa nini wee <u>haukujangi</u> kutuona siku hizi?*
SS: *Kwa nini [wewe] <u>huji</u> kutuona siku hizi?*
        Why don't you come see [visit] us these days?

Habitual tense *-anga*

Perhaps the most significant example of restructuring is the use of the typically Bantu habitual tense marker (suffix) *-aga/-anga* in KS/Sheng, instead of the prefix *hu-* prescribed by Standard Swahili. In fact the prefix *hu-* is unique to Swahili because the *-ag*a suffix (of which *–anga* is a variant) is the most widespread in the Bantu family to which Swahili belongs, linguistically.

KS/Sheng: *<u>Yee</u> hukuj<u>anga</u> hapa kila siku.*
SS: *<u>Yeye</u> <u>huja</u> hapa kila siku.*
           He comes here every day.
Sheng: *<u>Mi</u> ata <u>sijuangi</u> game <u>yake</u>.*
SS: <u>Mimi</u> sijui yeye hutaka/hutafuta nini.
           I <u>don't know</u> what he wants.
KS/Sheng: *Anafany<u>anga</u> kazi tu kwa ofisi ya gavaa.*
SS: *(Yeye) <u>hu</u>fanya kazi katika ofisi ya serikali.*
           He just works in a government office.

KS/Sheng: *Hawaku<u>jangi</u> hapa sana.*
SS: <u>Hu</u>wa hawaji hapa mara nyingi.
              They <u>don't</u> come here often.

The restructured *-aga/-anga* is a recovery/retrieval from older forms of Swahili, rather than a true innovation. It is not restricted to KS/Sheng and is found in other regional varieties of Swahili, including coastal ones. Tanzanian speakers mostly pronounce it as a velar frictative (*-aga*), rather than prenasalized velar stop (*-anga*) as in Sheng/KS.

Rule extension: plural suffix *-ni*

The SS suffix *-ni* (different from the previously seen locative) is typically used to mark plurality (i.e. 2nd person plural) in the imperative mode only, e.g. *karibuni* 'you (plural) welcome', or *sikilizeni* 'you (pl.) listen', etc. For example, in SS, *Karibu<u>ni</u>* 'Welcome (pl)' or *Simame<u>ni</u> tafadhali* 'Stand up/stop you (pl) please' (*simama* also means 'stop'). However, it is quite common in KS/Sheng to use the suffix *-ni* in non-imperative marked contexts, e.g. *hamjambo<u>ni</u>* and even *hawayu<u>ni</u>* (< English: how are you (pl.)?), in place of SS, *hamjambo?* which in fact is a question ('are you (pl.) well?'), not an imperative statement and therefore adding a suffix *-ni* to such non-imperative sentences or clauses is ungrammatical in SS. The over-generalization of the locative suffix *ni* extends, somewhat outrageously, to proper nouns, e.g. *Mambo vipi huko <u>Mombasani</u>?* '(How are things over there <u>in Mombasa</u>?)

Diminutive *ka-* and augmentative *ki-*

In SS the diminutive sense of a noun is expressed by applying the NC7 prefix *ki-* (plural: *vi-*) e.g. *kitoto* 'small little child' (< *mtoto* 'child'), or *kimeza* 'small table' (< *meza*). If the noun to be modified is monosyllabic, the diminutive prefix is *or kiji-/viji-*, for example *kijiti* 'small tree, branch' (< *mti*), or *kijitu* 'small person' (< *mtu*). In some cases, SS uses the same *ki-* to express the augmentative sense e.g. *kijua* 'lots of hot burning sunshine' (< *jua* 'sun').

KS: *Ana <u>ki</u>gari <u>ki</u>kubwa!*
SS: *Ana gari kubwa!'*
              She has a <u>big/huge/impressive</u> car! (NOT 'a small car' as in SS)
KS/Sheng: *<u>Ki</u>mtu <u>ki</u>likuja hapa jana.*
SS: *<u>Ji</u>tu <u>li</u>likuja hapa jana.*
              A big [bad, ugly, unpleasant, etc] person came here yesterday.

KS/Sheng overwhelmingly prefers the prefix *ka-* (plural: *tu-*) only, to express diminutive or affectionate meanings, and *ki-* alone for augmentatives. The diminutive marker *ka-* is not used in this way at all in SS, but it is very common in Bantu languages such as Gikuyu or Oluluhyia or farther afield in languages such as Otjiherero (Herero) of Namibia (Möhlig et al 2002). Therefore, *kitoto* (small child) in SS is *katoto* in Sheng/KS, and SS *kijua* (hot, unpleasant sun) seen above is in fact *kajua* 'little (pleasant) sunshine' in KS/ Sheng. The Nairobi Data Set contains numerous examples of this such as the following.

KS/Sheng: *Wachana na hako kamtu.*
SS: *Achana na hicho kijitu.*
           Leave that (silly) <u>little fellow</u> alone.
KS/Sheng: *Kalikuwa katoto kadogo!*
SS: *Kilikuwa kitoto kidogo!*
           It was a [mere] <u>little child</u>!
KS/Sheng: *Uzuri nilikuwa na kasimu kengine hadi hakana kifuniko.*
SS: *Kwa bahati nilikuwa na kisimu kingine kidogo hata hakina kifuniko.*
           Luckily I had a <u>little [cheap] phone</u> that did not even have a cover.

In sum, SS and KS/Sheng create amplicative meaning by different means. In fact, the prefix *ki-* (or *kiji-*) is the chief strategy used in SS to derive diminutive meaning, whereas KS/Sheng uses the same prefix to create amplicative sense.

Phonology

There are differences in articulation (pronunciation) and sound patterns (phonology) between KS and SS. Sheng loan words tend to be clipped (shortened), and to end in long, open syllables, e.g. *ɔchaa* (< Gikuyu: *gĩcagi*, 'upcountry'); *mtɔii* (< SS: *mtoto*, 'child'); *tichɛɛ/mtichɛɛ* (< English: 'teacher'); *mɔshenee* (< Gikuyu: *mũcene*, 'gossip'); *dɛree* (< SS: *dereva* 'driver'); *salɔɔ* (< English: 'salary'); *kijanaa/vijanaa* (< SS: *kijana/vijana*, 'youth/s'). The simplification of syllables extends across morphological boundaries, which affects syllable structure and causes the weakening of glides or 'semi-vowels' (y, w), e.g. *naeza/siezi* (I can/I cannot) instead of *naweza/siwezi*.

Prenasalization of the velar fricative /g/ is a common feature of Sheng, such that it is pronounced as *-anga* instead of *-aga* in the case of the previously seen habitual tense marker. A number of respondents believed that this was 'to make Sheng sound like Kikamba', a Bantu language that is widely spoken in Nairobi by a community of speakers who have a strong presence in the city's Eastlands housing estates. It make sense, because Sheng welcomes features of different Kenyan languages, as we have already seen, from Gikuyu, Luhyia and Dholuo. The prenasalization is strongly marked, almost exaggerated and therefore highly noticeable suggesting a conscious effort to create difference between Sheng and *Kisanifu*, rather than merely a question of mother tongue interference in Swahili. Sheng speakers take in stigmatized features of Swahili as a positive marker of difference.

-enye relative pronoun

A relative clause is one that is linked to its antecedent by a pronoun such as 'who', 'which', or 'that' and 'those', in English. For example, 'The person **_who_** wanted a motorbike taxi.' The SS relative pronoun is *amba-*, which takes an 'agreement' suffix (ending) such as *-ye* (NC1), which in this case corresponds to the antecedent or subject *mtu* (person), that is, '**Mtu** *ambaye alitaka boda-boda.*' Sitting at a high-end cafe restaurant in Nairobi, I overheard this question uttered by one waitress to another (25 January 2017).

KS: *Si uiangalie kwanza nisikupatie kitu yenye si poa?*
SS: *Si uiangalie kwanza [ili] nisikupe kitu ambacho si kizuri?*
          Why don't you look at it first so I don't give you something which is not good?

In KS/Sheng the relative pronoun *-enye* is most frequently used instead of the SS *amba-*. Many examples of these non-standard uses can be obtained in any short conversation, as when Mama Mboga said in the earlier conversation: *mtu mwenye alikuwa anataka pikipiki*, instead of SS *mtu ambaye alikuwa anataka pikipiki*. There are many more examples littered in interviews with Nairobians, such as the following:

KS: mtu *mwenye alikuja hapa*
SS: *mtu ambaye alikuja hapa*
          the person who came here
KS: watu *wenye walikimbizwa*
SS: watu *ambao walifukuzwa*
          those who were chased
KS: *kitu chenye sitaki*
SS: *kitu ambacho sitaki*
          [the] thing [that] I don't want

A peculiar form of *-enye* seems to have taken hold in KS, when it links a NC7 (*ki-/vi-*) noun, in a relative clause: the underlying form *ki-* remains unmodified ('unpalatalized') as it normally should in SS where the surface form of the prefix *ki-*is normally realized (i.e. actual pronounciation in SS) as *ch-* before vowels: Kitabu *ki+angu* > **cha**, e.g. kitabu **changu** 'my book', *ki + e* > **che**, e.g. *kitabu chenye picha* 'a book that has pictures', etc. This non-standard use can occur even in the beginning clauses which are truncated sentences, as in these examples obtained from a narrative told by a 17 year old secondary school student:

KS: ...*kenye nataka ni dɔɔ zangu*
SS: ...*nina<u>ch</u>otaka ni pesa zangu (<u>chenye</u> nataka)*
...<u>what</u> I want is my mo*ney*
KS: *<u>Kenye</u> tulikuwa tunangojea ni majibu.*
SS: *(Kitu <u>ambacho</u>) tulikuwa tunangojea ni majibu.*
<u>What</u> we were waiting for were answers.

Noun classification

KS 'deviates' a lot from SS in the area of agreement and concord system, which is typical of Swahili and most other Bantu languages: nouns and adjectives 'agree', i.e. the NC marker of the subject is mapped onto dependent nominals in an manner that produces some kind of alliteration, such as ***<u>Kitabu</u> kile kizuri kimenifikia*** (That nice book has reached me) or ***<u>Wazee</u> watatu walikuta <u>simba</u> mfu*** (Three elders came upon a dead lion). In these two examples, the head nouns (NC7 and NC2, respectively) are underlined. However, a common feature of KS is the invariable use of NC9/NC10 agreement markers *i-/ya-* which represents a drastic simplification of the elaborate noun classification (*ngeli*) of SS. Unsurprisingly, this is an area of focus (*ngeli*) in primary and secondary school Swahili textbooks, lessons and examinations – in effect trying the difficult job of trying to correct 'errors' that young Kenyans pick up daily from their immediate, natural environment such as the following:

KS: *<u>Hii</u> chama yetu itapigania <u>kiti</u> ya urais* [politician].
SS: *<u>Hiki</u> chama chetu kitapigania <u>kiti</u> cha urais.*
This our [political] party will fight for the presidential seat.
KS: *<u>kitu</u> yenye si poa* [young waitress]
SS: *kitu amba<u>cho</u> si **kizuri**/hakifai*
something unsuitable
KS: ***<u>Mashule</u>** zote zimefungwa sasa* [school headteacher].
SS: *<u>Shule</u> zote zimefungwa sasa.*
All schools are now closed.

It is too easy to assume that the deviations are a result of lack of 'competence' in SS generally, because they really are what Kenyans learn to speak from their linguistic environment. Perhaps it is also due to the effects of mother tongue interference especially among those who speak different Bantu languages with different noun classificatatory systems from SS. It is common to hear in Kenyan Swahili what are ungrammatical sentences such as *Chakula <u>hii</u> ni <u>mzuri</u>* (This food is good/tasty) instead of SS, *Chakula <u>hiki</u> ni <u>kitamu</u>.* A parallel sentence in Sheng talk would similarly use NC9 agreement markers (instead of NC7 in this case), but the adjective (-*zuri*) is replaced with the non-SS (Sheng) verb -*bamba*: *Chakula hii inabamba* (lit. 'This food is hitting [the spot]'). I also noted earlier that general KS has features originating from non-standard, native dialects of Swahili (i.e. non-Zanzibari) including noun agreements and adjective concords, such as the following examples obtained during a conversation with an elderly man in Siu, a native speaker of Kipate dialect of Swahili spoken on the Lamu archipelago in northern Kenya:

Kipate:	*Hiki ni kijana kidogo.*
SS:	*Huyu ni kijana mdogo.*
	This is a young person.
Kipate:	*Sisi hapa ni makulima.*
SS:	*Sisi hapa ni wakulima.*
	We are farmers here.

Locatives -*ni* and -*ko*

In SS, the idea of place or location is expressed by adding a suffix -*ni* to a noun. The derived noun then shifts to noun class (*ngeli*) 16/17/18, and subsequent concords (after adding -*ni*) must also change to 'agree' with the new noun. For example, the noun *nyumba* 'house' changes to *nyumbani* 'at/in a house' or less literally, 'home'. Therefore in SS *nyumba yangu* means 'my house' but *nyumbani kwangu* means 'at/in my house' i.e. at home. Note that the agreement marker in the first instance is *y*- but in the second instance, it is *ku*- (NC17) which becomes modified to *kw*- in speech and writing (*ku+a > kwa*). In another example, 'our classroom' is *darasa letu* but 'in our classroom' becomes *darasani kwetu.*

KS overwhelmingly uses a separate word, *kwa*, in place of the suffix -*ni* to describe location. In effect, the SS sentence *Kitabu kiko nyumbani* (The book it is at home) is expressed in KS as *Kitabu kiko kwa nyumba*. In KS *Mwalimu yuko darasani* (The teacher is in the classroom) is rendered *Mwalimu yuko kwa darasa*. In KS *Bado hajatoka kwa nyumba* is 'corrected' in SS as *Bado hajatoka nyumbani* (S/he has not left home) (cl 16). In a Sheng narrative, there are numerous examples of sentences such as *Nilikuwa na ma-coins kadhaa kwa mfuko* (SS: *Nilikuwa na sarafu kadhaa mfukoni*) 'I had a few coins in the pocket'.

SS also makes a clear distinction between the locative (place) particle -*ko* marked with a subject (e.g. *Niko nyumbani* 'I am at home') and the present tense form of the verb *kuwa na* (to be/have), e.g. *Kuna mtu nyumbani* ('There is someone at home'). However, Kenyan Swahili does not make this distinction and similar behaviour has been observed in the Kisangani and Bunia Swahili (Congo) varieties (Nassenstein 2015):

KS:	_Iko waruu?_
SS:	_Kuna viazi?_
	Are there potatoes?
KS:	_Uko na dɔɔ/pesa?_
SS:	_Una pesa?_
	Do <u>you have</u> money?
KS:	_Niko na watoto watatu._
SS:	_Nina watoto watatu_
	<u>I have</u> three children.
KS:	_Niko mgonjwa_ (also in KS: _Najisikia mgonjwa._)
SS:	_Ninaumwa._
	<u>I am</u> ill.

Contact influences on Kenyan Swahili

Kuna Sheng ya Kikikuyu, na Sheng ya Kijaluo, hivyo hivyo.
There is Kikuyu Sheng and Dholuo Sheng, and so on.

Male, 18 years old, Eastleigh, 9 February 2017

All languages are dynamic systems which are always in the process of change. Ultimately, the change is systematic and follows certain orderly principles. Some changes occur from within the linguistic system, but most linguistic change is induced by contact with other languages. Lexical innovations (word borrowing) is the most common phenomenon in multilingual situations, and such changes tend to be easiest to notice. KS shows influences from a variety of typologically different languages spoken in Kenya: Nilotic (Dholuo), Bantu (Gikuyu), Germanic (English), and so on. Grammatical changes are far less frequent, but some examples can be found in KS. In one instance, I overheard a man requesting another to call someone else on his (the speaker's) behalf in the following way: *_Si_ **_unimw_**_itie?_ by which he meant 'why don't you call **him/her** for **me**?'). This is ungrammatical (hence the asterisk) because SS does not permit the marking of two objects (in bold) in the same clause (-_ni_-, 1st person singular, and -_mw_- 3rd person singular). But this is possible in Gikuyu (**_mũ-nj-ĩtĩ-r-e_** -- OM1-OM2-call-TS-APPL-FV (call <u>him/her</u> for <u>me</u>) which as we shall see, has many influences upon Kenyan Swahili.

Conversely, Swahili also affects the morphology of other languages, especially among urban, bilingual speakers. For example, some use the invariable Swahili object marker -_ni_- (1st personal singular (NC1)) in place of the Gikuyu one which varies in different phonological environments created by crossing of morpheme boundaries. Among Nairobians and other urban Gikuyu speakers, I have observed the use of ungrammatical structures such as: *kũ-ni-ngũtha**(kũ + OM1 + verb), instead of *kũngũtha* (*kũ-n-gũtha*) 'to hit me' or *Ekwendaga kũ-ni*-test 'S/he wanted to test **me**' which in this case is parallel to the code-mixing in Kenyan Swahili, *Alitaka ku-ni*-test. Such mutual contact influences on the grammar of Kenyanese may become permanent features of it.

However it is true that most influences on Sheng come as loan words, the largest 'donor' languages being English, Gikuyu and Dholuo in proportionate order. To a lesser extent Luhya, Kamba and Taita influences are attestable in Sheng. SS itself has very many loan words from Arabic, Persian and a few other Asian languages (Lodhi 2000, Zawawi 1979). It has more recently borrowed heavily from English, and some from Portuguese and German earlier on. KS and Sheng have carried on this long tradition but the borrowing and code-mixing in KS/Sheng seems to consciously move away from English, Arabic and Swahili, and towards indigenous languages. The following are a few examples of common expressions in KS with SS equivalents:

KS/Sheng: *tupa mbao; noki*
SS: *enda wazimu*
lose one's mind

KS: *matatu*
SS: *gari la abiria (daladala* in Tanzania)
public service vehicle

KS/Sheng: *mathee/masa/mɔkɔrɔ*
SS: *mama*
mother

KS/Sheng: *Wanjiku*
SS: *kabwela (*also: *yahe* Tanzania*)*
ordinary citizen

KS/Sheng: *buda/budaa/mzaɛɛ/fathɛɛ*
SS: *baba*
father

KS/Sheng: *chanuka*
SS: *erevuka*
be smart/savvy

The expression *mundu khu mundu* (lit. 'man to man'; a face off, challenge) used in KS is from Oluluhya (Luhyia), as is the word *inghoko* for 'chicken' (Chimerah 1998). An interesting Luhyia influence upon KS is the addition of the suffix *-ko* to verb clauses, but this may simply be a devoiced form of the habitual tense suffix *–aga,* coupled with a common Kenyan habit of replacing the final vowel of Swahili with that of another Bantu language (**a** > **o**):

KS: *Tunakwendako hɔm.*
SS: *Tunakwenda/tunaenda nyumbani.*
          We are going home.
KS: *Si unipe* twenty bob *nikuangalilieko hiyo gari?*
SS: *Si unipe shilingi ishirini nikuchungie hiyo gari?*
          Why don't you give me twenty shillings I look after that car?

Dholuo

Dholuo (Luo) is known as *Kijaka* in Sheng, and *Kijaluo* in SS. It is a Nilotic language with numerous speakers in the heartland of Sheng among the residents of the Eastlands and Kibera and elsewhere that Sheng is vibrantly used at all times. As a result, Dholuo influences the language and cultural life of Nairobi, including food practices (fish, *ugali*), and music such as *Ohangla* style and *Benga* which is more broadly a Nairobian music style but with greatest influence from Luo music tradition. The common KS/Sheng phrase *mos mos* (also: *omole*) means 'slowly' and is from Dholuo *mos*, which also means 'slow'. It was popularized by a young musician (E-Sir) who produced a (2002) hit song titled, '*Mos mos*', with the choral lyrics, *Wacha presha... kuja mos mos!* ('Stop being in a rush... come slowly'). Another Dholuo word that is common in Sheng is *Jakom*, a term of respect used to mean 'leader' or 'chairman' generally. The Sheng word for 'calf' of the leg in Ofafa/Jericho area is *ɔngwarɔɔ*, of the same meaning with its original Dholuo source, the only difference being the lengthened final vowel in the Sheng version.

Perhaps the greater contribution of Dholuo to Sheng/KS is phonological. It seems that words borrowed from any language – Swahili, English, and Gikuyu – follow a common pattern found in Luo language – the prefixation of o/ɔ- to proper nouns, i.e. names of people and places (Okombo 1997). Examples of this in Sheng include words such as, *odukɔɔ* (<Swahili *duka*) 'shop'; *odush* 'bird' < Gikuyu *ndutura*); *orezɔɔ* (< English 'president'); *orifɔɔ* (English 'school prefect'); *Oriosh* or *Oriobaa* (< Kariobangi, a housing estate in the Eastlands); *ɔbakɔɔ* and *ɔnyatɔɔ* (Kibaki and (Jomo) Kenyatta, two former presidents); *ɔrismo* (<Christmas); *ɔrurɔɔ* (< *ndururu*, Swahili 'five (Kenyan) cents'); *ɔrwarɔɔ* (< Swahili *suruali*) 'shorts', and many more. Sheng's role in acting as bridge between Kenyan languages is best exemplified by Sheng word *ɔdherɔɔ* (also *ɔtheng'aa*) whose origin is the Gikuyu word *githeri* – a simple, staple dish made of boiled maize and beans that has grown very popular as it is affordable and readily available in markets and kiosks of Nairobi's low-income neighbourhoods. Similarly, /ɔkuyɔɔ/ the Sheng word for Gikuyu people, or individual (SS *Mkikuyu/Wakikuyu*) is made up of Dholuo morphology (ɔ- prefix), and Sheng's uniquely heavy syllables (long vowels) in word-final position.

Gikuyu

The Gikuyu language is known in Sheng as *Kisapere,* and *Kikikuyu* in SS. It has the most significant influence on Sheng regarding word borrowing and coinage, phonology and even morphosyntax. This is due to a predominance of speakers of this language who form a majority in the country, in Nairobi (see data counts), and in the peripheral metropolitan region of the city. Gikuyu speakers occupy ubiquitous occupations in Nairobi's small trade and service industry, in markets, streets and neighbourhoods – as *mama mbogas*, *mitumba* sellers, and in the *matatu* industry (Wa Mũngai 2013). The densely populated northern and western limits of Nairobi which spill over into Kiambu county are historically the residential areas of this community. As a result of these factors, there is a proportionately larger number of Gikuyu speakers among the city's residents, traders and workers of the *jua kali* industry. Of course, many non-Gikuyu speaking Nairobians live in these areas, to commute into the city, or work and trade within these rapidly expanding suburbs such as Kangemi, Uthiru, Limuru, Githurai, Kahawa, and so on. Many Sheng speakers who have grown up in the Eastlands understand Gikuyu to varying degrees of competence, as Gikuyu speakers themselves do of other languages such as Dholuo. They have had close interaction, living together and growing up together in a multi-ethnic neighbourhood, where a common socio-economic status works to de-emphasize ethnic and linguistic differences. At Mama Mboga's shop in Dagoretti Corner, the conversation continued to flow and shift with a different customer, middle aged, male. The Gikuyu word for potatoes (*war<u>uu</u>*) replaces the Standard Swahili *viazi* in one question in this conversation (*waruu*), with a final long (heavy) syllable which is common in Sheng, an innovation because that final syllable is short in Gikuyu. In the next line of the conversation, however, SS *maharagwe* (beans) is used. Such code switching with Gikuyu is common in KS and Sheng. Some traditional Gikuyu foods are popular nationally, such as *githɛri*, *mɔkimɔɔ*, and *waruu* which are known to Nairobians by those same Gikuyu names, now part of Kenyan Swahili:

Customer:	*Iko waruu?*
SS:	*Kuna viazi?*
	Are there potatoes?
Mama Mboga:	*Imeisha.*
SS:	*Vimekwisha.*
	They're finished.
Customer:	*Maharagwe?*
SS:	*Maharagwe?*
	Beans?
Mama Mboga:	*Iko.*
SS:	*Yako.*
	There are.

The Gikuyu word for 'grandmother', *cũcũ* (IPA: šɔšɔ) has taken such a hold in KS via Sheng (i.e. with an elongated final syllable, *shoshoo*) that it has practically replaced SS *nyanya* among Nairobians. The vowels in the *shoshoo* are different from those of SS, and mirror those of the donor language,

Gikuyu. We shall see many more examples of this phenomenon in the next chapters. Adult speakers also use *shɔshɔɔ*, especially when talking to children. In the following exchange, three Gikuyu loans that are very common in Sheng are highlighted: *mɔkɔrɔ* (parent, older person) which is another Gikuyu loan (*mũkũrũ*) which means 'elder' (not 'parent'), a term of respect, and *wera*, Sheng for 'work, place of employment', from Gikuyu *wĩra* of the same meaning.

Question	Response
Sheng/KS*: Ako wapi <u>shɔshɔɔ</u>?*	Sheng: *Ako hɔm.*
SS: *Yuko wapi <u>nyanya/bibi</u>?*	SS: *Yuko nyumbani.*
Where is grandmother?	*She's at home.*

Question	Response
Sheng: *Ameenda wapi <u>mokoroo</u>?*	Sheng: *Ako <u>wera</u>.*
SS: <u>*Mama/baba*</u> *ameenda wapi*?	SS: *Yuko <u>kazini</u>.*
Where is mom/dad?	She is at work.

The common KS word for 'upcountry or rural home' is *ushagoo* (IPA: ušaɣoo) with two variations in Sheng, *ochaa/ocha* (IPA: očaa/oča). It complements *moshadha* (IPA: mɔšaða) (< Mũcatha) the Gikuyu name of a village very near Nairobi's northern end, but it has acquired indefiniteness, to mean 'rural home' anywhere in Kenya. *Usapere* means 'kikuyuness', the abstract noun derived from the Sheng word for the language (Kisapere), using regular Swahili morphology of applying the prefix *u-* to create an abstract noun. The word *ngiri* ('thousand') also from Gikuyu is widely used in place of SS *elfu* (< Arabic), as is *thaɔ/thaɔɔ* from English 'thousand'. Other Gikuyu loans in KS/Sheng include *mokimo/mokimoo* (mashed potatoes and beans or peas), *gidheri* (boiled maize and beans), *ngwashɛɛ* (sweet potatoes), *madaha* (similar to *mokimoo*), and *ndumaa* (arrowroot) – all traditional Gikuyu foods which now enjoy wide popularity among Kenyans of all ethnic backgrounds. Other KS/Sheng loans from Gikuyu include *wathii* (< *athii* 'passengers'), *mɔkɔrɔ* (< *mũkũrũ* 'elder').

Gikuyu slang in Sheng

A significant proportion of Gikuyu loans in KS are slang words and expressions, reflecting the type of register of contact and subsequent borrowing. This links some registers of Sheng talk to operators of the *matatu* industry known as *manamba* or *makanga*, The latter is a word of Gikuyu origin in reference to 'tribal police (*makanga,* singular: *ikanga*) who, having no food allowance, used to demand food from those on whom they served warrants'

(Benson 1964:208). Today's *makanga* employ a rough, demanding manner of interaction with passengers, almost as if they are demanding loot rather than a bus fare; these men are frequently reported to have physically injured passengers. In Sheng talk *nduthi* is a motorbiker or a *boda-boda* (SS: *pikipiki*) from Gikuyu *nduthi* which is used among *boda-boda* operators who are predominantly (young) males. There are many examples of Sheng words not found in SS, which are drawn from Gikuyu: *mɔhahɛɛ* (< Gikuyu *mũhahĩ*, 'gossip'); *marimaa* (Gikuyu < *irima* 'drinking den'); *mɔkɔrɔɔ* (< Gikuyu *mũkũrũ* 'elder, parent'). The primary (literal) meaning of *guoko* in Gikuyu is (1) 'hand' (SS: *mkono*), but other secondary, metaphorical or figurative (slang) meanings have passed onto Sheng, (2) 'fight' and (3), 'five' or 'fifty'. Both extended meanings (2) and (3) are figurative, evoking a fist fight in (2) and the image of fingers folded into a fist to indicate the number 'five' or 'five tens', i.e. fifty or five hundred in (3). *Guoko* is also used in Gikuyu expression *'cookia guoko'* now a calque in KS/Sheng, *rudisha mkono* meaning 'to return a favour'. It also means 'to give back change to a passenger' among the *matatu* operators (*manambas/makangas*) while the plural *moko* (hands) refers to 'windscreen wipers' (Wa Mũngai 2013:237). Gikuyu slang words in Sheng also include *ngware*[2] (SS: *asubuhi mapema, alfajiri*, 'early in the morning, dawn'); *thɔka* (< Gikuyu *thũũka*[3] 'become, go bad, get rough, get worse, hard or difficult); *kɛrɛndɛ* (SS: *umati* 'crowd'), from Gikuyu *kĩrĩndĩ* 'crowd, a mass of people'. The verb *nyita* means 'grasp' in two senses in Gikuyu: a physical one, and a conceptual one (figurative) but in Sheng it is used only in the latter sense of 'understand', e.g. *Umenyita [rada]*? ('Do you understood [the plot/story]?'). *Marima* is Sheng/KS for a 'drinking den' (also *Mama Pima*) which comes from Gikuyu *marima*, (singular, *irima*, 'hole' and dim. *karima*). *Ngai!* or alternatively, *Ngai fafa!* or *Ngaatho!* (exclamation of shock or surprise) are used by female speakers, according to personal observations. The extent of their use in Sheng or general KS is so significant that they have acquired a text (SMS) orthography – NGFF – which is equivalent to English OMG (Oh my God!). It can be regarded as one of the many examples we shall see of Sheng's interaction with global influences and trends in social media.

The verb *ɔra* (SS: *enda, ondoka*) 'go, leave' is also a Gikuyu loan in Sheng (< *ũra*, 'run off/away'):

Sheng:	*Hiyo mathree ili*ɔ*ra kitambo.*
SS:	*Hiyo matatu iliondoka kitambo.*
	That matatu left a long time ago.

---

[2] Also: *rengwa* (transposition of *ngware*).
[3] SS: *chacha, haribika.*

The English loan 'class' in Gikuyu is *kĩraathi* [kɛradhi] and it has two meanings in the language: (1) classroom (2) socio-economic 'class'. The second meaning has passed into Sheng/KS in place of rarely heard SS *tabaka*, of Arabic origin. However, the clipped forms of *keradhi* (*ɔlasɔɔ, darɔɔ* or *dach* from SS *darasa*) refer to 'classroom' in Sheng. It is more complicated since the SS *darasa* is an Arabic loan where it refers to religious instruction/class (*madrassa*). *Kiwaruu* is also Gikuyu slang mainly among children to mean 'envy' or 'jealousy'. It is has been borrowed by Sheng with the same meaning, and it is frequently heard in place of SS *wivu*. Another Gikuyu slang word, *kĩrai*, means 'empty' in Sheng, with the additional meaning of 'free, freebie' in the same way as in its Gikuyu original meaning of 'free, gratuitous':

KS/Sheng: <u>*Mathrii ya first*</u> *ilikuwa* **kirai.**
SS: <u>*Gari la kwanza la abiria*</u> *lilikuwa* <u>*tupu*</u>.
             The first matatu was empty.

Some Sheng words for money are Gikuyu loans, including *mbao* 'twenty shillings' and *ngiri* 'one thousand [shillings]', < Gikuyu *ngiri*, 'thousand' (SS: *elfu moja*), also called *muti* from *mutĩ* which is another Gĩkuyu slang word for 1000 shillings. It is interesting how Sheng sometimes favours Gikuyu or other Kenyan indigenous language loans, instead of English or Arabic ones. For example, in Sheng talk, one may use *mbathi* (or *buu*) which are English loans via Standard Swahili (SS: *basi*, from English 'bus') instead of *basi*, for example, and *tenee*, also a Gikuyu word (adjective, *tene*) meaning 'old' instead of SS *-a zamani*, or the more common SS adjectival root *-zee* (old):

Sheng: *Ile* **mbathi** *ni ya* **tenee**
SS: *Ile basi ni ya zamani/ile basi ni nzee*
         That is an old bus.

Most Gikuyu loans in Sheng are nouns; there were only five verbs in the full list of Gikuyu loans obtained from our collected speech data (Table 10, Nairobi Data Set, 2002–2017), including some of the examples discussed above.

Table 10 Some Gikuyu loans in Kenyan Swahili/Sheng (NDS 2002–2017)

Sheng	Gikuyu	Gloss	Comment
dhuti	*thuuti*	suit	Gikuyu pronounciation of dh/th.
gecagi	*gĩcagi*	upcountry	Also: *oshagɔɔ, ocha/ɔcha, ochaa/ ɔchaa.*
gɛthaa	*gĩthaa/ ithaa*	time, period	e.g. *manze hii si githaa poa na waks.* 'Man this is not a good time to work' (example from GoSheng, Kamusi ya Sheng)

gidhɛri	gĩtheri	githeri	a simple traditional Gikuyu meal of maize and beans. Also: *odherɔɔ, odede, otheng'a*
gɔdha	gũtha	con (someone)	Gikuyu 'hit'. Informal/slang: 'con, cheat'
guoko (1)	guoko	(fist)fight	Gikuyu 'hand'. Informal/slang: 'fist fight'
guoko (2)	guoko	five shillings	'five', alluding to the fingers of the hand. Also *kɔbole*
shanɔra	canũra	make (street) smart	colloquial Gikuyu, e.g. *Sheng inashanɔra watu* 'Sheng makes people smart'
wɛra	wĩra		Gikuyu 'work'
kɛrɔrɔ	kĩrũrũ	alcoholic drink	traditional brew made with sugar cane, consumed widely in central Kenya and Nairobi. Another is *chibuku* made of millet/maize from western Kenya
kɛradhi	kĩraathi	social status ('class')	implies 'high' class in colloquial Gikuyu: *ũcio nĩ wa kĩraathi* 's/he is of [the] high class'
kɛwaru	kĩwaru	jealousy	colloquial Gikuyu. Fig. choked up feeling like a potato blocking the throat of a person filled with jealousy. Used by children to taunt each other
gɔrɔka	gũrũka	go mad, crazy	same meaning
thɔka	thũka	go bad, tough	same in [informal] Gikuyu registers, e.g *kumethɔka, jo!* 'things are bad, man!'
nyita	nyita	grasp, understand	'grasp, hold', physically, and figuratively, 'grasp, understand'
umɛra	umĩra	go/come out	same meaning
marima	marima	drinking den	literally 'a hole' and also fig. 'drinking den'
mbao/mbaɔ	mbaũ	twenty shillings	informal, same meaning
mɔhahɛ/ mɔhahɛɛ	mũhahĩ	gossip	same meaning
mɔkɔrɔ	mũkũrũ	elderly woman	same meaning

ndudhi	*nduthi*	motorbike	same meaning
ng'edhia	*ng'ethia*	stare, be idle	same meaning
ngiri	*ngiri*	a thousand shillings	same meaning
Ngomongo	*Ngomongo*	a housing estate	Gikuyu: hard rock; poor place. Also: *Ngomosh* in Sheng
ngware	*ngware*	early morning	same meaning. Also: *rengwa*
nudhu	*nudhu*	half	same meaning. < SS *nusu*
todhi	*tothi*	toast	from SS *tosti* (< English)
waruu	*waru*	chips	'potatoes'. Also *chipɔɔ, chibo, njiva*, etc.
wadhii	*athii*	passengers	'travellers'. The NC2 (plural) prefix *a-* is replaced by a SS one, *wa-*

Chapter 5
Features of Sheng

The chief characteristic features or markers of Kenyan Swahili (KS) and Sheng are lexical and phonological, the two main sites of exchange in any language contact situation. But the speech codes also demonstrate morpho-syntactic variation, with interesting implications for the direction and per-manence of linguistic change in KS. Variations in Sheng or KS also reveal substrate influences from different Kenyan languages. This chapter identifies some of those features specific to Sheng talk which exist alongside but are distinguishable from general KS.

Phonological innovations

Although all sounds of Sheng are also found in Standard Swahili's inventory, some occur with greater frequency in Sheng, and in places where they do not in Standard Swahili (SS). The consonant sounds /sh/ (IPA: [š]) and /ch/ (IPA: [č]. occur frequently in final position of Sheng words (e.g. *odush* /oduš/ 'dove' or *Kibich* /kibič/ 'Kibera'). This is different from SS (and all Bantu languages), which does not allow consonant endings. Sheng vowels also tend to be elongated when in final position (e.g. *ochaa* /ɔčaa/ 'village, rural area', *ndɔmaa* 'arrowroot', *shugee* /šugɛɛ/ 'sugar' and so on. Certain Sheng vowels are lower in articulation than their canonical counterparts, as we have already observed. Swahili's orthographic <e> and <o> used to write Sheng are pho-netically IPA: [ɛ] and [ɔ], respectively. This is possibly an influence from Dholuo and Gikuyu, since they are ubiquitous in both languages, which also dominate in Sheng's primary ecology (Nairobi). Syllable reduction is also quite common, particularly by deletion of glides (y, w) resulting in a diph-thong e.g. *naweza > naeza*; *siwezi > siezi* 'I can/I can't'; *yenyewe > enyewe*, etc. In many cases, bi-syllabic Swahili stems are reduced to monosyllabic ones in Sheng, e.g. *sikiliza > skiza* 'listen' or *jisikia > jiskia* 'feel for oneself'. Final syllables are also likely to be deleted or replaced with long-V (heavy) single syllables. A prime example is the SS phrase *sasa hivi* 'right now, just now', which is widely rendered as *saa hii* in all registers of both Sheng talk and KS. The same applies with personal pronouns, with the exception of *wao* 'they' which does not have a deletable onset for the second syllable:

SS	Sheng		Example + SS equivalent and gloss
mimi	*mi/mii*	I	*Mi ata sijuangi* game *yake.* *Mimi hata sijui nia yake.* I don't know even what he's up to.
wewe	*wee*	you	*Wee unajiskiaje?* *Wewe unajisikiaje?* How are you feeling?
yeye	*ye/yee*	she/he	*Ye hukujanga hapa* daily. *Yeye huja hapa kila siku.* S/he comes here daily.
ninyi	*nyii*	you (pl)	*Nyii mna-*do? *(Ninyi) mnafanya nini?* What are you (pl.) doing?
wao	*wao*	they	No reduction.
sisi	*sii*	we/us	*Sii hapa huongea tu Sheng.* *Sisi hapa huongea Sheng tu.* Here we speak Sheng only.

In other cases, when an existing final vowel is lengthened, stress shifts from the penultimate syllable to the final (long) one, thus syllable structure of some SS words is altered in Sheng by simplifying two syllables, and turning them into one 'heavy' syllable, i.e. one long vowel. Examples: *madha* > *madhεε* 'mother'; *vijana* > *vijanaa* 'youths'; *raiya* > *raiyaa* 'people'; *hivi* > *isivii* 'this way'. Some greetings and spatial expressions also provide some evidence of reduction of forms derived from SS, and influenced by English equivalents in a perfect recipe of Sheng e.g., *Walapaa!* casual greeting (< 'What's up!'); *Niwatize?* ('What's going on?'); *Niaje?* (< 'It is what/what's up?'); *asapaa* 'right here' (< SS *hapa hapa*).

Lexical borrowing

Word borrowing is perhaps the most salient feature of Sheng, and in the previous chapter we saw many loanwords and their sources in other Kenyan indigenous languages. Sheng words are also coined through meaning shift, polysemy and synonymy, but a major external source of Sheng borrowing is English. However, whatever the source, loan words are readily inserted into the morphology generally without affecting the template of SS grammar. In general, loan words (e.g. verbs) are inserted in the morphology of Swahili without altering the template or order of morphemes. For example, the 'Mijikenda' verb *-lola* is used in place of SS *-angalia*; *-kam* from English 'come' is used in place of SS -*kuja* and -*mada* from 'murder'; -*nyita* from Gikuyu instead of SS -*elewa*, are used in this way in the following examples:

Sheng:	*Ebu **lola** huyu **mresh**!* (*lola* < Giriama; *mresh* < *mroro* < Chichifundi)
SS:	*Hebu angalia huyu msichana!*
	Just <u>look</u> at this <u>girl</u>!

Sheng:	*Ali**kam**.* (< 'come' English)
SS:	*Ali<u>kuja</u>.*
	S/he <u>came.</u>

Sheng:	*Badala ya awashike, anawa**mada**.* (< 'murder' English)
SS:	*Badala ya awashike, anawa<u>ua.</u>*
	Instead of arresting them, he kills/<u>murders</u> them.

Sheng:	*Ume**nyita**?* (*nyita* < Gikuyu)
SS:	*Ume<u>elewa</u>?*
	Do you <u>understand</u>?

However, the meaning of some words may widen, narrow or change in another way. *Manyanga* for example, is a frequently used noun and adjective in Sheng which means 'beautiful, well-kept', for example [*dɛm manyanga*] 'beautiful girl' or *shɔshɔ manyanga* 'an older but well kept woman'. It can also be a descriptive noun for a flashily decorated *matatu* fitted with blaring music and giant flat-screen televisions. According to an informant, the word *manyanga* is from the Giriama language of the coastal Mijikenda group. However, in this language it refers to a musical instrument (*kayamba*, a seed filled, flat instrument). Sheng also borrows words simply to expand the semantic choices/repetoire available to its speakers:

Sheng:	*Twende <u>home</u>, **maze**.* (home < English)
SS:	*Twende <u>nyumbani</u>, bwana.*
	Let's go <u>home</u>, man.

Sheng:	*nikapata wamedɛdi (*dead < English)
SS:	*nikapata wame<u>kufa</u>*
	'[and then] I found them <u>dead</u>'

The word *Maze* entered KS in the mid 1980s, the title of a song by a popular Congolese (Lingala) singer, Tabu Ley Roucherou. It is frequently used as an exclamation, of surprise, disappointment, etc., in modern Sheng talk, where it is also sometimes pronounced as *manze* (different from *manzi* – 'girl') e.g. *eeh, manze jana tuliwaka!* (eh, last night we got lit up, man!). English adverbs such as 'any', 'so', 'like', etc., occur frequently in code mixing instances, and coined Sheng verbs such as *vuruta* (SS *kunywa*) are also common. The grammar of Swahili is never violated in all examples of Sheng; imperatives for example follow regular rules of SS where the object of the command takes the subject position, and the final vowel is duly inflected (*a > e*):

Sheng:	*Nibring'ie* (< English 'bring')
SS:	*Niletee.*
	Bring [it] to me.

Sheng:	*Sina <u>any</u> lakini nataka kuvuruta.*
SS:	*Sina <u>kitu</u> (pesa) lakini nataka kunywa pombe.*
	I haven't <u>anything</u> (money) but I want to drink.

Possible evidence of reduction is seen with plural ending *-ni* for imperatives (2nd pers. pl.), which is normally left out in Sheng:

Sheng:	*Twende **hepi*** (< English 'happy')!
SS:	*Twende(ni) tukajiburudishe!*
	Let's go be <u>happy</u> [have a good time]!

Sheng:	*Tuishie!*
SS:	*Twende (ni)!*
	Let's (all) go!

Meaning shift

Another common feature of Sheng is shift of meaning whereby referential meaning is reassigned. The Hindi word '*boza*' for example, originally means 'ale', or 'European type alcohol/beer' (*pombe la kizungu*) in Hindi and Gujerati (Bir 1902). But in Sheng, *boza* is one of the many synonyms of marijuana (see Sheng Glossary). In some cases, the meaning of existing SS words changes in Sheng, for example, *(ma-) hewa* 'music' means 'air' in SS, and *mchuma* (SS: 'iron-made') means 'gun' in Sheng, and *kago* from English 'cargo' refers to 'stolen property'. Such mutations are characteristic of speech codes used in closed registers for secrecy, at the same time rapid lexical innovations taking place to achieve the same purpose. The following is another example of Sheng talk used for covert communication among some groups:

Sheng:	*Saa ni <u>idhaa</u> ya <u>ketesh</u>.*
SS:	*Sasa ni wakati (wa kula) <u>miraa.</u>*
	Now it's <u>time to</u> (chew) <u>miraa</u> [khat].

In SS, *idhaa* means 'radio/TV broadcast, or 'period/service', e.g. *idhaa ya Kiswahili ya KBC* = KBC (Kenya Broadcasting Corporation) Swahili service. It is possible that the meaning of *idhaa* has shifted, while retaining the general notion of 'period of' which has narrowed in Sheng to one main interpretation:

a time for, period (SS *wakati wa*). It is also possible that it is a Gikuyu loan (*ithaa* < SS *saa*) which also means 'time of', a period for doing something (e.g. *ithaa rĩa kũrĩa* – 'time to eat'). Still on the above sentence, a shift of meaning has taken place with the word *ketesh*, whose origin is in the name of a popular tea brand, Ketepa, an acronym of 'Kenya Tea Packers. It is clipped to 'ketesh' in Sheng, and its meaning shifted to *miraa*, which like tea, is grown and consumed widely in Kenya.

Polysemy

Like all natural languages, Sheng has polysemy, giving multiple meanings to a single word, but the semantic relationship between the words is not always obvious. For example, *guoko* (< Gikuyu *guoko*) can mean (1) a fight (2) five shillings or (3) fifty shillings in different contexts. In Gikuyu the word *guoko* means 'hand' or 'to fight' in that language's slang, but in Sheng it is figuratively used to mean 'five' from the gesture of folding a fist to show five (tens). *Mbao* is Gikuyu slang for twenty shillings (< *mbaũ/kĩbaũ* < English 'pound'). In Sheng, this now means either (1) 20 shillings, (2) a slap, or (3) to go crazy, be confused, when used in the idiom *kutupa mbao*. These particular words and expressions are now widely accepted, and are prevalent in ordinary KS.

Synonymy

There is also plenty of synonymy in Sheng, when several words have the same referential meaning. Sheng has a propensity to borrow or coin words to co-exist or replace existing SS words, at times drawing on figurative meanings. This serves to add to its verbal repertoire, and also to establish difference, to mark the boundaries between Sheng and ordinary KS. Clearly, many Sheng words are 'unnecessary' loans in that they have common, ready equivalents in SS. Many Sheng innovations replace Swahili words of Arabic origin with those of English or indigenous Kenyan languages, as the following examples demonstrate. But why create a new word for 'teacher' (Sheng: *odijoo, mtich33*) instead of the usual SS 'mwalimu', or *ng3pa* for 'hat' (SS: *kofia*), or *Mngoso* for SS *Mzungu* (European) or *njeve* for SS *baridi*? The first answer could be that Sheng talk is meant to hide meanings from non-ingroup members and adult authorities (parents, police and teachers). Another one is that Sheng speakers see some SS words as archaic (old, unfashionable) and therefore unsuitable in projecting the modernity which Sheng desires. What is clear, however, is that Sheng avoids Arabisms associated with 'deep' coastal Swahili, in preference for coinages and loan words from English, or those sourced from indigenous African languages such as *waks, gange, janta, job*, etc., instead of SS *kazi*.

Transpositions (Pig Latin)

Pig Latin is used to describe word games or secret coded means which use a set of regular rules, usually that of syllable transposition (re-arrangement). Pig Latin-type innovations feature in many youth languages, where words rather than the phonological forms as above are distorted, e.g. nouns, verbs, adjectives are replaced by their semantic opposites – the 'man' for 'woman', 'up' for 'down', or 'overstand' for 'understand' in Rasta talk, etc. In some varieties of the language game, the tones remain as in the original with just the segments of syllables moved, and in another, the tones move with the syllable. It is also possible that the very word 'Sheng' is the result of transposition of the word 'English', with loss of one syllable, -li-. Sheng makes much use of 'pig Latin' in forming sentences or coining words, lending further weight to the claim that it can function as a secret language since the chief communicative goal of the speakers is to obscure meanings and intentions from non-members. Examples:

Sheng:	*Analaku.*
SS:	*Anakula.*
	S/he is eating.

Sheng	A: *Kiche leyu mudɛ.*
Sheng	B: *Cheki yule dɛm(u)*.
SS:	*Angalia yule msichana.*
	Check out [look at] that girl.

Table 11 Examples of Sheng transpositions – Pig Latin

Sheng	Source		Gloss
ndifu	< *fundi*	Standard Swahili	handyman
ngife	< *fɛgi*	UK English slang 'fag'	cigarette
jamo	< *moja*	Standard Swahili	one
mjamo	< *mmoja*	Standard Swahili	one (person)
tiplo	< ploti	English 'plot'	plot (residential unit)
zibɛ	< base	English	hangout
mbanyu	< *nyumba*	Standard Swahili	house
mbachu	< *chumba*	Standard Swahili	room
nyiaku	< *kunya*	Standard Swahili	defecate
nywaku	<*kuny*wa	Standard Swahili	drink (verb)
risto	<stori	English 'story'	story

Sheng verbs

In a vocabulary list of 534 items gleaned from the Nairobi Data Set (2002), 13.8 per cent of the total were verbs, but the proportion increased in the 2017 study to 24.8 per cent, in a corpus of 450 items. This may be an indication of a propensity for Sheng to increase its verbal repertoire as its roles and domains of use have expanded. In true fashion of a vibrant, living language variety, Sheng readily adds to its verbal repertoire through borrowing and coinage. English is the chief source of loans, but Sheng also borrows verbs from the other languages in contact. For example, Sheng talk makes use of three synonyms from three different Kenyan languages or dialects in addition to the SS verb *angalia* 'look'. These are: (1) *kukenga* from Taita language (2) *kusisia* from Kamba language with same meaning, and (3) *lola* which is attested in both Giriama (Githiora 2002), and in an unspecified Swahili dialect (Kamusi 2018).

The verb -*nyita* is a Sheng synoym of SS *shika*, e.g. Sheng: *Umenyita rada?* 'Do you get [grasp] the idea?' (SS: *umeelewa?*). It is an unmodified Gikuyu loan whose very basic meaning of 'grasp, hold, catch' can be extended to a wide range of related meanings such as 'capture, arrest, acquire, receive (e.g. wages)', and figuratively, 'understand an explanation or idea'. Sheng narrows the meaning of *nyita* to the extended (figurative) meaning 'understand' after which the Gikuyu verb becomes the base for an idiomatic/periphrastic Sheng verb, *nyita rada* (also, KS *shika rada*) 'get the point or idea, understand'. Another example is *gotha* lit. 'hit' 'cheat', 'trick' in Sheng (< *gũtha*, Gikuyu slang 'to hit [con]'); or *goroka*, 'go mad, crazy' (< Gikuyu *gũrũka*).

Sheng also sources loans from non-standard English, e.g. *bɛstɛ/mabɛstɛ* (< 'bestie'); *chalii* ('Charlie'); *fɛgi* ('fag'); *ku-chil* (< 'chill out'), or colloquial English expressions, such as *ku-kreki* ('crack up, go mad') and *ku-shoot* ('shoot'). Verbs can also be derived form English nouns, e.g. *ku-dishi* ('to eat', from 'dish'), *ku-heng* ('hang [out]') and *ku-bugi* (< 'boogie: US slang, 'dance''), etc. To have a chat with friends is *ku-piga stori*, also *ku-piga risto* (and *chapa stori*) coined from *piga*, a 'light' verb in SS with a basic meaning of 'hit', but which can predicate many different meanings depending on the noun used in conjunction, e.g. *piga simu* 'to telephone'; *piga chafya* (sneeze); *piga domo* (complain); *piga chapa* (type or print), etc. Other innovative cases where an English word is turned into a verb using Swahili morphosyntax include the Sheng verb *filisha* 'make someone feel emotional or touched' from English 'feel' with an SS causative suffix –*isha* which adds a causative meaning to a regular SS verb, i.e. 'make/cause a feeling'. Sheng speakers overwhelmingly prefer this particular coinage to describe emotion over SS *hisia* or, KS *sikia* which is indistinguishable from the sensory 'hear'. The verb *fastisha* 'speed up, hurry up' is also derived from English loan 'fast' + SS causative suffix *-isha*:

Sheng: *Stori yake <u>inafilisha</u>.*
SS: *Hadithi yake <u>inafanya hisia.</u>*
  His/her story is touching/emotive.

Sheng: *<u>Fastisha</u> ndio twende* home *mapema.*
SS: *<u>Harakisha</u> ili twende nyumbani mapema.*
  <u>Hurry up/do faster</u> so that we can go home early.

There are a number of unique Sheng verbs which are coinages and of very high frequency in Sheng talk (see narratives in the next section). Many of them, such as *kaa masaa* (be alert, on the lookout) and *kaa square* (sit properly/tightly in a *matatu*) and *kosa network* (be clueless, lit. 'to lack network') are widely used outside youth registers i.e. they are so present in general KS that some students sometimes confuse them with SS verbs when writing compositions or in Swahili debating club, according to teachers we interviewed.

Table 12 Examples of Sheng coinages – verbs

Sheng	SS	English
chora noma	*fanya mpango*	make a plan
chuna ngoma	*cheza ngoma*	dance
kaa masaa	*kaa macho*	be alert
kaa rithi	*kaa chonjo*	be alert
kaa square	*kaa vizuri*	sit properly (in a matatu)
kosa network	*duwaa*	be clueless, lost
kudɛma	*kula*	eat
kudhanya	*kupiga*	beat, hit
kuhai	*kuiba*	steal
kukaba	*kujificha*	hide
kumanga	*kula*	eat
kung'am	*kuona; angalia*	see
kupeleka honda	*kuendesha; kuhara*	have diarrhoea lit. 'to drive a Honda'
kusanya	*kuiba*	*steal*
kutoka tara	*kutoroka*	take off, run away quickly
kutomisha	*kuwa mkali*	be mean or stingy
ku-mada	*kuua*	kill, murder

Sheng also tends to use SS verbs that are not frequently used, for example, *bamba*: 'to seize, arrest, hold by force', instead of the more common SS verb *shika*, e.g. *amebambwa na makarao* (s/he's been arrested by the police), or *jimbambie na M-Pesa* (grab it for yourself on M-Pesa). The meaning of *bamba* is extended in Sheng to mean figuratively '[get] hold [of]','understand,' e.g. *unabamba*? (do you get it/understand?), or even to express an adjectival sense, *Hii chakula inabamba!* (This food is really good!) Another frequently used verb in Sheng which does not exist in SS or any dialect of Swahili known to us is *bonga* (speak, talk, converse). It is the most frequently heard one in Sheng talk, not its SS equivalents such as *ongea* or *sema*. In order to indicate a larger volume of talk, Sheng is more likely to use *piga risto* (talk, chat) instead of SS *zungungumza*.

There are a number of possible reasons for these lexical shifts: prestige of new forms, perceived difficulties of recall of certain standard Swahili words, and the inevitability of change that languages undergo to reflect changing circumstances. What is evident, however, is that there seems to be a deliberate attempt to move away from *Kisanifu*. An analysis of our data indicates that Sheng applies three main strategies of lexical innovation, in an effort to 'deviate' from SS, which is perceived by some Sheng speakers as alien as English itself:

(1) modifying existing words to make them sound or appear new (e.g. *risasi > rithεε* 'bullet'; *busu > mbuthu* 'kiss'; or *darasa > darɔɔ* 'classroom'

(2) replacing Arabic loans with those of modified English, e.g. mwalimu > *tichεε/mtichεε/odijɔɔ* (< teacher); *rafiki > beste* (friend, 'bestie'); *biashara > bisnaa* (< business); *ndugu/dada > brathee/sistee* (< brother/sister); *pesa > dɔɔ* (< 'dough' [money]); *serikali > gavaa* (< government); *kitabu > mbuku* (< book)

(3) replacing Arabic loans with with those of borrowed from an indigineous African language, e.g. *wakati (gidhaa; idhaa)*; *kofia (ngεpa)* 'hat'; *mzungu (mngoso/mlami)* 'European'; Kiingereza *(Kingoso/ Kilami)* 'English language'; *baridi (njeve)* 'cold'; *filisika (sota)* 'be broke'; *pesa (chapaa)*; *thumni (chwani)* 'fifty cents'; *pesa (ganji)* 'money'; *elfu (ngiri)* 'one thousand'; *keradhi (tabaka)* 'socioeconomic class'; *tajiri (sonko; mdosi)*; *matajiri (matapεε)*; *ishirini (mbao)* 'twenty [shillings]'; *kibiriti (nare)* 'lighter/matchbox'; *dhahabu (ndechu/mandechu)* 'gold, jewelry'

Table 13 Examples of Sheng coinages – nouns

Sheng	Standard Swahili	gloss
chwani	*thumni*	fifty cents
darɔɔ	*darasa*	classroom
gεto (<ghetto)	*mtaa*	neighbourhood, estate
gidhaa/idhaa	*wakati*	time, period of
bestε/beshtε	*rafiki*	friend
kuchil	*kupumzika*	relax, rest
mbuthu	*busu*	kiss
odijɔɔ/mtichεε	*mwalimu*	teacher
ndechu (ma-)	*dhahabu*	gold
ngεpa	*kofia*	hat
ngiri	*elfu*	one thousand
salɔɔ	*mshahara*	salary, pay
teɔ	*mtihani*	exam
Mngoso/Mlami	*Mzungu*	European/White person
Kingoso/Kilami	*Kizungu/Kiingereza*	English language
kuzɔɔ	*binamu*	cousin
ganji/dɔɔ	*pesa/fedha*	money
ushagɔɔ/ɔcha/ɔchaa	*kijiji(ni)*	village
njeve	*baridi*	cold
matapεε	*matajiri*	rich people
morenga/ndaε/dinga	*gari/motokaa*	car
rithεε	*risasi*	bullet
kusota	*filisika*	be broke
vako	*subira*	waiting period
mdhii/wadhii	*msafiri/wasafiri*	passenger

Narratives of local experience

Ni venye hawa makarao humadanga majamaa huku.
It's how these cops kill guys around here.

Sheng narratives yield many fascinating insights into the day-to-day experiences of those young residents of the underprivileged section of Nairobi's population. It also gives narrators – all teenagers and students – an opportunity 'to demonstrate their verbal skills, their command of complex syntax, and their creative powers' (Labov 1972). The narratives are very useful in giving us information about the social context in which narrators are involved, thus providing us with an additional source of sociocultural data for understanding Nairobi city. Sheng narratives are also valuable sources of vernacular speech because they are spontaneously produced. Speakers demonstrate a level of sophistication of verbal expression and creativity that would be hard to produce or sustain in English, SS, or the indigenous language available to different individual speakers. After providing a few illustrating examples, I shall turn to look at structural aspects of the Sheng narratives and how these relate to the attempt to understand the nature of Sheng as one of the many ways of speaking KS.

I collected a number of narratives from Nairobians aged 13–17 years, and these were recorded in both audio and video, and later transcribed using standard sociolinguistic transcription conventions (e.g. CAPS for loud or breathy/animated voice, etc). Some Sheng narratives describe activities that are prohibited for the youth, or socially stigmatized (e.g. chewing *miraa*, going to all night discos, etc.) and are therefore to be kept away from parents. '*Sheng pia ni ya kuficha mokoroo*' – 'Sheng is also for keeping secrets from the mother/parents.' Therefore among other communicative functions, Sheng is instrumental in exchanging private, in-group information, and adds to one's repertoire of street survival skills or 'street cred' (Mose 2012). However, this particular function is not my focus or interest, rather I was interested in the broader social and linguistic features of Sheng narratives.

I have used an analytical framework established by Labov (1972) in his study of Black English Vernacular (BEV), also known as African American Vernacular English (AAVE), or 'Black English' in Harlem, New York City. His analysis of narratives of personal experience among urban youths and adults of (mainly) African heritage proved an excellent means to capture sociocultural information, and linguistic data. The results of the study demonstrated the uniqueness, as well as the universality of African American narratives. These were enriched by the particularity of AAVE grammar, which Labov established as different in significant ways from that of Standard American English (SAE) while sharing certain sociolinguistic characteristics.

I hoped to overcome the 'observer's paradox' by obtaining samples of language that most approximated natural speech, by trying to elicit strong emotions which would produce spontaneous, vernacular speech. To achieve this, the investigator must minimize the degree of self-consciousness or inhibitions of the respondent on matters of language. The 'danger of death' approach (Labov 1972) yielded animated, spontaneous and therefore more natural speech samples:

> …because they occur in response to a specific stimulus in the interview situation, they are not free of the interactive effect of the outside observer, the form they take is, in fact, typical of discourse directed to someone outside of the immediate peer group of the speaker. However, because the experience and emotions

involved here form an important part of the speaker's biography he seems to undergo a partial reliving of that experience, and he is no longer free to monitor his speech as he normally does in face-to-face interviews. (Labov, 1972:355)

This technique or device was developed from Labov's work on vernacular speech in inner city New York, in an attempt to overcome the constraints of a face-to-face interview. In our Nairobi study, we conducted many of our interviews in schools where the presence of teachers may have provided additional monitoring effect. To limit that effect, I did the interviews away from the teachers' presence during a special period allocated for the interviews on particular days. We encouraged the students to be as free-spoken as possible, by adopting a relaxed and even jocular group atmosphere. The strategy resulted in less monitored speech, in which KS/Sheng vernacular forms emerged naturally and plentifully and fluently since the narrator was in full control of the language in which he or she is most fluent. The vernacular is definitely the means by which a speaker is best able to demonstrate their verbal skill and emotive capabilities. This Labovian technique ensured the production of near spontaneous speech and emotional narratives. His observation that the speaker becomes deeply involved (animated) in rehearsing or even relieving the events of his past was all too evident in every instance during our Nairobi study, as in the following two examples.

Narrative A: male, 17 years old, Ainsworth Primary School, Eastlands, 21 September 2002

A: *siku moja nilikuwa...nilikuwa huko* **ochaa** *tukiona* **masangu** *pamoja na* **mbuyu** *wangu. sasa tulipowasili pale Machakos na.. na..kuchukua* **buu**..*tu..tu..tulianza safari yetu* *fiti na nili-* **nilicheki** *mbele ya safari nikaona, nikaona tu ni* **poa**..*lakini tulipofika na huko..karibu tufike* **ochaa** *tulikutana na* **mangosa** *wengine waliposimamisha* **buu** *na kuanza* **kuhanda** *watu..wakaambia watu warushe walipo--walichokuwa nacho...asanteni... walinyang'anya kila mtu kile alichokuwa nacho ..kama ni* **thaɔɔ,** **mbaɔ**....*halafu tukawachwa hivi.*[1]

---

one day I was..I was over there in <u>village</u>, admiring the <u>country-side</u> with my <u>Dad</u>. now when we arrived there at Machakos [bus terminal] and.. and to take the <u>bus</u>..we...we started our trip <u>okay</u>

[1] 13 of 62 words in Sheng, no code-swtiching, one instance of code-mixing. No structures of KS.

and I loo- ..I <u>looked</u> ahead of the trip and saw…I saw it would be all <u>fine</u>..but when we got there…before we got to the <u>village</u> we met some other <u>gangsters</u> then they stopped the <u>bus</u> and started <u>robbing</u> people…they told people to bring out all they had…thank you…they robbed everybody of what they had…if it's a <u>thousand</u> [shillings], <u>twenty</u>…then we were left like that.

Narrative B: female, 15 years old, Ainsworth Primary School, Eastlands, 21 September 2002

*siku moja nilikuwa **naendanga** na hapo hivo **Dandoo**, tukaku-tana na **mangosa** wengine hapo- EH! hao **mangosa** walikuwa na **<u>ma-guns</u>** zingine hapo hivo KAALII! ehh! wakaanza **<u>ku-shoot</u> watu..walikuwa wamepelekesha watu ndwathe!!** HE! HEE! HE! wacha nikUAMBIE MIMI SIKUONEKANA KWA HIYO NJIA TENA!! Nilikuwa **nimeKATA** he! ata kama ungeniona! ungesema hata huyo si mtu, haki!..asanteni!*[2]

one day I was <u>going about</u> there in <u>Dandoo</u> [Dandora estate] we met some other <u>gangsters</u> there -EH! those <u>gangsters</u> had some other <u>TOUGH guns</u> ehh! they started <u>to shoot</u> people…they <u>were really making people run</u>! HE! HEE! HE! let me TELL YOU ME I WAS NOT TO BE SEEN ON THAT ROAD AGAIN! he! I <u>RAN</u> he! if you had seen me! you'd have said that really is not a human being, I swear! ..thank you all!

Labov described narrative as 'one method of recapitulating experience by matching a verbal sequence of clauses to the sequence of events that actually happened' (1972:375). In his studies among African Americans in New York City, he attempted to correlate language features such as syntactic forms (e.g. comparatives and intensifiers) and age, with particular components of the narrative. Signalling devices include syntactic features such as tense or aspect and discourse markers such as hedges, overlaps, and repetitions. These features have a significance in the analysis and interpretation of a narrative. He also identified six parts in the overall structure of the narrative, and each part is characterized by distinctive grammatical, prosodic or other patterns. I will summarize them very briefly and then show where and how they fit in with the

---

[2] 5 out of 53 words in Sheng, two code-mixed (ma-guns, ku-shoot) and two Sheng idioms (e.g. *pelekeshwa ndwathe, kukata*).

following sample narratives in Sheng. The first two (Narratives A and B) were collected in 2002, and the other two (Narratives C and D – see pp. 119–223) in 2017. The gap in time provides insights into changes or innovations that have taken place within that period of time, for example new words and coinages, and a higher degree of code-switching.

Analysis of Sheng narratives

In a narrative, the *abstract* is normally a clause that summarizes for the listener what the narrative will be about. Both narrators in A and B started out with such a clause, recurring to a formulaic narrative device: '*one day…*' The abstract is usually followed by an *orientation*, which provides background information about the narrative (time, place, etc.). Again, in both cases, the orienting clause was followed by an identification of the location in which the narrative took place:in A: *ochaa* – countryside, village, and in B: *around about Dandora* [estate]). In Narrative C below, the abstract is clear and succinct: 'it's [about] how cops kill guys around here' and the setting is the immediate neighbourhood, *huku* 'around here':

A: *Siku moja nilikuwa…nilikuwa huko ochaa*
    One day I was…I was out there in the rural area
B: *Siku moja nilikuwa naendaga na hapo hivo Dandoo*
    One day I was going about there in Dandoo [Dandora]
C: *Ni venye hawa makarao humadanga majamaa huku*
    It's how these cops kill guys around here

The abstract in Narrative C is then quickly followed by an orientation which gives the now attentive listeners the background to the events that follow in the narrative, including the name and profession of the protagonist, and place where he committed his deeds, which are at the core of the narrative:

C: *Ah…Ilikuwa Disemba 2015 polisi mwingine anaitangwa hapo Rashidi…aliingia Kiamaich akamada vijana kumi na mbili*
    It was December 2015 [when] another cop known as Rashidi…went to Kiamaich (Kiamaiko) and murdered twelve youths…

A *complicating action* follows to give detailed description of the actual sequence of events which occurred in the narrative; a reversal in the order of the narrative clauses for example, would change the entire meaning of the narrative. Since narratives rely heavily on sequenced description, a minimum number of complicating action clauses is required in order to identify a narrative as such. Narrative A provides ample support for this analysis, constituting at least six, well sequenced complicating actions; any change in that order would obviously damage the narrative's coherence or effectiveness:

Narrative A:

(1) *sasa tulipowasili pale Machakos* (now when we arrived at Machakos [bus station])
(2) *na…na…kuchukua buu…* (and…and… took the bus)
(3) *lakini tulipofika na huko…karibu tufike ochaa* (but when we arrived there… before we got to the village)
(4) *tulikutana na mangosa wengine* (we met some gangsters)
(5) *waliposimamisha buu* (when [then] they stopped the bus)
(6) *na kuanza kuhanda watu…* (and started robbing people…)

In Narrative C, the orientation, which took place in the past (December 2015), is brought forward in a single clause to the present for greater dramatic effect:

Narrative C:

(1) *hadi jana nilikuwa <u>nakam</u> hivi jana nilipata majamaa wengine pale wamedɛdi*
      even *yesterday* when I was coming this way I found more dead guys
(2) *walikuwa wanafyatuliana <u>marithɛɛ</u> na <u>makarao.</u>*
      they were [had been] exchanging bullets with cops.
(3) *wengine bado nikitoka home nikapata mwingine <u>amedɛdi</u> bado*
      still [more] others since when coming from home I found another dead one

Comments about the universe of the story from the outside are referred to as *evaluation.* For example, embedded within the first complicating actions in Narrative A, we find a remark such as: *tu…tu…tulianza safari yetu <u>fiti</u> na nili-nilicheki mbele ya safari nikaona, nikaona tu ni <u>poa.</u>.* (we…we…we started our journey and I looked ahead and saw it would be just fine). The evaluation or summary in Narrative C is quite dense, reflecting the depth of emotion felt by the narrator; it consists of as many clauses as the narrative itself:

(1) *hata unashindwa ni nini…*
      you just wonder what's going on…
(2) *mi ata <u>sijuangi</u> game yake [Rashidi]*
      I don't know what's his *game* [Rashidi]

According to Labov, such evaluating remarks occur in the narrative to tell or remind the listener of the significance of the story such as, 'I thought the trip would be alright but little did I know that danger was forthcoming' and 'these things [killings] happen a lot around here and in Mathare North where I live'. Evaluations may therefore be intertwined in the story at different sections, especially if the narrative is longer. The *resolution* marks the end of the complicating action, and may be the prelude to a *coda* or that section of the narrative that brings the author and listener back to the present world.

Resolution: Narrative B:
                 *walinyang'anya kila mtu kile alichokuwa nacho.kama ni
                 thaɔɔ, mbaɔ....*
                 they robbed everyone of all they had, if it was a thousand
                 [shillings], twenty...

                 Narrative C:
                 *...eeh..mi naishi Mathare North... eeh, huko hutokea sana
                 sana.*
                 ...eeh I live in Mathare North, these things happen there a
                 lot...

Coda: *halafu tukawachwa hivo.*
                 and then we were left like that [robbed]

                 Narrative C:
                 na ni vijana WADOOGO...iko wengine nilikuwa nawajua
                 and they're YOUNG kids...I knew some of them...

                 Narrative D:
                 hayo ni ma- maneno tumezoea...ni ya mtaa
                 these are thi- things we're used to...they happen in the
                 streets/neighbourhood.

It needs to be mentioned that indeed oral narratives are best appreciated within their cultural context of performance. The context gives the audience a picture of the implications of the narrative itself, and in the performance paralinguistic features such as movement, facial expression and so on, enhance the messages contained in the language used. For example, the speaker in Narrative C was visibly distressed, and the audience responded to his facial expressions by creating a sombre and thoughtful mood in the usually boisterous groups of secondary school classmates. As such, transcriptions of narratives such as the ones above present only part of the performance; significant aspects of rhythm, prosody, or interaction with the audience are not readily represented and may also be lost, but they are obvious in both the audio and video versions of these recorded interviews, even to one not familiar with Sheng.

It is interesting to note that while Narrative B told by a teenage girl (15 years) contains all the components described above, its complicating action section comprises only three, rapidly sequenced clauses. The emotion by the narrator is much more evident in the raised, animated voice MIMI SIKUONEKANA KWA HIYO NJIA TENA! (*I WAS NOT TO BE SEEN ON THAT ROAD AGAIN!*) and Sheng idioms (*walikuwa wamepelekesha watu ndwathe*! – they [robbers] were making people run [flee]). The narrative ends with another vivid metaphor (*ata ungeniona! ungesema mimi si mtu, haki!* – if you had seen me you'd have said I am not human, I swear!). Notably, she does not resort to any evaluating comments such as seen in Boy A's narrative, indicating a more straightforward, highly animated story that effectively makes full use of her Sheng verbal skills and idiom. This gender bias was noted earlier in Chapter 3 (the section on attitudes towards different languages), where we found female respondents to be more eloquent, and to use more sophisticated descriptors than male respondents.

Grammar in Sheng narratives

An interesting aspect of these narratives is that, other than the use of Sheng words underlined, all of the grammatical structures used to narrate are well formed SS sentences as highlighted by italics in the text. Many of them actually are complex structures involving a combination of tenses, relativization and contractions etc, as the following examples clearly show:

Narrative A:
Sheng: _wenye hawakuwa wamedema_, _wakadema_
SS: _(wale)_ _ambao hawakuwa wamekula_, _wakala_
            those who had not eaten, (then) ate

Narrative C:
Sheng: ni _venye_ hawa makarao _humadanga_ majamaa huku
_SS:_   ni _vile/jinsi ambavyo_ polisi _huua_ watu huku/sehemu hizi
            it's how police kill people around here

Correlations – or lack of them — between grammatical elements and parts of the narrative are found in many languages. For example many Bantu languages such as Swahili and Gikuyu employ a special tense known as the 'consecutive' or 'narrative' tense (C-tense), which is used only in sequenced narrative clauses. The tense does not occur in English where its closest equivalent would be '...and then...'. In Swahili it is achieved through use of an infix -_ka_- as underlined in the example above, and in those that follow below, highlighted in bold letters. The C-tense naturally dominates in narratives for obvious reasons, and because it is also used for pace and dramatic effect. In all Sheng narratives and other data samples, we find that Sheng speakers applied the C-tense in their discourse in the same way as prescribed by SS grammar. Furthermore, the context of their use in narratives corresponds, as expected, with the complicating action where most sequencing takes place, naturally:

A: _watu...wakaambia watu warushe_
        and then they told people to throw down...
        halafu tukawachwa hivo
        and then we were left like that...

B: *tukakutana na mangosa wengine*
        and then we met some gangsters
        wakaanza ku-shoot
        and then they started to shoot

During such spontaneously produced, animated speech, one may expect features of a reduced, pidginized variety of Swahili to become apparent. However, samples of Sheng vernacular do not reveal any such reduction of grammatical form. In fact, many of them are as complex and used in same ways as in SS, for example, the use of infixes in relativized clauses, such as when A says, ...*kile alichokuwa nacho*... (that which she had*)*. In another instance, the narrator self corrects, and uses the correct (SS) relative marker *-cho-* which agrees with *kitu* (thing) the default object in relative sentences in SS '...*walipo--walichokuwa nacho*...'. This is clearly an indication of a conscious awareness and knowledge of SS grammar. Despite Narrator B's use of non-standard expressions or loan words, she similarly demonstrates a clear ability to use correctly those complex forms of SS such as compound tenses, e.g. *walikuwa wamepelekesha watu ndwathe*! (they had been making people flee), or *nilikuwa nimeKATA, he!* (I had taken off running!); conditional past tense, *ata kama ungeniona! ungesema* (had you seen me you would have said...). In the last example, the narrator uses the *-nge-* marker for the modal 'would' where SS dictates the use of *-ngali-* representing a past 'regret' marker, of actions that can no longer be experienced or witnessed. This difference of modality markers is found throughout KS upon which Sheng is based, therefore it is an 'error' only if determined against SS, which is not much used outside the classroom in Kenyan.

Content of Sheng narratives

The content of Sheng narratives provide us with key insights into the social context in which the young Sheng speakers live. They are urban and far removed from the traditional 'African' folk story, which dominates the study of oral narratives in Africa. Many Sheng words have been coined in recent times to describe various 'new' methods of urban crime such as *kuhanda* (hold up), applied to an encounter either with police or robbers (e.g. *jana tulipoachana maze nilihandwa na makarao jo!* – 'last night after we parted, man, I was held up [robbed] by the police!'). The *ngeta* tactic is common in alleys of Nairobi. It involves the sudden use of a vicious arm hold around the victim's neck, using a wooden stick or iron bar tied around the arm and hidden in the robber's coat.

    I recorded the following narrative from a 17-year-old male secondary school (Form 3) student who volunteered to tell a story in response to our challenge of 'danger of death'. He was clearly distressed by the nature and freshness of the events, but he seemed relieved to have shared it with an attentive audience of his peers:

Narrative C: male, 17 years, 9 February 2017

Ni venye hawa makarao humadanga majamaa huku. Ah…Ilikuwa Disemba 2015 polisi mwingine anaitangwa hapo Rashidi…aliingia Kiamaich akamada vijana kumi na mbili, hadi jana nilikuwa nakam hivi jana nilipata majamaa wengine pale wamedɛdi… walikuwa wanafyatuliana marithɛɛ na makarao, wengine bado nikitoka home nikapata mwingine amedɛdi bado, hata unashindwa ni nini… mi ata sijuangi game yake [Rashidi]…na ni vijana WADOOGO…iko wengine nilikuwa nawajua…Eeh…badala ya awashike, anawamada…eeh…mi naishi Mathare North… eeh, huko hutokea sana sana.

It's how these cops kill guys around here. Ah…it was December 2015 [when] another cop known as Rashidi…went to Kiamaich (Kiamaiko) and murdered twelve youths, even yesterday when I was coming this way I found more dead guys…they were exchanging bullets with cops, and still others, when coming from home I found another dead one, you just wonder what's going on…I don't know what his *game* [Rashidi]…and they're YOUNG kids…I knew some of them…eeh, instead of arresting them he kills them…eeh..I live in Mathare North, these things happen there a lot…

The depth of emotion expressed by the verbal as well as non-verbal language of the young narrator was readily evident. Nairobi, and in particular the Eastlands area, has high crime levels; some is petty and poverty-related, but also gangsterism, drugs and violent robbery are extremely common in the city. So is police violence against the residents of the Eastlands, especially the young and unemployed or out of school. It is not surprising that the vocabulary of violence is prevalent in Sheng; practically all the narratives we collected were about bad experiences, some perhaps because we asked for narratives of 'danger'. Some of the stories were jocular, and less traumatic (e.g. Narrative D) although no less troubling in other ways.

Narrative D – *Kuhandwa mtaani* 'Being robbed in the hood': male, 17 years, Eastleigh, 9 February 2017

In this longer narrative, there is also a markedly higher frequency of Sheng words and phrases or idioms (highlighted in bold in the Sheng text and in the SS translation), e.g. '*So, ile kuhandwa ni lazima*' (In fact/therefore/indeed being mugged is a must [expected]); 76 out of 290 (26.2 per cent) of the total words in the narrative were of the youth register or 'deep' Sheng, compared to 9.5 per cent (5 out of 53 words) in the narrative recorded in 2002. The change in percentage frequency might indicate an increased use of Sheng lexicon and more code-mixing in Sheng vernacular speech that may have taken place during the intervening 15-year period.

---

eh..nilikuwa nimetumwa na *mathangu*..**saa** vile mimi nilitumwa, **mi** nikaenda…**saa** huko kwetu unajua **maodinari** [ni] wengi…. **MAODINARI** *so* huko kulikuwa na **maodinari** wengi. *So*, ile **kuhandwa** ni lazima…*so* mi nikaenda nikanunua *SAPA* (*supper*), **saa mi** natokea- narudi **saa kejani**, napatana NAO **wananihanda, saa** vile **wamenihanda** wananisimamisha wanasema '**Kijanaa** toa kile uko nacho'…**enyewe** nika…*at the moment*, eeh ilikuwa tu **NGORI JO**, ili- enyewe ((chuckles)) …**enyewe**…waka- wakani- ingia MFUKO, wakaniingia **MBOSHO wakanitoa** simu…uzuri nilikuwa na kasimu kengine **hadi** hakana kifuniko…bado nili- kuwa natumianga kiJITI…eeh, **saa** unajua… Walijua tu hakuna kitu ningefanya- ningefanya. *So* **mi**, waka- wakaninyang'anya, wakachukua **dɔɔ**. **Walihepa** nazo. Ilikuwa kitu **kaa rwabe** na *macoins* kadhaa hapo sikumbuki zilikuwa ngapi kwa mfuko. **saa** wakachukua, **saa mi** nikaenda **kejani**, kwenda **kejani** napata **hadi** funguo sina..nikashangaa eh, kwani kumeendaje tena…**saa** naita **beshte** yangu fulani […] unajua kunakuwanga na **maboi** wengi, *so* wenye wenye walinihanda si wenye- si wa huo mtaa, unajua **maboi** wanakujua hawawezi **kukuhanda**…lakini ni WAMOJA tu, ni kama [ ] moja. Lakini **wenye wanakuhanda** si wa hapo, ni wa mahali pengine lakini **wamekam** kutembe- lea **mabeste** WA- **mabeshte** wao. **Saa** nilienda nikapata sina funguo, ah, naenda na[…?} **dEm** fulani wa hapo kwetu, eh **mi** nimenyang'anywa, nimenyang'anywa *key*, na **yee ananionye- sha kam uchapie Jose**…tukaenda **tukachapia boi** fulani huko mtaa…**ye** hukuwanga tu **nare**, anaenda **anabonga** nao **anawao- nyesha 'kijanaa** rudishieni huyu **chalii** mumemwibi- mmem- wibia.' Ah **vijanaa** wanaanza kutetateta, Jose ameitana, ah saa hii imekuwa ni **kaa** jeshi mbili, nikaona hakuna maana ya vita,

huyo **dɛm anawachapia,** 'leteni tu fungu- funguo.' <u>Saa venye</u> **mi**
nilikuwa natembea hapo tukijaribu *ku-consult* hiyo maneno, ndio,
wakakam…saa *wakakam*..tukaona funguo chini…ni **kaa venye
walisikia** waliangusha funguo chi- chini… **sa venye niliona**
wameangusha *key* chini, ah **mi** nikachukua tu na nikasema hiyo
maneno nimemali- nimemaliza hiyo *stori* nikamalizia tu hapo…
hayo ni ma- maneno tumezoea…ni ya mtaa

Narrative D: Standard Swahili (translated Sheng in bold and KS underlined)

---

eh..nilikuwa nimetumwa na **mamangu**…**sasa** vile nimetumwa,
mimi nikaenda tu. Sasa unajua huko kwetu wakora ni wengi…
WAKORA, kwa hivyo kulikuwa na **wakora** wengi..kwa hivyo
kunyang'anywa ni lazima, basi mimi nikaenda nikanunua
chakula cha jioni, sasa nimetokea…narudi sasa **nyumbani,**
napatana nao, **wananisimamisha**, sasa vile **wananisimamisha**
wanasema, '**Kijana** toa kile uko nacho'…enyewe **wakati huo**
nilikuwa na **WASIWASI BWANA**, il- -- **basi** ((anacheka))
enyewe wakaniingia mfuko, wakaniingia **pochi wakatoa**
simu… **kwa bahati nzuri** nilikuwa na **kijisimu kingine** hata
hakina kifuniko…bado <u>**nilikuwa natumia** kijiti [ ]</u>…sasa
unajua walijua **nisingeweza kufanya kitu**… basi, mimi, waka-
wakaninyang'anya, wakachukua **pesa**. Wakatoroka nazo. Ilikuwa
kitu **kama mia mbili** na **sarafu** kadhaa hapo sikumbuki zilikuwa
ngapi <u>mfukoni</u>. **Sasa** wakachukua, **sasa** mimi nikaenda nyumbani, kwenda nyumbani napata **hata** ufunguo sina, nikashangaa,
eh, kwani kumeendaje tena…sasa naita **rafiki** yangu fulani […]
unajua <u>huwa na</u> **marafiki** wengi , kwa hivyo <u>wale ambao</u> **walin-
ipokonya** si wa huo mtaa, unajua **vijana** wanakujua hawawezi
kukunyang'anya…lakini **ni WAMOJA** tu, ni kama [ ] kitu
kimoja. Lakini <u>wale ambao</u> **wanakunyang'anya** si wa hapo [huo
mtaa] wametoka mahali pengine lakini wame**kuja** kuwatembelea
rafiki zao. **Sasa** nilienda nikapata sina funguo, ah, naenda na […?]
msichana fulani wa hapo kwetu, eh **mimi** nimenyang'anywa
kii – nimenyang'anywa *key*, **basi yeye** <u>akaniambia njoo umpigie Jose simu</u>…tuakenda **tukampigia rafiki fulani simu** huko
mtaani…**basi yeye** huwa [**moto**] **mkali**, akaenda **akaongea** nao
akawaambia, 'rudishieni huyu **kijana** [kile] <u>mmemnyang'anya</u>.'
Ah, **vijana** wanaanza kutetateta, [wakati huo] Jose ameitana, ah,
sasa zimekuwa ni **kama** jeshi mbili, nikaona hakuna maana ya
vita, huyo **msichana anawaambia**, leteni tu fungu- funguo. **Sasa**

kwa sababu **mimi** nilikuwa hapo tukijaribu **kushauriana** hayo
maneno, ndio **wakaja**...sasa **wakaja**..tukaona funguo chini...
ni **kama** vile walisikia/walikubali [basi] wakaangusha funguo
chi- chini...**sasa** nilipoona wameangusha *funguo* chini, ah **mimi**
nikazichukua tu na nikasema hiyo maneno nimemali- nimemaliza
hayo maneno, nikamaliza tu hapo...hayo ni **mambo** tumezoea,
ni ya **mtaani.**

In this longer narrative, we find plenty of English borrowing and code-mixing typical of Sheng talk such as *mathangu* (< English: 'mother' + Swahili possessive *–angu*, i.e. 'my mother' or *mamangu* in SS); *ma-coins* (< NC6 *ma* + English 'coins, loose change' – SS: *sarafu*); *wakakam* (< NC2+ka (consecutive tense) + English 'come' – 'and then they came' – SS: *wakaja*); *ku-consult* (verb infinitive marker *ku* + English 'consult' – SS: *kuomba ushauri*). Sheng: *dɛm anawachapia, leteni tu funguo* – SS: *msichana anawaambia: leteni tu ufunguo* – 'The girl tells them, just bring out the key'. Sheng: *yee ananionyesha, kam uchapie* Jose – SS: *yeye ananishauri, njoo umpigie Jose simu.* 'She *advises* me, you come and *give Jose a ring [phone call]*,' and so on, as highlighted in the text and its translation. It is of interest to note that the narratives we collected in 2017 have a higher rate of code-switching compared to those we collected in the 2002 narratives, for example the English words 'key' (SS: *ufunguo*); 'supper' (SS: *chakula cha jioni*); 'at the moment' (SS: *hivi sasa/wakati huu*); 'so' (SS: *kwa hivyo*) are indicated by the underlined sections. These are also many instances of non-standard Swahili forms which are of widespread use in general KS, in all registers, including the following:

- *ka-* diminutive, e.g. *kasimu kengine.* ('another (little, old) phone')
- use of habitual *-anga* suffix to indicate habitual tense/iterativity instead of the SS *hu-* prefix, e.g. *nilitumianga* (SS: *ambayo nilikuwa nikitumia* 'that which I used to use')
- use of *-enye* in place of *amba-* relative, e.g. *wenye wanakuhanda.* ('those who rob you').

Narrative D in English translation.

[Eeh...I'd been sent by my mom...so because my mom sent me, I just went. Now you know out there in my area thugs are many... THUGS, so there are many thugs, therefore to be robbed is a must, so I went and bought our supper/dinner, so I am off, now going back home, I meet them, they stop me, so because they stopped me they say, 'young man bring out all you have,' in truth at that moment I was really frightened, man! so (chuckles) *anyway* they got into my pockets, they got into my wallet/bag and got out my phone...luckily I had a really [little] old phone that did not even have a cover, I was still using that... now, you know they knew I could not do a thing, so they robbed me, they took [my] money. They got away with it [the money] it was something like two hundred shillings and some coins, I can't remember how much there was in my pocket. So they took it, and so I went home, on getting home I find I don't even have the key [for the house], I was flabbergasted, eh, what's going on now...so I call a certain friend of mine [...] you know I have many friends, but those who robbed me are not from that neighbourhood, they've come from elsewhere but they've come to visit their friends. You know youths who know you cannot rob you...but they are ONE [together], they are like one thing [one group] but those who rob you are not the area, maybe they have come to visit friends. So now I realize I don't have the key, I go to [...?] a certain girl from my area, eh, 'I've been robbed of my key/s,' so she tells me come and ring Jose...we went and called a friend from the hood by phone...so, he is *hot* [tough], he went and told them [thugs], 'give this young man whatever you stole from him.' Ah, the youths start to protest [by then] Jose has called [for backup], now it is like two armies but I decided there's no need for a fight... the girl tells them, just bring out [return] the key – keys. Now because I was going back and forth trying to resolve this matter, that's when they came... they came...then we saw the key/s on the ground...it's like they heard/agreed/backed down [to the threat] and dropped the keys dow- down...now when I saw they've dropped the keys on the ground, ah I just took them and said that matter is over, I ended it right there...these are things we're used to, they are the ways of the streets/estate.]

Summary

It is very interesting how Sheng oral narratives reveal similar structural features as those obtained in New York City in the late 1960s. This fact alone demonstrates the universality of oral narratives and their structure, and is reflective of convergences between the social experiences and linguistic behaviour of urban youth in two geographically distant locations. Indeed, some verbal arts practised by Sheng and African American youth are comparable speech events: Githinji (2010) has described *mchongoano* in detail as a type of aggressive verbal contest practised in Sheng, comparable to African American ritual insults known as 'sounding' or 'signifying' (Labov 1972). These similarities could be a result of (African) transnational influences, or merely indicative of the universality of certain speech events across cultures. However, among people of African origin everywhere in the world, there is always the possibility of 'diasporic semblances and biological remembrances' (Hamilton 1995). In fact some features of AAVE can be linked to the Atlantic Creole Continuum and ultimately to their African origins, but it is beyond the scope of this study to make further comparisons or link AAVE to Sheng linguistically.

One more observation is that the abundance of crime and violence in Sheng narratives should be a cause for concern about the reality of the life that young, underprivileged people who live in Nairobi. Crime levels and unemployment are quite high, and the apparent antagonistic relationship between young Nairobians and the police authorities results in a lack of distinction between their (police) actions and those of violent criminals. For example, the Sheng verb *kuhandwa* makes no disctinction between being stopped and robbed ('attacked') by gangsters, or by the police. Such blurry distinctions can bring about a lack of empathy with authorities in general, or even an attraction to criminality, including radicalization of various sorts. It may also lead to a situation where the police service attracts people who see in it an opportunity to break the law with impunity. Sheng narratives demonstrate a troubled relationship between the police authorities and the underprivileged youths of the Eastlands.

Chapter 6
Expanded domains and global influences

The concept of the linguistic domain is an old one which refers to areas of use of a language, an area of human activity in which one particular speech variety or a combination of several varieties is regularly used (Fishman 1972). In this framework, the choice of language during an interaction is related to roles (e.g. teacher–student, among peer friends), place (e.g. at home, in the street, classroom or school playground), and topic of conversation (e.g. business, family affairs, politics). There are reservations about a concept of rigid 'domains' or spheres of language use, but it is still useful as an idealized construct for the purposes of establishing parameters of language practices. The languages of formal and informal domains have always been starkly demarcated in Kenya: English is the language of mainstream print media, international business, higher education and government at the policy-making level, including parliamentary debates. Kenyan Swahili (KS) is the 'national' language (of the masses, of popular expression and social solidarity), and in lower level commercial activity and inter-ethnic social interaction and communication. Its standard variety (SS) is the language of school textbooks, news broadcasts and public information, and co-official with English since 2010. The rest of Kenya's 60 odd languages and dialects in vernacular forms are used in situations in which they dominate within their respective communities, in relatively more linguistically homogenous rural areas, or in some urban homesteads. Indigenous languages of Kenya have received a generous boost and rejuvenation since the 1990s when they entered with vigour into media broadcasting on both radio and television. They have created a vibrant industry which provides employment to journalists, newscasters, translators, administrators and infrastructure maintenance workers. It also encourages the development of those languages as their utility enters financially rewarding domains of the linguistic marketplace. It has also made individual Kenyan languages more familiar to citizens of other communities, and of course, they now receive even greater mutual influences due to their greater contact with Swahili, English and other indigenous languages.

More recently, Sheng has found its way into the media, creative and entertainment industries. Its role in these domains of mass media, and the sheer weight of its numbers of users, has begun to influence the speech habits of the rest of the Kenyan population. Most Nairobians today can be said to speak or at least understand some Sheng, which they use every day in the marketplace, at the corner kiosk, on the streets, at home, inside the *matatu* on their daily commute, in schools and universities, and even in formal contexts such as at work. Consider the following exchange between two clerks at an upmarket, privately owned Kenyan bank located in Karen, a wealthy suburb of Nairobi. One speaker is a man, the other a woman, both aged approximately mid to late 20s, or early 30s. The underlined forms are in Sheng, and the second line is a Standard Swahili (SS) translation of the same, followed by an English gloss:

Teller 1: Nipee, one-twenty K.
Nipe elfu mia moja na ishirini.
Give me one hundred and twenty thousand.

Teller 2: Eeeh, uko na dɔɔ?
Sawa, una pesa?
Ok. Do you have [that amount of] money?

The conversation took place in a formal register (bank) which ordinarily requires a formal style of speech in the form of 'Standard Swahili' (in italics) or Standard (Kenyan) English (KE), but it was not. The English loans 'one-twenty' and 'K' meaning 'thousand' [shillings] are in common use among upwardly mobile Nairobians when discussing money, and *dɔɔ* we already know, is a calque of American English slang ('dough'), a word which has been used in Sheng since the 1970s.[1] The elongated final syllables by both speakers are typical of Sheng words, as we saw earlier in the Introduction, and also noted by Ogechi (2005). Of course the grammar of the two sentences is Swahili, which is laid bare by simply replacing the English loan words with Swahili ones.

During his first official visit to Kenya on 25 July 2015, US President Barack Obama greeted his large audience in Nairobi in Sheng, when he rose to address an entrepreneurship conference in Nairobi. He immediately followed his Standard Swahili (SS) greeting (*Hamjambo*!) with quintessential Sheng greetings, *Niaje, wasee*?, whose closest equivalent would be African American Vernacular English (AAVE), 'Yo! whassup, guys?' After a dramatic pause, he added, *Hawayuni*? ('How are y'all?'), to the delight and amusement of delegates and viewers of the live broadcast. A seasoned politician, it was clear that President Obama understood correctly that Sheng is an important identity marker of modern Kenya, especially to the globalized Kenyan youth who are also in the forefront of entrepreneurship and innovation. He used

[1] Another example is the word *beste* (sometimes *beshte*), from UK English slang *bestie*, or *bae* to mean 'best friend'.

Sheng to appeal to his audience by reducing the social distance between them, by deploying a language of youth solidarity. Obama was not the first politician to recognize Sheng's appeal to a youthful audience they wish to court. It may have started in the 2002 presidential campaigns when a popular song '*Unbwogable*', a Sheng word coined from English suffixes and the Dholuo word *bwogo* 'defeat', hence 'unbeatable', was adopted by one of the political parties/candidates that eventually won the presidency. A decade later, during the 2013 general elections, a Kenyan presidential candidate coined the campaign slogan '*Tunawesmek*' (*tu-na-wes-mek* – 'we-TS-Present-can-make [it]'), which means in Sheng, 'We can do/make it.' In a similar effort to identify himself with the youth electorate through language choice, another senior politician famously described himself as a fellow *hustler* to convey solidarity with the poor under-employed masses largely made up of youth, and to distance himself from the political elites.

There were 178 registered FM radio stations recorded in 2017, an astonishing 28.06 per cent increase on the previous quarter (CAK 2017:8). Radio broadcasting closely reflects the reality of Kenya's multilingualism, according to our survey of 47 FM radio stations which live broadcast through the internet (www.radio.or.ke). Of these, 22 broadcast in English, representing 47 per cent of the total, while 15 of them (32 per cent) are designated 'community' radio stations because they broadcast in a Kenyan Indigenous language, although some programming (e.g. interviews with national figures, advertisements, and infomercials) can be in Swahili or English. Seven radio stations broadcast in Swahili only (15 per cent) while one, Ghetto Radio FM – 'The Official Sheng Station', focuses on a Sheng audience with significant success, judging by the vibrancy and popularity of its shows, hosts and deejays. The name of this radio station appeals to an association with the inner city ('ghetto,' *mtaa*), which is a large constituency of Nairobi's population of four million. At least one radio station (Sound Asia FM) broadcasts in Nairobi and Mombasa in Hindi, Gujarati, Punjabi and English.

The 1990s saw early commercial uses of Sheng in advertising (Kariuki et al. 2015), and the new millennium oversaw a rapid expansion of Sheng in public domains such as media, politics and creative arts. Kenya's vanguard literary journal *Kwani?* was an early entrant as it has been publishing fiction and poetry in Sheng alongside English since 2000.[2] The name of the publication itself is a KS expression akin to 'So what?'. Currently, the chief promoters of Sheng use include local hip-hop music (*genge*), music videos, *matatu* operators, and the media. Radio and TV lead in this area, and a lot of social media communication is done in Sheng. Many radio and TV stations

---

[2] See for example the Sheng poem '*Mapinduzi*' (Revolution), by Kijana Ngala in *Kwani?* (2010:15)

also broadcast some of their programming in Sheng, while those hosts doing their shows in SS cannot prevent callers from expressing themselves in Sheng or in a form of KS. One radio station which we shall discuss in some detail is Ghetto Radio FM, whose motto is 'the original Sheng station'; it broadcasts entirely in Sheng, including news. Mobile technology is key in digital communications not only because mobile phones are widely accessible to the youth, but also because it offers a unified platform for radio, internet, music, and video. Phone texting (SMS) is the least expensive way of using a mobile phone; therefore it plays an important role in propagating Sheng or other linguistic innovations. Mobile penetration in Kenya at large stands at 39.1 per cent, with 86.2 mobiles phones per 100 inhabitants (CAK 2017). They are now so prevalent among Kenya's 'generation text' that they are becoming perhaps the only means by which many users practise any form of literacy.

The Nairobian newspaper

Sheng has entered a domain that has until recently been the carefully guarded preserve of standard versions of Swahili and English: print media (i.e. newspapers and magazines) which are overwhelmingly dominated by English. The entry of Sheng in print media is parallel to a notable decline in the readership of Kenya's main Swahili newspaper, *Taifa Leo*, which also now uses popular KS and Sheng in some of its content. Since March 2013, a popular weekly newspaper called *The Nairobian* has broken the frontiers by publishing a weekly column in Sheng.[3] The rest of its content, including some headlines and feature stories, is creatively written in 'Kenyanese'. We have already seen samples of a regular column called *Story za Mtaa* ('Stories from the Hood'), written purely in Sheng by two popular Sheng artists, King Kafu and Mbusii. *The Nairobian* is in the vanguard of Kenyan mainstream print media which consists of four daily English language newspapers – *The Daily Nation, The Standard, The Star,* and *The People*, which publish in carefully edited, educated KS – and *Taifa Leo,* which publishes in SS. The following is a short text of the Sheng column, *Story za Mtaa.*

'Ma-teacher *Msiwaguse* **watoi** *wetu*'
The Nairobian, 5–11 July 2013

lipeni walimu warudi shuleni, watoto wetu hawawezi endelea bila walimu. Wazazi hawatoshi kuwa walimu wa watoto wao bila usaidizi wa walimu. <u>I wonder how our children will prosper</u>

---

[3] *The Nairobian* is published by The Standard Media group, which also publishes *The Standard* newspaper.

without teachers in class. *Serikali lipeni walimu watoto wasome bila* **mbrrrrrrcha** *yoyote.* Male teachers *pia muache za ovyo,* I have two daughters M*** and J***,16 but *siwezi wapeleka shule wakuwe mabibi za waalimu.* Why do you teachers take advantage of our girls? Imagine *ni mtoto wako anadhulumiwa na mwalimu mwanamume,* **utafeel** *aje?*

'Teachers don't touch our children'

Pay [striking] teachers so they return to schools, our children cannot continue without teachers. Parents are not fit to teach their own children without the help of teachers. I wonder how our children will prosper without teachers in class. Government [should] pay teachers so children can study without problems. Male teachers also stop misbehaving, I have two daughters M*** and J***, but I cannot take them to school to become wives of teachers. Why do you take advantage of our girls? Imagine it is your child who is being abused by a male teacher, what would you feel?

Typical Sheng code-switching has taken place in the passage, that is, insertion of full units (words or sentences) of English placed into Swahili sentences (underlined), and one instance of code-mixing, that is, embedding of linguistic units into the morphology of Swahili:

u-ta-feel-aje?
you(sg)-FUT-feel-how?
how will/would you feel?

Note that the future tense marker (*-ta-*) is here interpreted as a modal 'would', which is quite common in KS. Some of the units are idiomatic phrases of English such as 'take advantage of' and 'I wonder why…' that are frequently interspersed in ordinary conversations in Kenyanase, and have now found a place in written language. The column may well horrify journalists who write mainstream Kenyan newspapers, as well as columnists and occasional commentators on culture, society, education and politics. They are generally Kenyans of high socioeconomic status (SES) – prominent and well paid senior journalists, politicians, lawyers and academics above the age of 50. Experts of all sorts in all areas of knowledge but especially politics also get space to make commentary of Kenyan politics and culture and society. Their language is English, and whenever a popular KS expression is inserted, e.g. *mwananchi* (ordinary citizen), it is placed in italics, and translated into English. Clearly, the intended audience is foreign to Kenya's linguistic reality.

June 5–11, 2015 / The Nairobian / Page 37

THE NAIROBIAN
STORY ZA MTAA
MBUSII Twitter: @mbusii facebook: mbusii email: githis83@yahoo.com

MA3 CULTURE

Uzee uheshimike

Vijana wengi hudharau wazee eti juu wamezeeka, lakini hakuna kitu ya maana kama kuzeeka. Watu wengine hata hudharau wazazi wao eti kwa sababu ya uzee, lakini mzazi, hata kama ni mzee, lakini ako uhai, ni poa kuliko ule mzazi myoung na ako kwa kaburi. Watu wengi hawajuangi maana ya wazazi wakiwa hai, wanajuanga umuhimu wao wakishasonga kwa Sir Jah. Unapata watu wengi hawaheshimu uzee, saa zile mzee ako hai anaoneshwa madharau but saa zile amededi ndio wanasema vile huyo mzee alikua ameheshimika lakini wapi. Heshimu mzee na uzee wake, na kama wewe ni mzee heshimu uzee wako juu siku hizi unapata mzee mzima amekunja katotoise kwa kona anataka kukapiga kuni. Unataka kulala na mtoto wa rika moja na mtoto wako halafu unaexpect huyo mtoto akuheshimu. Totoise anakwambia daddy don't touch me there, nabado unainsist lazima akuanikie ikuss. Wamama wazee pia wachaneni na vijana wadogo. Mnamalitzia wasichana wazee wao na wazee wenu wako. Wanaume wazee na nyinyi muachane na tu totoise tudogo. Mnaharibia vijana wadogo ma bibi zao. Yaani in short heshimu uzee yako ndio uheshimike kwa kijiji.

Ukilewa tulia

Kuna tabia zingine watu wengine wakilewa wanafanyanga na hazileti bidii hata kidogo. Ukikunywa tei uhothloliwe, unafaa kujua sio kila mtu umekunyuia. Usianze kupayuka kwa bar mzima ni kama ni wewe tu umatel hapo. Ukilewa tulia, unaweza bongesha mtu pole pole na asikie. Walevi wengine nao ni wale akilewa lazima asumbue, lazima atoe vita. Wengine nao akionge lazima akugongagonge; akukaribie kwa maskio na saa hizo anakuuulia rushia mate. Ukilewa behave. Wengine eti juu mtu amelewa anaongea bila brakes anaongea matusi hata mbele ya watoi nani ile matusi haiwezi andikika kwa Nairobian. Walevi wote kueni wapole mkishahothloliwa.

NYAHUNYO NYAHUNYAHU

Nyahunyo nyahunyahu kwa wale watu wote wenye hawajjoendi. Unapata mtu amejaribu ku commit euicide mara karibu tano na hafaull. Mara amepanda kwa post ya slima anataka kujipigisha shock. Mara amekunywa peison, mara ako na kamba ya kujinyonga na bado hafall. Unasahoo Mungu ndie kupanga life ya mtu. Kama hajasema ukufe hauwezi kufa, na kama unajua uko na tabia kama hio tafadhali rekebisha tabia na upokee nyahunyo.

Ahmed Darwesh
Falsafa za busara

Utu uzima dawa

Mapenzi yakiwasibu watu wawili ndiyo mapenzi. Asikuambie mtu, raha ya mapenzi umpate mtu mzima sio vijana, wao vijana wana nguvu nyingi kuliko akili. Lakini mtu mzima dawa. Utamsikia mzee akibembeleza penzi: "Binti haraka ya nini raha ya ngoma ufuate mdundo. Ngoma yataka matao ati!" Wazee wanajua kulea na kudekeza, wazee wanajua mabaho na kuenganenga. Wazee wanajua kurai na kubembeleza, wazee wanajua kukata pochi bila ya hiyana. Wazee wanajua 'malavidavi' ya kuitana 'honey na sweetheart'. Tofauti na vijana ambao vyao havliki bure, na ukivipapata vitakutoka na puani, kwani atafanya juu chini kuhakikisha amekukomoa kwa njia moja ama nyengine. Namaanisha mtu aliyekomaa kiakili hata kama ni kijana, lakini awe amekomaa. Kwani wengi hujisoza katika ulimwengu wa mapenzi bila ya wao kuwa tayari kuingia kwenye safari hii yenye milima na mabonde, wakitarajia kuwa kila kitu kitakuwa tambarare. Katika kujisoza huku wengi hujikuta wakivunja mahusiano yao mapema mno, na hata kuishia kutengana kwa sababu hawakuwa tayari kwa hili, ila walikuwa tu wakiyajaribu maji kama yapo moto au yako baridi. Kulingana na uvuguvugu au ubaridi uliokuwepo waliamua kila mtu awe baidi kama ardhi na mbingu. Farakano likajiri. Ni hulka ya kibinadamu kuwa ngoma ya watoto haikeshi. Lakini utu uzima una ukomavu wake wa kuyafahamu mambo kwa weledi na uzoefu wa muda mrefu, tena kwa mapana na kwa maerfu. Wazee hawana haraka katika kufanya mambo yao. Hawana pupa katika kula zabibu na kama fursa ipo basi huliwa kwa umakini na kwa kujinafasi. Kila mmoja anafurahia safari kwa kuwa pande zote mbili husika zimeridhiana. Isiwe mambo ya kitoto ya kutoana nishai na kuumbuana pale mambo yanapokwenda segemnege. Kama ni zawadi iliyotolewa wakati wa huba zimeshamiri basi itasalia kuwa hidaya siku zote. Hapatakuwepo na kushikana mashati na kulazimishana katika kurejesheana mulichopeana pindi itakapotokea sababu na mukorofishane. Utu uzima unakataza hili, badala yake unatoa fursa ya kufahamiana na kuelewana. Usikubali kamwe kudhalilishwa na kukomolewa kwa vile umekula nyama choma na bia za mpenzi wako. Kama ameamua kukufurahisha atwe amekurikhisha kwa dhati ya nafsi yake 'isiwe ni mambo ya nipe nikupe'. Kama ni kupeana iwe ni kwa raha zenu, pasiwepo masharti na kushikiana shokoa. La sivyo, itakuwa munafanya biashara. Ni mawazo yangu tu.

Wasiliana nami kupitia darweshahmed@yahoo.com ama thenairobian@standardmedia.co.ke

Lopha, no chewing miraa here

[PHOTOS: PKEMOI NG'ENOH]

the latest, which is less than two weeks old, is Ndenderu."

With more than 300 members now Lopha Sacco, the sacco has never changed the name Latema, Odeon, Parklands, High ridge, and Aghakhan, (LOPHA), despite their growth into other City routes.

Stanley Kimure, the sacco chairman says: "Some of the routes we have introduced include Ruaka, CID headquarters, Ruiru, Thika Road and Juja,

He reveals drivers and conductors are bound by set rules and anyone caught smoking or chewing miraa is punished by suspension, after which they will write an apology letter before their fate is decided.

"We don't discriminate those joining with old matatus but the vehicle must be in good condition," he said.

He added that they are expanding to out of Nairobi routes like Thika, Muranga, Nyeri and Isiolo.

—Pkemoi Ng'enoh

Send your feedback with the word NAI to 22840

Star of the week

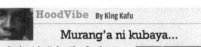

As the chairman of NCPWD one of the major challenges facing our members is public transport. Every day, this matatu crew picks our staff with disabilities, at ABC Place and drives them to their homes at normal bus fare rates. This saves them the agony of crossing the busy Waiyaki Way and also saves them the hassle of bus drivers leaving them stranded at bus stops.I wish to request more champions in the matatu industry to support our journey in accessing public transport.

—David Ole Sankok

HoodVibe   By King Kafu

Murang'a ni kubaya...

Squad ya mtu kumi inahangaisha malion mbaya area za murang'a. Imefika mahali ukichapa tei umachapa ukiwa radar sana. Inakuwa design ata beshte yako pia usimuamini sana. Ukiwasha kimandazi ni kama ya mwisho, nanga (ass) inamulikwa (sodomise). Kivingine kuna vile imefanya malion wa hizo area wamepunguza tei juu hizo ndio area tei imekuwa ikimada walevi sugu mbaya. Hiyo story ya malion kudecodiwa wakiws tei, wamegwaya mbaya. Lakini hiyo ni story haileti bidii. Kama wako roho juu mbona wanakuta walevi peke? Kama unajua hauwezi ji-control itabidi ukae radar. Raiya waungane na makarao wamalize hiyo maneno.

Big up

Big up ma single mother's na ma single fathers wote kwa kulea watoi wao vizuri na kuwa-support ki-education bila kufikiria mob. Big up sana na musichoke kuwachunga vizuri.

Matapeli River Road

Juzi niko nje ya Family Bank jamaa anatoka ndani ya ngive (bank)ananza story hazileleweki. Zake ni matension ati 'oohh nimeshinda dhow kwa wale watu' lakini hasemi ni watu wagani. Zake tu nikumambia nimpeleke akatoe na nikiangalia jamaa mwenyewe ametoka ndani ya ngive, nika jam na yeye nikamtolea za ovyo. Nikamudiiza kwani mimi ni customer care jamaa? Alitoka teke mbaya, ndio kuna matha alitokea akadai huyo jamaa bado alikuwa amemkuta akakataa story yake. Ukikutana na msee kama huyo na ako na problem usijidai Yesu. Kusaidia sio mbaya lakini jua form ni gani ama utosho pahali yake.

SHENG WORD YA LEO: Ting
ting
ENGLISH: Bling
Wewe unaitage bling mtaa yako?

Send us your feedback via mail to: thenairobian.standardmedia.co.ke or tweet us @NairobianToday. You can also like our Facebook page, Nairobian Today or follow us on instagram @nairobiantoday

Tuma jibu kwa: thenairobian@standardmedia.co.ke

Figure 11 *The Nairobian,'Heshimu Uzee'* ('Respect Age')
(© and reproduced by permission of *The Nairobian*)

The Nairobian weekly newspaper has made a brave, innovative departure from that conservative position of journalism in Kenya by embracing Sheng and KS and its speakers, and making efforts to provide content that is more inclusive of Nairobians. The 'Asian Arena' for example occupies a whole page, and is written every week by two female Asians. It is dedicated to news and commentary about the Asian community in Nairobi and its diaspora especially that of the UK. It informs and educates readers about the ordinary life of that community, demystifying knowledge about their daily lives, culture and society. The expatriate community is given a voice too, by two columnists, one British (NaiNotepad) the other an (African) American (Expat Talk), to provide commentary and viewpoints about Kenya and Kenyans, their lives as expatriates, and comparisons and insights about their own countries of origin. They are interesting and valuable to Nairobians because these writers are long-term residents and well-grounded in Nairobi, and are therefore in a position to engage with Kenyan readers effectively. There are sections targeting university students ('Campus Vibe'), the artistic community ('ArtsLounge') and ('JazzLounge'), the inner city ('Hood Vibe', 'Stori za Mtaa'), the *matatu* operators ('Ma3Culture') and in news ('Capital News', 'Country news'), and features ('Nai Indepth'). It also carries sports news, job advertisements and tenders. The 'Engsh' audience is addressed by a column called 'Nai Notepad'. A content analysis of *The Nairobian* shows an extensive use of Sheng, English or KS – Kenyanese - in practically every page, such as the following taken from a single issue of *The Nairobian* published on Thursday 4 June 2015.

Table 14 Sample Stories from *The Nairobian*

---

(1) '*Mheshimiwa* [Honourable, MP] on fresh scandal' (front page)
(2) 'I have worn my *mtumba* [used] shirt for over ten years.'
(3) 'Married city MP busted in Naivasha with a '*clande*' [clandestine girlfriend, cheating] (in quote marks, unlike the Swahili insertions).'
(4) 'Men who can't *nguruma* [lit. roar] in bed.'
(5) '[President] Uhuru na *kangum*u [cheap doughnut]: so, the president walked into a *kibanda* [roadside kiosk] in Machakos and ordered a soda and a *kangumu*.'
(5) '*Mboch* [househelp] and sister deny Sh 2.9 million theft' (p. 19).
(6) 'I clean human *matumbo* [lit. offal] medic says procedure washes away all leftovers from the food path, freeing the body of common illnesses.'
(7) '*Janta* [job] Corner' for *job* adverts (p. 20).
(8) 'You could soon sing anthem in *Kisapere* [Gikuyu] or *Kijaka* [Dholuo]' (p. 33)
(9) '*Kyuks* [Gikuyu] and *Luos* [Luos] will cease to exist in 50 years' (p. 38, *Engsh* column)
(10) 'Sheng word of the day' which in this particular issue was *mneti* ('jailbird') (p. 37) in the *Stori za Mtaa* section (by King Kafu, another Sheng columnist).

(© and reproduced by permission of *The Nairobian*)

The Nairobian seems to aim at being inclusive and innovative, where the mainstream newspapers are dominated by conservatism and exclusion by their strict adherence to standard (English and Swahili) language norms. *The Nairobian* uses popular language (Kenyanese), that is KE and KS spiced up with Sheng and popular KS words and phrases to appeal to the large, critical mass of Nairobians who do not have the interest or competence to read mainstream newspapers in 'textbook' English or Swahili.

Sheng in social media

Sheng is the language of millennials, who are the most prolific users of social media, which facilitate the rapid spread of peer trends. WhatsApp is more popular than Facebook or Twitter and is probably the most effective for its ease of use and ability to transmit photos and videos. According to the Communications Authority of Kenya's 3rd Quarter Annual Report, mobile penetration stands at 86.2 per cent (CAK 2017). Subscription to and use of Facebook leads the pack, distantly followed by LinkedIn, Instagram and Twitter in that order. However, their use is uneven since about 85 per cent of Facebook users, for example, are in Nairobi, while Mombasa accounts for only 3 per cent and Eldoret and Nakuru only 0.9 per cent each, Kisumu 0.6 per cent (Miller 2017). YouTube is also very popular for all types of expression and commentary using Sheng: music videos by Kenyan artists, short documentaries (e.g. *Sheng Talk: Kama Kawa*), and film. Some current Sheng expressions are indicative of the central role of Facebook in the lives of modern Nairobians (see the Sheng glossary).

Although it is beyond the remit of this book to examine all forms of social media in detail, a few examples are sufficient to illustrate the point that Sheng is central in social media communication. It is also fundamental to e-commerce and the creative industry: it is the means through which modern Kenyan entrepreneurs conduct their sales and advertising, particularly on Facebook and WhatsApp. The following comments in Sheng are culled from responses to three YouTube videos by three well-known personalities in the Kenyan media and entertainment industry: Buda Boss ('Boss Man', in Sheng) runs a popular YouTube show by the same name, and Octopizzo, a prominent hip-hop (*genge*) artist. The comments have been anonymised by removing the account information such as email address and accompanying photograph.

Budaboss' Episode 68 'Sheng Itolewe?' ('Should Sheng be Banned?') https://www.youtube.com/watch?v=0ulTj-sMUNU

- 'Sheng to the world...*manze imebidi ii sheng ifike adi france bana...lazma..ntacheki io maneno*'
  'Sheng to the world, man! This Sheng has gone all the way to France, man, for sure...I'll check that out...

- *'Enyewe hii **kamaneno** nilikuwa nimefikiria juzi nikaonelea usishangae ukipata kuna* bill *itapelekwa parliament kuifanya iwe* national language.'
  'By the way I put some thought to this **issue** the other and I saw it should not surprise if you see a bill taken to parliament to make it [Sheng] a national language.'

- *'it's too late for that* [ban] *coz sheng **isha kita** mizizi...*
  'it's too late for that [to ban Sheng] because Sheng **has put down** [deep] roots...'

- *'Haiwezi **buda**.. kwanza ikuwe introduced kama subject **masystem joh**.'*
  'It's impossible **man** [to ban Sheng]...it should actually be introduced as a [school] subject in the **education system, man.**'

- *'aah **bazengaio h**aiwezi Sheng ni lugha ya mtaa so **kuchorea** ati sheng itolewe itakuwa **mezesha noma***
  'aah ? it's not possible Sheng is a street language so **to plot** its ban will be **useless'**

- *Sheng nitamu*
  'Sheng is sweet'

Commentary on *Red Namba Plate* song by Octopizzo (https://www.youtube.com/watch?v=TzvOmYtPNE8, accessed 16 June 2018, 696,125 views)

- *hey octopizzo **maze** eka io ngoma mdundo, **maze tutadownload***
  Hey Octopizzo, **man** put some rythim into that song **man, we will download** [it].

- *Kama **unafeel** hii ngoma **ngonga** like hapa*
  If you love this song, hit 'like' here.

- *Kijaka na Swah Fuq Kingereza.....!!! Waaapi nduru...!!! King KING ... GVNG GVNG_*
  Dholuo and Swahili F*** English....! Scream out!

Commentary on *Baba Yao* song by Jua Cali (https://www.youtube.com/watch?v=jc8_0XGI880, accessed 6 June 2018)

- *hii video ni kali sana jo_!*
  This video is too tough [good] man!

- *big up mtu wangu poa sana ..universe is the limit....hivo hivo_*
  Big up my man, great...universe is the limit...keep on that way
- *[wewe ni] moral icon wa ma youths*
  [you are a] moral icon for the youth
- hey im nigerian and juacali says "au sio" a lot what does that mean?
- Mean [sic] "isn't that right!?"

GoSheng

In its press release, GoSheng presents itself as the 'leading curator of the Sheng language and culture'. Their activities revolve around inclusion and empowerment of the youth using Sheng language as their platform. According to its founder, Duncan Ogweno (pers. comm., email), they recognize that 'Kenyan culture is evolving, diverse and at the same time aspires to advance national unity'. Through funding by both international and local agencies, they have created both physical and digital platforms to engage in a discourse, expression, and broadcasting in Sheng. GoSheng claims to have a network of 60,000 members spread through various platforms linked to the organization's official website (www.sheng.co.ke). Their Sheng online dictionary boasts of over '14,000 words, idioms, phrases and, similes of Sheng'. It is an impressive work of amateur lexicographers, easy to navigate and is cross-referenced. It also features *mchongoano*, a verbal game that showcases participants' wit, humour, originality and speed of thinking (see Githinji 2010). The moderated dictionary invites online participants to contribute new words, examples and possible etymologies of words, thus engendering a community spirit and sense of ownership among Sheng speakers or enthusiasts. GoSheng also runs Sheng Nation (bonga.sheng.co.ke), an online discussion forum with over 13,000 members that provides an open platform for debate with members on issues ranging from governance, society, constitution, human rights, and so forth. The organization also runs Shengwear, an online store for distributing merchandise containing content about Sheng language and culture, such as tee shirts, wristbands, tea and coffee mugs, key holders, and such.

GoSheng not only demonstrate creative entrepreneurship but also serves as a good example of how Sheng can be used to reach out to the constituency broadly known as 'the youth'. They engage the youth in civic affairs through their 'language' to 'further cement the position and need for the use of Sheng as a medium for addressing topical issues facing the youth population' (ibid). GoSheng participated in the consultation process that led to the crafting and promulgation of a new constitution in 2010. They also did an unauthorized translation of the Kenyan Draft Constitution's Bill of Rights into Sheng, and parts of the Traffic Act. In other activities, they participated in the 'Tuvuke Peace Initiative on Fair and Peaceful Elections in Kenya', a nationwide peace campaign whose overall objective was to push for peaceful, free and fair elections during the 2013 national elections. These efforts can empower those who conduct their lives in Sheng, and GoSheng was rightly recognized by the Ford Foundation as 'Champions of Democracy' in 2012, specifically for their participation in 'advancing Peace and Participation through Technology'.

In GoSheng's 'news and information' section of their website, they publish Sheng translations of material from news outlets from around the world. On 30 March 2015, an article discussed the topical issue in the UK of Jeremy Clarkson, host of *Top Gear* show, who had been recently fired from this job.

Jeremy Clarkson anaishia Netflix?

Hii mwezi imekua **jamo ya aajab** *kwa* **husuyu mdabus**, *Jeremy Clarkson. After wakorofishane na* producer *wa* show *yake huko BBC, Top Gear, alibaki* **amechujwa waks** *kutoka kwa hio* show ya **vungu** *na* umati imekua ikisema *hio* show *watakua na shida ku-get msee mwingine ka yeye. Jeremy naye* on the other hand *inasemekana hata* after **kuchujwa waks,** *ni ka hatakaa mtaani* **kubangaiza**...*ashaanza kupata* offers *kadhaa kutoka kwa* **kampu** *zingine, moja yao ikiwa* **kampu** *inajiita Netflix. Netflix ni* **kampu** *ya* **ku-stream mamuvi** *na* **progi** *kwa* telly *na* online *kutoka huko* **majuu.** *Inasemekana Jeremy akiishia huko Netflix, anaweza pewa* full control *ya kitu yoyote atadaisha kuunda kwa hio* **kampu,** *yaani ako na* freedom *kuunda* **progi** *ingine ya* **mandae ka ana- jiskia.** *Wacha* **tuyebi** *ka ataitikia kuishia Netflix na aataamulia nini. Unaona* **future** *yake iko* **jea,** *kwa* **mandae** *ama* aishie *tu* home akatulize?*

Jeremy Clarkson Atahamia Netflix?
(SS translation)

*Mwezi huu umekuwa wa ajabu sana kwa **huyu mtu** Jeremy Clarkson. Baada ya kukorofishana na* produce*r wa kipindi chake huko BBC, Top Gear,* **alifutwa kazi** *yake ya kuendesha hicho kipindi lakini warazamaji wengi wamesema itakuwa vigumu **kupata mtu** mwingine **kama** yeye. **Kwa upande wake,** hata akifutwa **kazi** Jeremy Clarkson hatakaa sana mtaani **akitafuta** kazi nyingine... ameshaanza **kualikwa** na **kampuni** nyingine, moja yao ikiwa ni **kampuni** ya Netflix. Netflix ni **kampuni** ya **kuoenysha filamu kwenye runinga na mtandao** kutoka **ng'ambo.** Inasemekana Jeremy akienda Netflix anaweza kupewa **mamlaka yote** ya kuendesha kazi zake katika hiyo **kampuni,** na uhuru wa kuunda **kipindi kingine** cha **magari/motokaa,** kama akipenda. Acha **tuone** kama atakubali **kwenda** Netflix, ama ataamua nini. Unaonaje maisha yake ya mbele: kwa **magari,** ama aende tu nyumbani akapumzike?*

Will Jeremy Clarkson Move to Netflix?

This has been an **interesting** month concerning **this guy** Jeremy Clarkson. Following a quarrel/fight with the *producer* of his show at BBC, *Top Gear,* **he was fired** from that **popular show,** and people have been saying that it will be hard to get someone else **like** him to do that show. *On the other hand,* it seems that even **after being fired,** Jeremy will not spend time **roaming** the streets [unemployed] … he has already received several *offers* from other *companies* one of them being Netflix. Netflix is a company that *streams* **movies** and **programs** on t*elly* and *online* from **abroad.** It is said that if Jeremy **ends up** at Netflix, he could be given *full control* of whatever he **proposes** to start, that is he will have the *freedom* to start another program/show on cars if he feels like it. Let us see if he agrees to **move** to Netflix or what he decides. Do you see his future in **cars** or should he just **go** home and **relax**?

Underlined items are code-switched English words or expressions, or those embedded in Swahili morphology (for example, *ku-stream ma-movie* 'to stream movies' or *ku-ge*t 'to get'). Highlighted in bold (in both original and translation) are Sheng words or expressions whose knowledge and use is likely to be restricted to an in-group, for example, *husuyu mdabus* ('this guy'), *kampu* ('company'), *ndae* ('car'), etc. The rest is in KS characterized by the usual non-standard features such as irregular noun subject agreements and word order (e.g. *Hii mwezi* instead of *mwezi huu* 'this month') and irregular adverbial concords, for example, *kitu yo yote* instead of *kitu cho chote*. The code-mixing and lexicon used in this passage suggest that the target audience is not only fluent in English and Swahili and Sheng, but are also well informed, and globally interconnected by participating in current debates and trends as illustrated by the last sentence which is in the form of a question: do you see his [Jeremy Clarkson's] future in cars or should he just go home and rest? The targeted audience may be the 'youth' but clearly, they are not a marginalized, youth underclass of Nairobi.

Sheng and the *jua kali* economy

Sheng is the vernacular Swahili of the urban proletariat, including adult men and women working in the 'informal sector' of the *jua kali* industry, street hawkers, *mitumba* sellers and market traders, and of course *matatu* public transport operators. *Jua kali* literally means 'hot sun', but the two words mean much more in KS. The phrase has already found its way into the online Oxford English dictionary where it is defined as: 'a mass noun, usually as a modifier (in Kenya), small craft or artisanal work such as making tools or textiles'. However, *jua kali* in Kenya is much more than that: it is an entire mode of small-scale production and manufacturing, a very large 'informal industry' of micro-enterprises that provides employment and income for millions of Kenyans who make a living by small manufacturing in temporary structures built along major roads and streets of Nairobi. Certain areas and sections of markets are specially reserved for *jua kali* workshops, foundries and welding spots where not only artisanal work or making textiles takes place. These are sites for the production on all kinds of tools and household items such as charcoal and gas burners, wood and metal furniture, panel beating and auto mechanic services, electrical and car spare part shops and so on. The *jua kali* industry including manufacturing, construction, wholesale and retail, hotels and restaurants, transport and communications, and community, social and personal services employed 13.3 million persons in 2017, up by 5.9 per cent from 2016 (KNBS 2017:84). King (1996) described the 'juakalification of Nairobi', in reference to the centrality of this sector to the Kenyan economy:

> Originally from its meaning of 'hot sun' it had first come to refer to work predominantly done by male blacksmiths and metalworkers out of doors in the open air. It seems to have been extended to car and lorry mechanics next, and it became commonplace for many lower middle and middle-income clients to

talk of appreciating *jua kali* skills and very competitive prices. The term took on overtones of creativity and improvisations. Finally, the term broadened to stand not just for a particular form of micro-enterprise, but for a Kenyan version of capital accumulation to be contrasted with that of the multinationals or Kenya Asians. (King, 1996:24)

King's observation about the broadening of the meaning of *jua kali* industry in the mid-nineties has definitely come to pass. It is still a small-scale, improvised business model now extended to many other types business and services (including e-commerce) that provide employment to thousands of enterprising Kenyans. *Boda boda* operators, deejays, musicians and artists, producers of YouTube shows, taxi drivers, will describe themselves as *'jua kali'* people to mean self-employed, improvised, undercapitalized but most of all, creative. Bodash is one example. The 52-year-old director of the delivery start-up business which owns an app of the same name decided to name it in Sheng because 'all my employees speak Sheng at home and work' while packing and preparing deliveries to all parts of the city. He thought that the name *Bodash* and the slogan *Teketeke* (Sheng for 'speedy') capture the image of a youthful, fast, modern service that he wishes his company to project while doing their rounds in Nairobi.

'Sheng is the medium of communication for our company,' explained Mr Charles Muriuki during a personal interview (10 February 2018). 'Our company deals a lot with e-commerce businesspeople who are generally Sheng speakers (millennials), therefore we must use Sheng which used to be restricted to the ghetto [social housing estates] but not any longer.' The Nairobi based start-up delivery company which Mr Muriuki proudly described as a 'definitely *jua kali*' enterprise uses mobile technology and *boda-boda* motorcycles

Figure 12 *Bodash Teketeke*: Logo and uniform of a small delivery company (Photo © Chege Githiora)

to deliver goods in an easy and affordable manner. According to him, the name was coined after much brainstorming, and consideration of a number of proposed names such as '*Twende*' and 'Bike Rider'. To demonstrate the seriousness of the naming task, he gave out a questionnaire to a local technical university seeking opinions from students about a suitable brand name for a business involving *boda-boda*. 'Bodash' came up and was selected as the most appealing to the target market of Sheng users, while rejecting the SS '*Twende*', and the English 'Bike Rider'. 'Bodash' is a typical Sheng coinage involving the clipping of a long word (*boda-boda*), and applying the suffix *-ish* which is popular in Sheng words as we saw in Chapter 4.

The concept of Bodash, and its operation, is a good example of the intersection between Sheng, social media and *jua kali* creativity and enterprise. It works by using an app (Bodash) which is available on all apps stores, and very easy to download onto a mobile phone within in a few minutes. Bodash motorcycles are flexible and safer than those parked on the street because they are centrally monitored and regulated by the company headquarters or its agents. One can order, say, a book from one of the major bookshops in Nairobi, and have it delivered to someone in another part of the city by means of a 'pick and delivery' service through the Bodash app. The Bodash rider nearest to the bookshop will be located by means of Google geolocation service and sent to the client who will receive the delivery upon confirming a passcode issued to the client in the first step of the process. Although there is a cash option, the entire transaction is cashless, with payment made through M-Pesa mobile banking service. The delivery could be medicines ordered at a pharmacy 100 miles from Nairobi to be delivered to an elderly or sick person, which is obviously an important service in rural areas where distances to the nearest services are long. The Bodash app was designed in Nairobi, but coding was done in India due to 'shortage of capacity' in Nairobi – the knowledge was available but the process proved too slow – according to Mr Muriuki. Bodash currently has 500 riders in the Nairobi area, with plans to expand throughout the country. Bodash is not tied to any particular product or service, instead they adapt to the local ecosystem. For example, if the region of operation produces avocado or French beans, their local agent will look for local orders for his team. In Nairobi, currently they deliver cooking gas cylinders to households and businesses. The entire process is conducted predomantly in KS/Sheng marked by code-shifting between *Kisanifu* and Kenyan English during pick up or delivery.

Sheng and corporate advertising

Mutonya's (2008) study of language use, tone and theme in contemporary Kiswahili printed advertisements showed that using non-standard Kiswahili such as Sheng in advertisements helped to associate the products with desirable traits of novelty, change, urban sophistication and youthfulness (ibid: 56). The notions of modernity, uniqueness and globality associated with Sheng explain its popularity in all types of advertising by local small businesses and multinational corporate entities. This is nicely captured by one respondent's statement that 'Sheng *ina*-make *wasee wa*-stand out' ('Sheng makes guys stand out'). Mutonya also noted that non-standard Swahili can be used as a face-saving tool to engage the youth in public dialogue on taboo topics. In this domain, Sheng has been particularly useful in various campaigns by government and NGOs, for example in sexual health campaigns and sensitization of the public on various matters of national interest, such as the constitutional review process (2002–2010), or anticorruption as well as political campaigns etc. A youth magazine, *Shujaaz*, whose express aim is to reach out to the youth of Kenya and enhance their participation in national matters, is published in Sheng. More recent studies observe that the choice of Sheng words or expressions by multinationals in advertising and media is a common strategy; for example, 'there are a number of words meaning "win", which are used in various advertisements, to evoke excitement, chance, good fortune, risk-taking, etc.' (Kariuki et al. 2015:239).

Consider the following examples which illustrate how Sheng is used in corporate advertising, especially but not only that which targets the 'youth'. In some of the advertisements there are subtle orientations of code-mixing structured to appeal to specific sectors of the population. We also observe that the main messages of the advertisements are constructed as informative or instructional, rather than mere praises for products; they seem to assume that the audience is already convinced of the importance of the product. The two main features that define Sheng and KS used to construct these advertising messages are code-switching, code-mixing and special words placed on a Swahili or English matrix. For example the main message in Figure 13a '*Pata chapaa* around the corner' only one word (*pata*, 'get') is in Swahili, with a Sheng word (*chapaa*) inserted for effect. The rest are in English, which means that the imperative statement used to advertise is fundamentally an English sentence (matrix). In Figure 13c we have another imperative statement in which a Sheng word (*msupa*, also: *msupuu, msupu, mshii, dɛm, manzi*, etc.) is inserted in a Swahili matrix (*Rembesha **Msupa** Ushinde* – 'Beautify a **lady** and win'). In Figure 13e, it is code-switching, with English grammar: *Digitize masomo* – 'digitize [upgrade your] education'. Such mixing of Sheng and KS – Kenyanese – in advertising for a variety of products engenders familiarity and solidarity because it is a truer reflection of the language that Kenyans use in everyday communication.

Advertisments on radio are in a different style from print media. They tend to be longer than the short, catchy statements such as we saw above;

Figure 13a *Pata Chapaa* around the corner ('Get cash around the corner'), Barclays Bank ATM at University of Nairobi. (Photo © Chege Githiora)

Figure 13b Uber *chap chap* – *Fika* Faster Faster, save *chapaa* (Photo © Paul Munene)

BCLB No. 001991

Figure 13c Rembesha Msupa Ushinde ('Beautify a lady and win', Venus hair product advert for prize draw, *True Love* magazine)

Figure 13d *Masupuu* dishes, Eastleigh 'Hotel'

Figure 13e Digitize Masomo ('Digitize [Upgrade your] Education', Kenyatta University advert for online courses, *Daily Nation*)

obviously there is more space and time. In addition to the traditional formats, corporate advertising on radio takes two styles: (1) testimonials, in which selected citizens describe how the product or service has changed their lives, how happy they are, etc. and (2) a dialogue between two radio hosts. Radio deejays and co-hosts are paid to read scripts advertising different products, services or public information. Bonoko Deh, whose profile is in the next chapter, is a popular radio deejay who airs his show entirely in 'deep' Sheng peppered with Gikuyu words on Ghetto Radio FM ('The official Sheng station'). During one episode of the popular *Goteana Show* of the same radio station[4] he engages with a co-host (DJ Lin) to advertise for Coca Cola and M-Kopa, a credit giving branch of the giant mobile service and mobile money provider M-Pesa:

DJ Lin: *Na wee Bonoko Deh una*feel *aje ukikunywa Coke?*
SS: *Na wewe Bonoko Deh husikiaje ukinywa Coke?*
               And you Bonoko Deh, how do you feel when you drink Coke?
Bonoko Deh: *Aah..mii nikikunywa Coke najiskianga joto imeisha kabisa, life inakuwa rada kabisa! Inanifungua kwa maik [mike] kuongea na watu.*
SS: *Aah mimi nikinywa Coke husikia joto imeisha kabisa, maisha yanakuwa na raha kabisa! Inaniwezesha kuongea na wasikilizaji kwa maikrofoni.*
               Aah...when I drink Coke I feel nicely cool, life becomes totally great! It helps me talk to my listeners on the mic [microphone].

Features of KS/Sheng are underlined: loan words and code-mixing, and non-standard use of a monolysllbic verb where the infinitive marker *ku-* is retained (*ukikunywa* instead of SS *ukinywa*). KS/Sheng in the next dialogue between the same deejays uses a similar strategy by creating solidarity with the listener using Sheng talk to praise the product, in this case a banking app that promises to give instant credit (loans) to customers without need for collateral which ordinary banks require. The only requirement is for the applicant to have a Facebook account, and an M-Pesa mobile money account, which many Kenyans of all ages have on their phones anyway. Clearly, this product is aimed at the generation which is more likely to run a Facebook account, but not just 'youth' because it also explicitly appeals to parents who may need a quick loan to cover their children's school fees:

---

[4] 16 January 2018, 14.00–18.00 GMT.

DJ Lin: *ukitumia M-Kopa* **ganji** *inakuja kwa M-Pesa yako, enda kwa Google App Store, type BRANCH..hii App..click hiyo ndiyo App ya branch....* If/when you use M-Kopa money comes to your M-Pesa [mobile account], go to Google App Store, type BRANCH..this App...click that BRANCH App...

Bonoko: *Kabisa!*

DJ Lin: *Lazima uwe na akaunti yako ya facebook...ukiweka...* promotion code *ni 'goteana' utapata* **thaɔ** *mbili ukimaliza* installation process...*kila* **msee** *una-invite unapata* **soo** *tano, uki-invite wawili, hapo unapata* **ngiri***, uki-invite* **mabestɛ** *wakumi...hivo hivo* You must have a Facebook account... when you put [in] the promotion code 'goteana' [name of the show, 'Big up')] you will get two thousand [shillings] when you finish the installation process...[for] everyone you invite you get 500 shillings, if you invite two you get a thousand if you invite ten friends...and so on.

Bonoko Deh: Respect!

DJ Lin: *...hakuna* security*, hakuna eti leta mabarua* **mathɛɛ** *aliandikiwa na* **kanjɔɔ***...*
               ...there's no security [collateral], like bring letters your mother received from the [city] council...

Bonoko Deh: *Kabisa!*

Cohost: *...twenty seconds unapata* **ganji** *yako...kaa ni* **ngiri** *tano,* **ngiri** *kumi,* **uko rada** *Bonoko Deh?*
               ..in twenty seconds you get your money....if its five thousand, ten thousand, do you understand Bonoko Deh?

.

Bonoko Deh: *Niko rada kabisa!*
               I fully understand!

DJ Lin: *Hakuna tena kukimbizana na ma-*landlords*, ma-*caretakers*, nini!*
               No more running away from landlords, caretakers and whatnot!

Bonoko Deh: Respect!

DJ Lin: *Kama wewe ni* **budaa** *unahitaji* school fees *ya* **watoii***...*
               If you are a father, and you need school fees for your **children**...

Bonoko Deh: *Kabisa!* **Wazi jo!**
               Absolutely! **That's right, man!**

DJ Lin: *Kila kitu ni* **poa***.*
               Everything is **cool**.

Sheng in rural areas and schools

The expansion of Nairobi into a metropolis is a result of a natural increase in population (currently 4 million) and improved infrastructure, which encourages circular urban–rural migration, as well as commuting (Owuor 2007). The result is an expanded metropolitan region, and stronger links with rural areas further afield – networks which also facilitate Sheng's use in other towns and cities of Kenya, Nairobi's peri-urban and rural areas (see Jua Cali's *Kuna Sheng* lyrics in Chapter 7). The (covert) prestige that Sheng enjoys as a dynamic urban youth language has also contributed to its breaking urban frontiers. The results of a study in Table 15 show that Sheng has a significant presence, where a decade ago it may not have been heard.[5] A questionnaire was completed by 235 respondents, students in a small secondary school located 65 kilometres north of Nairobi city.[6] The aim was to find out the domains of use of the languages Swahili, English, Sheng, and the vernacular, which in this case was Gikuyu, a Bantu language we have already highlighted. Although the school is accessible to Nairobi, 65 kilometres away on a newly expanded highway, its location and student body is typical of a linguistically and culturally homogenous Kenyan rural community where a 'lingua franca' is unnecessary. Some people commute from this village to work in the capital, while those who reside in the capital have strong family and personal links to this community.

Table 15 Language use among students of a rural secondary school (average age: 16 years)[7]

	Swahili	Sheng	Gikuyu	English
Mother tongue	9.4%	0%	88.5%	2.1%
Homestead	17%	0.4%	81.2%	1.4%
Street	26.4%	34.9%	36.6%	2.1%
Solidarity	38.3%	28.1%	23.4%	10.2%
School	27.7%	1.7%	1.2%	69.4%

[5] Notably, that the category 'Sheng' was introduced by students when asked to name the languages they spoke in various domains, revealing a conscious awareness of the speech code.

[6] June 2014.

[7] N= 235, Boys: 110 and girls 125 but there are overlaps e.g. work/school language is both Swahili and English, hence some over/under-reporting. Also a number of N/As were in the raw data. Thanks to participating students of Mutuma Secondary School in Kiambu county, their teachers and head teacher, Mr Moses Muiruri.

Gikuyu, the vernacular ('homestead') language of the area, is spoken as the mother tongue by a majority (88.5 per cent) according to the data. Teenage secondary school students in this rural community speak an average of three languages, just like their Nairobi conterparts. Although English and Swahili have equal, official status, the former is the language of instruction, and most students (69.7 per cent) claim to use it during school time, probably because it is mandatory and its use strictly enforced. KS is used as a language of solidarity, i.e. informal talk among peers, in and outside the school grounds (38.3 per cent). Significantly, Sheng is used for solidarity (28.1 per cent) outside the school more than the local vernacular, Gikuyu (23.4 per cent), and has a nearly equal role (34.9 per cent) of 'street language' as the local vernacular (36.2 per cent). Personal observation confirmed that Sheng is the code of choice among youths of this rural community when they congregate at the local shopping centre, at video dens, pool bars, village halls, local bars or eateries, and football matches. This is especially true among young students home on holiday from boarding schools.

Formal schools are an important space for the socialization of modern citizens, and the acquisition of language (and culture) is an integral part of that process (Duranti 2012). Kenyans still lay heavy emphasis on the education of their children as the principal means of upward social mobility, of achieving a 'better life'. The spread of Sheng in rural areas is linked to schools, where much Kenyan youth of different sociocultural and linguistic backgrounds first come into close contact with each other during a formative period of life, and where they expand their personal and social networks (Milroy 1980). Sheng plays a central role in the daily lives of young students since group reference or 'talking like' is critical as with all other matters affected by 'peer pressure'. Sheng is associated with characteristics which they wish to project as their personal identity, such as modernity, urbanity, 'coolness'. Boarding schools are popular in Kenya because students generally perform better, presumably because students can focus more on their studies. They also play an important role in the spread of Sheng on one level, and in perpetuating class differences on another; they cost more because of the additional boarding fees and prestige they enjoy for their academic success, therefore they are a marker of socio-economic class, even though they are likely to be physically located in rural settings. Thus the boarding school environment mirrors the larger, economically stratified, multilingual Kenyan society where indigenous languages are stigmatized, and even prohibited on school grounds. Similarly, Sheng and 'Engsh' take centre stage among adolescents and teenagers, as they do in the homesteads, streets and neighbourhoods of Nairobi. Students from rural areas may take home during the holidays the prestigious Sheng vernacular that they have acquired in school and introduce it to their rural networks; urban-based students take back to the city new varieties and words, even as they pick up new trends during the holidays and bring them back to school.

Sheng and the diaspora (*majuu*): transatlantic influences

So, Sheng iko kila mahali, Sheng inaskika mpaka majuu, Sheng utaipata mpaka kwenye countries zingine, unaeza ongea hivi tu Mkenya atajua wewe ni Mkenya.

So, Sheng is everywhere, Sheng is heard even abroad, you will find Sheng in other countries. You speak this way and a[nother] Kenyan will know you are Kenyan.

DJ Jemedari, interview September 2017

Sheng is the language of Kenya's modern, cosmopolitan face in urban music, fashion, and lifestyle. It is also a recipient of global cultural influences, especially those of the African diaspora. Many products of US black culture enter Nairobi's sociocultural space through Sheng in popular hip-hop and reggae music, film, television, and of course the internet. 'Globalization' has enabled international capitalism to penetrate corners of the world, facilitated by modern communication, accelerated by internet technology especially through mobile phone technology. There is also greater circulation of people between Africa, Europe, and America despite recent effort to build a 'Fortress Europe', Trump's Mexican wall, Brexit, and such. Remittances or money sent home by Kenyans in a foreign land are now recognized as an important contributor to the country's growth and development due to the vast sums involved. Kenyans in Western Europe and North America bring the largest inflows of cash to Kenya, with the United States and Canada accounting for more than half of remittances. Europe accounted for 29 per cent of the US $1.9 billion (Kenya Shillings 190 billion) in 2017, for example (CBK 2017). The following examples of social media comments are illustrative of the connections between Nairobians at home and abroad, mediated by Sheng:

niko hapa pande ya maine [sic] United states kukaza tu ata sasa hivi ndio naelekea job.

I am out here in Maine United States hustling in fact right now I am heading to work.

Nafurahia sana hizi videos manake naona nyumbani na watu wake maridadi kabisa mimi nakazana ngambo pesa sio shida namis mabesty familia huko Nairobi siku moja tuu nitatokea mtaani nikule hizo chapo,nyama, madado manzy.

I am so pleased with these videos because I see home and the beautiful people I am hustling abroad money is not a problem [but] I miss friends and family there in Nairobi one day I will appear in the hood and eat that chapati, [roast] meat, beans, man! [sic]

Musicians and other artists – young and not so young – use Sheng as their expressive language, including prominent Kenyan artists such as Jua Cali, for example, who produces his music almost exclusively in 'deep' Sheng (see Chapter 6). Others like Octoppizzo rap in Sheng with more English code-mixing and orientation to popular expressions of African American Vernacular English (AAVE), such as 'yo!', 'whassup?', 'bling', 'blane', and so on. Mose (2012) described the centrality of Sheng in Kenyan *genge*, the Kenyan variety of US hip-hop music, noting that rappers such as Abbas Kubbaff have a 'unique style of rapping, infusing English with street slang Sheng'. All these different infusions work together to create a uniquely 'African' language hip-hop or reggae that can today stand on its own within those genres. The use of Sheng in Kenyan rap has increased since then, with many more artists, big and small, rapping their way to money and fame in Sheng. Kenyan artists regularly perform live shows in front of diaspora audiences in Europe and USA, and artists from those places regularly perform in Nairobi venues.

Sheng culture and lifestyle is also influenced by Rastafarianism, also with roots in Jamaica. Of course, there are other convergences underlain by the history of the two nations which have in common the English language in its many localized varieties. There are also shared values and traditions as members of 'the Commonwealth' of 52 independent states that are former territories of the British Empire. The group of states is also part of the 'outer circle of English ' (Kachru 1985), which are united by much more than English, their common official language and lingua franca. Indeed, there are strong connections in legal systems based on English common law, education, and religion (e.g. the Anglican Church), and the basic values of the Westminster model of a parliamentary democracy.

Other similarities are particular to the two nations but still derived from their common British colonial heritage. For example, Kenyans like Jamaicans before them, waged a guerrilla war of resistance against British slavery and subsequent colonialism. The insurgents – Maroons of Jamaica and Mau Mau of Kenya – captured the imagination of many black peoples around the world. A radical group Youth Black Faith in 1940s Jamaica, for example, deliberately kept dreadlocks as a political statement of defiance against what they saw was a corrupt system. But for Rastafarians, dreadlocks are a religious ('Nazarene') vow to reject shaving of the hair (Anderson 2018, personal interview). Dreadlocks were a symbol of resistance of Mau Mau freedom fighters who saw in them a statement of protest about the harsh times they lived in Kenya of the 1950s. Images of Ethiopian patriots who fought successfully against the Italian invasion of their country just before the outbreak of WWII also show them wearing dreadlocked hairstyles, and of course, many east African peoples wear dreadlocks as part of their traditional body adornment: Maasai men, Turkana men and women, Samburu peoples, and many others around Africa. All these images are at the centre of Sheng universe among millions of Kenyan youth and adults who are fans of reggae music. They dance and sing along to popular songs, and watch videos which are widely available in *matatus*, pool halls, in private homes and in public spaces such as bars, restaurants, cinemas and video arcades all over Nairobi.

Sheng in reggae

The popularity of reggae music in Nairobi is unmistakable. It blares out inside bars, *matatus*, market stalls, *marima* (drinking dens), kiosks, on large fancy speakers mounted on flashy *boda-boda* motorbikes used to transport people or luggage and goods for a fee, and on millions of earphones plugged into mobile phones and electronic devices. Kenyan artists such as Wyrie and Nazizi produce reggae of international standards, which won the former an International Reggae Award in Miami in 2014. Others produce their music in 'dancehall' form, or in 'reggaeton' (*reguetón* in Spanish), which has Latin American (Puerto Rico) roots. In these two formats, artists rap rather than recite or sing their lyrics, which draws out verbal skills to their maximum, following a much faster tempo than classical reggae. Studio mixes of original soundtracks with highly creative Sheng lyrics and hyperbole are often heard in nightclubs and on Ghetto Radio FM. Swahili, English and Vernacular radio stations play reggae at many different times of day and night, and many Nairobians also listen or watch reggae on (cable) television and internet on televisions sets, computers and mobile phones. Frequent live concerts take place, by local bands and international music bands including Grammy Award winners such as Ziggy Marley, Morgan Heritage, Burning Spear, and other internationally known reggae musicians. Many young Kenyans go by 'Rasta' names or tags such as *Rasta/Mrasta, Ras, Mnati,* and such. Some Jamaican reggae artists themselves have adopted names such as 'Black Uhuru' ('Black Freedom' English/Swahili) or 'Burning Spear' after Kenya's first president, Jomo Kenyatta. Dreadlock hairstyle is quite popular and widely tolerated in Kenya society today, unlike a decade or two ago, and Sheng talk is littered with 'Jamaicanisms', that is words that are rooted in the culture of far away (from Kenya) Caribbean island of Jamaica. Sheng helps transmit these cultural and linguistic influences from the African diaspora.

Jamaicanisms in Sheng

Cassidy (1961), who conducted a comprehensive study of what he termed 'Jamaica Talk' in the 1950s, described 'Jamaicanisms' as the 'dialectal element in Jamaica's language which evolved within the island's population and away from the *standard British English* [my emphasis], from local elements of Jamaican rhythm and intonation' (ibid:32). The distinctiveness of Jamaica talk in relation to British (Standard) English is that:

> Of non-British influences it is obvious that the African is the largest and most profound; it appears not only in vocabulary, but has powerfully affected both pronunciation and grammar. We may feel fairly certain of about two hundred and thirty loan words from various African languages; and if the numerous compounds and derivatives were added, and the large number of untraced terms which are at least quasi Africa in form, the total would easily be more than four hundred [words]. Even at its most restricted, the African element in the vocabulary is larger than all the other non-English ones together. (ibid:394)

A few Jamaicanisms – words and expressions as earlier defined – are frequently used in Sheng talk. They enter Kenyanese mainly through reggae music, 'a cultic expression that is both entertaining, revolutionary and filled with Rastafarian symbolism' on which Bob Marley stamped his personality and popularized worldwide, no less in Africa. Rastafarianism is an 'indigenous movement, of Jamaica which has the philosophy and structure capable of providing a rallying point for the masses in search of social change, in USA, Canada, UK and Africa' (Barrett 1997).

It is an appealing cult to many in Kenya, and most Nairobians know a '*Mrasta*' or *Mnati* – someone (generally male) who wears dreadlock hairstyle, likes reggae music and probably lives an independent lifestyle, a Rastaman. Reggae discourse resonates with Nairobi's proletariat, especially the youth who identity easily with the poverty, violence, discrimination and oppression that the music talks about. Most of these images linked to the musical lyrics ('*ma-teachings*') are spread through reggae, which also inspires a desire for social change and social justice. Of course the African based rhythm of the music is also very appealing.

The following examples were obtained from questionnaires and interviews of the Nairobi Data Set, and from the column *Stori za Mtaa,* which is published in Sheng in the weekly newspaper *The Nairobian.* I then compared their original meanings and contextual interpretations from available literature, and with the assistance of a Jamaican scholar who is also a Rastafarian elder resident in London. It was clear that Jamaicanisms are borrowed by Sheng with their meanings intact and slightly modified pronunciation such as the following:

Table 16 Jamaicanisms in Sheng.

Sheng	Jamaicanism
airee	*Iree*! Something good, e.g. *the man iree*? 'is he alright?'; *feel iree*, 'feel good' (2) as a superlative, *it iree man* 'it's the best' (3) a salutation.
babi (ma-)	*Babylon*. The oppressive, dominant 'system', in Rasta talk.
-deh, e.g. Bonoko Deh	A Sheng coinage, modelled after, but different from the Jamaicanism *deh*, e.g. *A mi deh* 'I'm here' or *Is Maxi deh?*
-dem e.g.	*-dem*. Jamaican plural suffix of Akan origin (Cassidy 1961), e.g. *man-dem* ('men'); *pikni-dem* (children < *pikni* 'child').
didre	*Dreddy, dread* (a transposition of *dredi* 'dreadlocks')
doba	Dub 'dub music', 'rub a dub'. 'Dub' is militant, revolutionary, the pumping beat, employing cymbals etc to create intense reggae music.
empress (ma-)	Woman, lady. Ethiopian Emperor Haile Selassie and his wife Empress were crowned together for first time in history, and in this way elevated a woman to dignity.
hasura (ma-) (hustler), and ku-hustle.	*Hustler*, which is related but older than 'a scuffler [who] can do anything, even pick pocket; a hustler is a bit more honest... scuffling means 'making the best of life by any means possible' (Barrett 1997:88).
kuchi	*Cutchie* different from the (bigger) chalice (water pipe) for smoking 'herb'.
kushumpeng	*Kushumpeng* 'good herb' (marijuana).
layon (ma-) < Lion	Brave (< 'Lion of the tribe of Judah', in Rasta talk) e.g., he's lion! (he's brave, strong) or 'humble lion' (a brave and strong but humble man). Also a salutation, exhortation: Lion!
ma-teachings	Precepts teaching of Jah/Rastafarianism, from the Bible etc.
mathaland (Kibera)	Motherland (Africa, 'Home').
ma-youth/mayut	(1) Youth especially young males (2) children, e.g. *mi youth-dem* ('my children'). Also used in place of 'boy', which is now a derogatory way to address a young man.
nati/mnati	*Natty*, 'person with dreadlocks'.
safara (ma-)	*Sufferer*, 'the struggling masses' (Austin 1984).

(Ma-)Babi

The Sheng word *babi* (plural: *mababi*) is borrowed from Jamaican English 'Babylon', and is used to embody a socioreligious concept propagated by Rastafarians. It describes the dominant power structure or 'system' and by extension, members of that system, including the socioeconomically dominant classes (Campbell 1985). The word was introduced by Rastafarians to refer to Jamaica and Western society in general as the 'land of oppression' in which Black people are imprisoned, and can only escape through divine intervention. Maxim Anderson adds that there is a 'moral angle' to Babylon: it is an evil place, oppressive, hence 'oppressor' (police, authorities), an oppressive system in general. In Sheng talk, 'Babylon' too embodies all oppressive forces but principally the police, *babilon* (plural: *mababilon*), who are notorious for harassing vulnerable *wananchi*, particularly young male adults and teenagers. We saw earlier how Sheng narratives reflect this reality of the fear and hostility between the youth and police in Nairobi and Kenya at large. The clipped version, *babi* (plural: *mababi*), refers to another class of powerful Nairobians: the upper classes, the well-off ('uptown') who live in leafy suburbs and mainly speak KE at home or in their socials circles (also known as *ma-punks*). Barasa & Mous (2017) suggest that *babi* may be derived from 'Barbie' (the doll), but while this might be true in reference to 'upper classes', it certainly does not evoke the image of police, or the 'system'.

Their counterparts are the *masafara* or those on the opposite end of that spectrum: the poor and victimized masses who speak Sheng or vernacularized varieties of KS. In Jamaican English, 'sufferer' is widely known to denote '[Jamaica's] poor, and particularly the young, unemployed in Kingston; an innocent victim' (Austin 1984:241). In both cases (*mababi, masafara*), the Swahili noun class marker *ma-* (NC6) is used instead of NC2 (*wa-*) to denote a collection, mass, (socio-economic) class of people, rather than a sum of numbered individuals. Such examples of Sheng talk reflect the awareness of social structures based on socio-economic class divisions and borrowing from distant languages and societies. Kibera (Kibra) is the largest 'informal settlement' of Nairobi, where many thousands live or have grown up since its beginning in the first half of the 20th century (see Chapter 1 on 'Kinubi'). Sheng speakers call it 'motherland', an allusion to the Rastafarian belief of Africa as the 'motherland' or the natural home of all Black people. Kibra, therefore, is not a 'slum' as Standard English would describe it, but rather a 'home' or 'roots' that one yearns for even long after they have made it in the big world. Jamaicanisms, and in particular Rasta Talk, in Sheng are examples both of 'counter language' and of the 'unceasing circulation' of peoples and ideas within the African diaspora (Hamilton 1995). Two more examples may underscore this point.

'Big Up'

The following example is a sentence uttered by the host of *Goteana* show on Ghetto Radio Online (Live stream, 15 January 2018):

Sheng: *Nataka kuwa-<u>big-up</u> ma-lion wote mtaani*
SS: *Nataka kuwapa <u>salamu zangu za dhati</u> vijana wote mtaani*
        I want to '<u>big up</u> all the guys in the hood

'Big-up' singular and the plural is an expression of acknowledgment, support, approval or encouragement. It is also a greeting, or a shout out. In South Asian and Caribbean informal English 'big-up' refers to a person of high status or great wealth (*mdosi* or *sonko* in Sheng). Maxim Anderson, a Rastafarian elder, expanded this notion during an interview:

> 'up' is an English term used to mean elevation, therefore the term 'big up' literally means to elevate highly or to a superlative degree. It is a salutation, and a term of endearment as in, 'I want to big up everyone who has shown me support over the years' or 'Big up on that excellent performance.'

Consider the following passage by Mbusii, a Sheng newspaper columnist and popular radio host on Ghetto Radio FM. Reading it, Maxim, who does not speak Sheng, could understand most of the code-switched sections of the text, and he easily understood and even provided further interpretation of other sections of the following text published in Sheng in a weekly column of *The Nairobian* newspaper. In bold are Sheng words, while underlined items highlight elements of non-standard KS grammar. The code-switched in English parts are in ordinary print:

---

*<u>**Inasemekananga**</u> ya kwamba* fear of the Lord is the beginning of wisdom, but *hapa Kenya sioni* wisdom. ***Sio poa** wewe* ku-trust *tu kila kitu* prophet *anadai. <u>Kua</u> kama wa Rasta* — we don't trust in prophet, in Jah we trust. *Kuna watu wengine huchukulia wengine* advantage. *Unapata kazini <u>ule</u> mtu anafanya kazi mob ndiye anapata **chedas** kidogo.* But you have to start from somewhere ***juu** hivyo ndivyo **kunaendanga**. <u>Wakikuchukulia</u>* advantage*, **uskonde**, wewe **chapa waks** yako na <u>Sir Jah</u> atakubless.*

Standard Swahili (*Kiswahili Sanifu*)

***Husemekana** kwamba <u>kumhofu Mungu ndio mwanzo wa busara,</u> lakini hapa Kenya sioni busara. **Haifai** wewe kuamini kila kitu <u>anachodai</u> nabii. Kuwa kama Warasta – hatumwamini nabii,*

*Mungu tu ndiye tunayemwamini. Kuna watu wengine wanaodan-ganya wengine. Unapata kazini yule mtu anayefanya kazi nyingi ndiye hupata **pesa** kidogo. Lakini ni lazima uanze mahali fulani, **kwa sababu** hivyo ndivyo ilivyo. <u>Wakikudanganya</u>, **usife moyo,** wewe **fanya kazi** yako, na **Mungu** atakubariki.*

English

It is said that the fear of the Lord is the beginning of wisdom, but here in Kenya I do not see wisdom. It is not right for you to trust everything that a prophet says. Be like a Rasta – we don't trust in prophets, in God we trust. There are some people who take advantage of others. You find that at work the person who does most is the one who gets less money. But you have to start from somewhere because that is how things go. If they take advantage of you, do not fear, you just go on do your job and God (Sir Jah) will bless you.

Rastafarians believe that a prophet is a man after all and man is fallible: 'You see a man face but not his heart,' explained Anderson. Therefore he agreed with Mbusii[8] that one should not trust everything a 'prophet' says: '*Sio poa wewe ku*-trust *tu kila kitu* prophet *anadai*' (It's not right for you to trust/believe everything a prophet says). He explained the same idea using another Rastafarian saying, 'Man to man is unjust you do not know whom to trust.' His interpretation of the Sheng statement, '*Wewe chapa works yako na Sir Jah atakubless*' (You just do your works, and God will bless you) proved to be an eye-opener to one uninitiated into Rastafarian philosophy. The same message is expressed in another saying that 'Words without works is death' (i.e. meaningless), where 'works' (Sheng, *waks*) is used in the archaic/biblical sense of 'good works' or 'good actions' in life. Cassidy (1961) noted that one of the features of Jamaica Talk is the use of old words or expressions (archaisms) which are no longer used in Standard (British) English. Rastafarians have many such sayings for example, 'Jah works spread goodness', that is the good actions of an individual bring goodness to the world (and therefore must be encouraged).

---

[8] Mbusii here refers to the many self-proclaimed 'prophets' who flourish in Kenyan evangelical churches among gullible congregations.

Sheng: *Wee <u>chapa waks</u> yako na Sir Jah atakubless.*
SS: *Wewe <u>fanya kazi</u> yako na Mungu atakubariki.*
              Just <u>do your work</u> and God will bless you.

A notable Sheng innovation unknown to the Rasta Elder nor in the available literature is the prefix 'Sir' in 'Sir Jah' of Sheng talk, alternating between God and *Mungu* (SS). Indeed, the *genge* artist Jua Cali in the lyrics of his signature his song *Kuna Sheng* (see Chapter 7) asserts that *Mungu mtaani si humwita <u>Sir Jah</u>* (In the hood we call God 'Sir Jah'). Many Sheng words and expressions, as well as the style of dress, body adornment, hairstyles, reflect its ongoing and dynamic linkages to a larger cultural universe of the Western world (*majuu*). Sheng supplements English as another face of a globally interconnected Kenya, while retaining an African authenticity at the level of language and some of its imagery. Sheng therefore plays the role of linking Kenyan 'youth' to the African diaspora (*majuu*) through hip-hop and reggae music.

Chapter 7
Sheng in practice

'Kuna Sheng' lyrics by Jua Cali [1]

The song *'Kuna Sheng'* (literally, 'There is Sheng') by Jua Cali captures a number of key elements of the Sheng phenomenon. Its main theme is that there are different 'Shengs' in Nairobi, and beyond, *'lakini sii [sisi] wote tunaelewana'* (but we all understand one another). I reproduce the words below, but for the sake of brevity, I have cut all but the first and last of 39 lines and four refrains, which are sufficient to illustrate my point. Jua Cali makes reference to localized (in-group) varieties of Sheng ('deep Sheng') that are marked by use of different words or expressions according to area of residence (*mtaa*) of the Eastlands housing estates of Nairobi where Sheng is the primary language of interaction, e.g. in Line 3, the underlined words mean 'one hundred shillings' in different parts of the city: *nikikuitisha <u>ing'ang'a</u> nakuitisha <u>sɔɔ moja</u>* (If I ask you for <u>*ing'ang'a*</u> I am asking you for <u>*sɔɔ moja*</u>). The four refrains in between the stanzas of the song mention 20 specific neighbourhoods of Nairobi (highlighted in bold) whose names are typical of Sheng coinages in two ways: clipping of words or names, and favouring the ending *-ish/-ich*, if not a heavy syllable (long vowel), e.g. *Okongɔɔ* for Makongeni or *Isich* for Eastlands, *Kibich* (Kibera) or *Eldii* (Eldoret). With the exception of *Westii* (Westlands), all those mentioned are low income, densely populated, housing estates; some are called 'slums' in Kenyan English, e.g. Kibera (Kibich), Kawangware (Ongwarɔɔ) and Korogocho. The rest are old council or low to mid income, civil servant quarters of the city which are strongly identified with Sheng talk. Nonetheless, the singer is aware of the Sheng community beyond Nairobi: five of Kenya's main cities are mentioned in this Sheng anthem: Mombasa, Kisumu, Eldoret, Nakuru, and Thika. These are big cities with large, multi-ethnic populations comparable to that of Nairobi, although to a lesser degree in terms of multilingualism, and where Sheng is widely spoken. In between the choruses, the singer educates the listener about different expressions and words of Sheng, and what they mean in other varieties of

---

[1] Source: https://www.youtube.com/watch?v=Urxhkjh45ck, accessed 7 February 2018.

Sheng, e.g. Line 6 *kutia blanda ni kujiingiza* (make a mistake, blunder), or in general Kenyan Swahili (KS), e.g. Line 2: *kutoka chwa ni kutoka mbio* (run off fast). Other lyrics point at how Sheng vocabulary has changed with time, how older words may have been replaced with new ones, e.g. Line 1 of Stanza 1: these days *wangodi* are called *mandingo*, or 'to be called a *dwanzi* [these days] is the same as being called *fala*', an old Sheng word. These Sheng synonyms are underlined in each line of the transcription below, and the 20 estates mentioned in the song are highlighted in bold, with their full names in square brackets. Jua Cali's song '*Kuna Sheng*' is indeed a story of Sheng. Through it, the listener learns about 50 Sheng words in pairs of synonyms, a majority (40, or 80 per cent) consist of the following verbs: wait; escape; be scared; make a mistake; pay attention; be broke; share; be left out; be evicted; to be cool; compare; stink; eat; attend to business; be trusted; be clueless; stay in place. The rest are nouns including the following: gangster; one hundred shillings; mobile phone; girl; fool and God. These vocabulary are quite ordinary words of daily usage, they do not suggest secrecy or illegal activities. But they give clues about the life of 'hustling' which is experienced by the *masafara* of the city, the main theme of many of Jua Cali's musical lyrics.

'*Kuna Sheng*'

Introduction: *Kanyeria! Jua Cali!*

REFRAIN 1

> *Kuna sheng ya Calif lakini sii[sisi]²wote tunaelewana*
> There is <u>Calif</u> [**California**] Sheng but we all get along [understand one another]
> *Kuna sheng ya <u>Buruu</u> lakini sii wote tunaelewana*
> There is Buruu [**Buruburu**] Sheng...
> *Kuna sheng ya <u>Dandora</u> lakini sii wote tunaelewana*
> There is **Dandora** Sheng....
> *Kuna sheng ya <u>Okongɔɔ</u> lakini sii wote tunaelewana*
> There is Okongɔɔ [**Makongeni**] Sheng....

STANZA 1

Line	Sheng synonyms (underlined)	gloss
1	<u>*Wagondii*</u> *siku hizi wanaitwa* <u>*madingɔ*</u>	gangster
2	<u>*Kutoka chwa*</u> *ni* <u>*kutoka mbio*</u>	run off fast
3	*Nikikuitisha* <u>*ing'ang'a*</u> *nakuitisha* <u>*sɔɔ moja*</u>	one hunderd shillings

---

² See Chapter 5, 'phonological innovations' in Sheng. While '<u>*sisi wote*</u>' is normal in KS, it is '<u>*sisi sote*</u>' in SS.

4	*Nikikuambia <u>nitegee</u> nakuambia wee <u>ngoja</u>*	*wait*
5	*Una<u>shtuka</u> nini wacha <u>kujitisha</u>*	*be scared*
6	<u>*Kutia blanda*</u> *ni <u>kujiingiza</u>*	*make a mistake, a blunder*
7	*Niki<u>ongea</u> na wewe poa naku<u>skiza</u>*	*listen, pay attention*
8	<u>*Kupigwa na makarau*</u> *ni <u>kuvaliwa</u>*	*be beaten up by police*
9	*Unajaribu kupiga <u>simu nangos</u> sina kitu*	*mobile phone*
10	*Chali yangu <u>umechar</u> hauna kitu*	*be broke*
11	*Baadaye tunakuona <u>umebambwa</u> kwa <u>mbulu</u>*	*be in trouble*
12	<u>*Ku-share kitu*</u> *ni <u>sulu bin sulu</u>*	*to share*

REFRAIN 2

*Kuna sheng ya **Isich** lakini sii wote tunaelewana.*
There is Isich [Eastleigh] Sheng *but we all understand one another.*
*Kuna sheng ya **Kibich** lakini sii wote tunaelewana.*
There is Kibich [Kibera] Sheng....
*Kuna sheng ya **Embaa** lakini sii wote tunaelewana*
There is Embaa [Embakasi] Sheng...
*Kuna sheng ya **Marish** lakini sii wote tunaelewana*
There is Marish [Maringo] Sheng....

STANZA 2 Vocabulary

REFRAIN 3

*Kuna sheng ya **Ongwarɔɔ** [Kawangware] lakini sii wote tunaelewana*
*Kuna sheng ya **Pangɔɔ** [Pangani] lakini sii wote tunaelewana*
*Kuna sheng ya **Salem** [Salem] lakini sii wote tunaelewana*
*Kuna sheng ya **Ungem** [Kangemi] lakini sii wote tunaelewana*

STANZA 3: Vocabulary

REFRAIN 4

*Kuna sheng ya **Bahaa** [Bahati] lakini sii wote tunaelewana.*
*Kuna sheng ya **Jerii** [Jericho]...lakini sii wote tunaelewana.*
*Kuna sheng ya **Bangla** [Bangla] lakini sii wote tunaelewana.*
*Kuna sheng ya **Korogocho** [Korogocho] lakini sii wote tunaelewana.*
*Kuna sheng ya **Westii** [Westlands] lakini sii wote tunaelewana.*

*Kuna sheng ya **L.A** lakini sii wote tunaelewana.*
*Kuna sheng ya **Githurai** [Githurai] lakini sii wote tunaelewana.*
*Kuna sheng ya **Madaa** [Madaraka] lakini sii wote tunaelewana.*

STANZA 5 Sheng outside Nairobi

Line

33   *Siezi sahau watu wangu wa **Eldii***
        I can't forget my people of Eldii [**Eldoret**]
34   *Eehhh!*
35   *Siezi sahau watu wangu wa **Nakuru** (watu wa nguvu)*
        *Can't forget my people of **Nakuru** (strong pepole)*
36   *Eehhh!*
        Sheng ya Kisumu (ni noma sana)
37   **Kisumu** Sheng is 'bad'
        Sheng ya Mombasa (mambo mbaya)
38   **Mombasa** Sheng (tough stuff)
        Sheng ya Thika (noma sana)
39   **Thika** Sheng (cool stuff)
        eehhh!
        Au sio (au ndio)
        Aha ha ha ha...!
        Ehhh TUGENGE YAJAYO
        Kanyeria, Juacali!
        GENGE Au sio...
        End.

Ghetto Radio FM: 'The official Sheng station'

Ghetto Radio FM is a live FM radio station that has been broadcasting out of Nairobi in Sheng since 2007, and more recently online. On its website it describes itself as: 'Your No. 1 Sheng station, with local and international news, sports and lifestyle'. Ghetto Radio FM was set up 'to reveal the fuller picture of urban African ghetto [low income estates, *mtaa*] life and culture by being a channel for youth living in those spaces, artists can tell their own stories through music, comments, news items, stories, poetry'.[3] Online

---

[3] Ghetto Radio Foundation assists with the setting up of FM radio stations in Africa's urban slums, with the 'aim of providing radio broadcasting training to motivated and

Figure 14 Sheng billboard, Nairobi (Photo © Paul Munene)

they also aim 'to offer an international audience a more complete picture of urban slums/ghettos and its inhabitants than the relentless misery normally portrayed in mainstream media'. Their programmes offer features and commentary on the social environments in which the participants live every day. On the commercial side, Ghetto Radio FM serves as platform for infomercials and commercials sponsored by large corporations including Coca Cola, Safaricom, mobile banking services, as well as mainstream ones such as Equity Bank. They also advertise for public agencies such as the university placement service, advising young people how to apply for university, in Sheng. I have listened in to many of the daily radio shows which feature relevant issues to the youth and general public such as the psychology of addiction, drug and alcohol rehabilitation programmes available in the city, HIV and safe sex education and such. They also discuss topical issues such as corruption and police harassment, youth unemployment, and daily challenges facing ordinary Nairobians. There is a steady stream of callers offering different opinions on the topic of the moment, in Sheng. The radio station also offers what they call 'street credible' news, views and entertainment by people 'from the urban ghetto, to an audience within and beyond the ghettos' – in 'deep' Sheng. The following news item was recorded and transcribed from live streaming internet radio Ghetto Radio FM broadcasting from Nairobi:

Sheng news item on Ghetto Radio FM (online), 16 October 2017

Mansansee wanamsakanya...mansansee wamemcheki base zake zote lakini hawajamwahi....hii ni after interior cabinet secretary *Matiang'i alisema **gavaa itam-charge**...Matiang'i anataka* wasee wote *walipoteza* **ma-properties** *kwa hiyo **demo wa-rekod statement** kwa **makarao**....ningependa kusema shukran sana kwa **ma-lion** wote na **empresss** wote **wame-keep locked** na Ghetto Radio FM....**ka-evening kawambambe**.*

Standard Swahili translation

Polisi wanamtafuta, wamemtafuta mahali pote anapoweza kuwa lakini hawajampata...hii ni baada ya waziri wa mambo ya ndani kusema serikali itamshtaki kortini...[waziri] Matiang'i anataka watu wote waliopoteza mali katika hayo maandamano warekodi

(contd) talented youngsters, thus enabling them to fill all the roles at 'their' station and broadcast to the entire city the music and news that resonates with ghetto inhabitants.' https://www.ghettoradio.co.ke/about-us/, accessed 28 June 2018.

malalamiko yao kwa polisi. Ningependa kusema asaante sana
kwa vijana wote na wasichana wote ambao wanasikiliza idhaa
hii ya Ghetto Radio...muwe na usiku mwema.

English translation

Police are looking for him. They have searched all his whereabouts
but they have not found him...this is after interior cabinet minister
secretary Matiang'i said that the government will charge him...
[minister] Matiang'i wants all persons [who] lost property during
that demonstration to record a statement with the police...I'd like
to say thanks to all Lions and all Empresses who are keeping
locked on Ghetto Radio FM...have a good evening.

Ghetto Radio has been awarded and nominated multiple times for best
show (*Goteana* and *Gospel Nite Live*), best station and best presenters over
the period 2008–2013. In the following section I will discuss an example of
the work, inspiration and role of Ghetto Radio in uplifting Nairobi youth using
Sheng. Bonoko Deh is one of the radios station's popular hosts and provides
a great example of how the radio station has attained some of its objectives
of using Sheng to help young people achieve their dreams. Another example
is that of deejay and host Mbusii, who moved on to become a regular Sheng
columnist (*Story za Mtaa*) at *The Nairobian* newspaper (see Chapter 6).

Bonoko Deh

'Bonoko Deh' is a well known deejay at Ghetto Radio FM where he hosts
a regular radio show called *Goteana na Bonoko Deh* (*Big Up with Bonoko*
Deh). The inspiring story of his life and how he became nationally famous
thanks to Sheng and radio, is well known, as is his style of speaking Sheng
with a strongly marked (Gikuyu) vernacular accent. Bonoko Deh was once
one of the thousands of street people (children as well as adults) who lived
off the streets with his mother and brother at what was a popular squat for
homeless Nairobi street families at Ngara roundabout, which marks the entry
into the city coming from the north. The large roundabout was 'my home and
ochaa' (village or rural home, in Sheng) says Bonoko Deh in his YouTube
interview. He was in every way a street child for 'whom the street – in the
widest sense of the word – has become his or her habitual abode and source
of livelihood, and who is inadequately protected, supervised or directed by

responsible adults' according to the Undugu Society of Kenya, an NGO dedicated to the welfare of street children.[4]

Most Nairobians, especially the youth, as we saw in the narratives of personal experience, and the most vulnerable of street people, are afraid of the police and often do not dare to confront or report them for misconduct. But one day in 2011, an outraged young street boy named Peter Kang'ethe Kimani (Bonoko Deh) did the unusual by coming forward as a witness on live TV to the fatal shooting of an innocent *muturaa* (Kenyan sausage) seller by a policeman. The policeman went on to plant a fake gun (*bonoko* in Sheng) on the body of the victim whose only crime had been to urinate in a public space, an unfortunate but common habit in the alleys and streets of Nairobi where public toilet facilities are few and far between. Soon after giving his witness account to TV journalists, someone produced a song by mixing Bonoko's original TV interview into a soundtrack. The remix became very popular and was followed by numerous remixes in both audio and video, which are available on YouTube. Meanwhile, Kimani's life went back to normal – abusing drugs and rummaging through garbage. Luckily for him, the artiste and shareholder at Ghetto Radio, Julius Owino, known as 'Maji Maji' and creator of the famous '*Unbwogable*' song we saw earlier in this book, took him off the streets, and gave him an opportunity to join the radio station after successful drug rehabilitation. Today, about five years later, Bonoko Deh has established his successful career as radio host, deejay and producer of infomercials for various products.[5] He also runs a homeless children's foundation called *Masafara Foundation* (Sufferer's Foundation). The dramatic story captured on television and posted permanently on YouTube is transcribed below.

Bonoko Deh interview[6]

BONOKO DEH: *Huyo si mwizi, anauza nyama pale Ngara. Sasa amekutiliwa akikonjoa hapo barabarani na hao maaskari, sasa kuona hawatangonjea akatoka mbio, sindio akapigwo risasi, saa kupigwo risasi, akauliwa, sasa kuuliwa, wakakunja na kitu inaitwo 'bonoko' wakamwekelea. Hata njuzi wamemwekelea mwenzetu hapa usiku, na watu wa soko walikuwa wamejaa hapa wote, na wanamujua…Huyo si mwizi, si mwizi -- huyo siyo mwizi,*

---

[4] http://undugukenya.org/index.php/stories-and-events/23-definition-of-street-children, accessed 18 June 2018.

[5] His story can be read at: http://www.mediamaxnetwork.co.ke/people-daily/159778/maji-maji-bonoko-the-unbwogable-bond/

[6] Available on YouTube in audio format.

ata wewe utauliwa bure uwekerewe bonoko. Na ni bure, na siyo kuiba umeiba.

He was not a thief, he sells meat at Ngara. He was found urinating on the street by those *askari*, and he was not going to wait for them so he took off running, that was when he got shot, after being shot, he got killed, and after killing him they came up with something called a '*bonoko*' and planted it on him. Even recently they planted the same on one of our colleagues here at night, even the market people were all over here still, and they know him... he is not thief, he is not a thief, he was not a thief, even you will get killed for nothing and have a *bonoko* planted on you. And for nothing, you have stolen nothing...

INTERVIEWER: *Bonoko ni nini*?
What is a bonoko?

BONOKO DEH: *Bunduki* fake *na hiyo ukipigwa unawekerewa, na hiyo ukiwekerewa unjue huezi jitoa.*
A fake gun, and when they shoot you they then plant it on you, and if they do, you can't get away with it.

INTERVIEWER: *Kwa nini alikimbia?*
Why did he run?

BONOKO DEH: *Alitolewa mbio akakunja kama amepotea. Si unanjuwa wee huezi ngonjea **askari** juu na wewe hauna pesa juu utaenda jela. Na unanjua njera pia ni pesa, sasa inabidi hata wewe ujizuie, JUU ukienda njera utateseka bure. Tuseme huko, huko hukuli na unapi...*
He took off, you know even yourself cannot wait for the police because you have no money [to bribe] and you will go to prison. And you know if you are taken to jail it's just money, so you have to ask yourself, BECAUSE if you are taken to jail you will suffer for nothing. Let's say over there, you don't get to eat and you get beaten...

INTERVIEWER: *Anaitwa nani?*
What was his name?

BONOKO DEH: *Jina ndiyo sijui lakini ananiuzia**nga** mutura, kama ya mbao, ya kumi, anauzanga kanyama na mitura pale Ngara, kwa soko.*
The name I don't know, but he sells me *mutura*, like for twenty shillings, ten shillings, he sells meat and *mitura* at Ngara, at the market.

INTERVIEWER: *Sasa alikuwa akikimbia ahepe* city council*?*
So he ran off to escape the city council [wardens]?

BONOKO DEH: *Si unanjua ata mimi wakinitokea saa kama hizi*
siwezi wangonjea, juu watanipiga halafu wanipeleke ndani.
You know even if it were me, if they appeared here now, I would
not wait for them, because they will beat me up and then take me
inside [to jail].

Why did Bonoko Deh hit Nairobians' soft spot? His courage to speak out no
doubt, and the sense of outrage that could clearly be felt in his voice as he
spoke in 'vernacular' - in the most profound sense of the word as we defined
in Chapter 1. The anger and danger he felt made him speak the unaffected,
natural and spontaneously produced Kenyan Swahili, with a very marked
(Gikuyu) vernacular accent, even though he was being interviewed by journalists in what would ordinarily be a formal register. In his vernacular speech,
one can feel the immediacy of the incident, and the emotion he obviously felt
at being witness to the loss of a friend and benefactor in the hands of a corrupt
police officer. The topic was emotive and sharply relevant to the daily lives
of Kenyans, and the 'language' he used to express that outrage is the most
familiar to the masses of Kenyans and Nairobi's urban proletariat. It was a
narrative of the type instigated by the 'danger of death' scenario, which produces the most natural, unmonitored vernacular speech, in this case Kenyan
Swahili/Sheng, that most powerfully appeals to people's sense of solidarity.
The story of Bonoko Deh is a story of Sheng success: from the streets of
the city to success in the entertainment industry as radio host, the support
he received from the creators of the first nationally prominent Sheng song,
'*Unbwogable*', and finally his commitment to others like himself through his
charitable foundation which works to assist homeless youths of Nairobi. It is
a story of solidarity and networks driven by Sheng, the common language of
Nairobians, artists, *jua kali* workers and all *masafara* of Kenya regardless of
ethnicity.

Shujaaz

Another example of Sheng in practice is *Shujaaz*, a free comic distributed
monthly through Kenya's *Daily Nation* newspaper. It is produced in Sheng
and is described by its producers as 'the brash mix of Swahili and English that
is the lingua franca for millions of mainly young Kenyans'. It was launched
in 2010, 'out of the nationwide reflection that followed that descent into chaos
of the 2007/08 post-election violence that shocked the country'. Its aim,

according to its producers, is to 'educate and entertain Kenyan youths, giving them tips on everything from planting maize seeds to nutrition and the role they can play in society'. According to a statement on its website, *Shujaaz* uses the medium of Sheng because it is an 'aspirational language for the 60 per cent of Kenyans who are under 30, but have little spending power…it speaks for the youth…our idea is that we hold the mirror up'.

The name *Shujaaz* means 'heroes' coined from the Standard Swahili (SS) word *shujaa* 'hero' (singular and plural) with a modified English plural suffix (-s), which is pronounced and written as -z. The coinage *Shujaaz* is characteristic of Engsh, which borrows words mostly from Sheng (Barasa and Mous 2017). The suffix is a phonetic mirror of its English equivalent and is meant to match the actual sound of -s in speech when it occurs before certain voiced and fricative sounds in the final position of English words, for example in words such as 'bees' /biiz/, 'cheese' /čiiz/ and 'shoes' /šuuz/ where it sounds exactly like -z in 'squeeze' /skwiiz/ or 'bushes' [bušez/.[7] It follows that of *Shagz* (< Sheng: *ushagɔɔ*), or *bunduz* (< Luhyia/Sheng *bundu,* 'upcountry') or *waruz* (<Sheng/Gikuyu: *waruu/waru,* 'potatoes, chips'), or *njumuz* (< Sheng: *njumu,* 'shoes') etc. Such cross-overs between Sheng and Engsh are meaningful because they reflect shifting identities or social personae.

Shujaaz enjoys a large circulation through free distribution and multiple readings through sharing. As well as appearing in the *Daily Nation,* Kenya's most widely distributed newspaper, the comic is distributed at Safaricom's mobile money M-Pesa kiosks countrywide for free. According to the information available on their website, their audience is 70 per cent rural and 30 per cent urban, which happens to be same proportion of the general rural and urban population of Kenya (KPSA 2013). *Shujaaz* is funded by the UK Department for International Development (DfID), Kenyan mobile phone giant Safaricom and USAid; 40 per cent of its funding comes from the commercial sector through advertising.

Shujaaz and Ghetto Radio FM represent the current practice of using Sheng to intervene in the lives of the 16–26-year-old demographic that is more likely to be out of school than in it.

---

[7] The plural maker -z also doubles plural marking in Engsh where it is applied to some nouns that are already marked as plural, e.g. *Wahindiz* (< *Wahindi,* 'Indians'); *junguuz* (< Swahili: *wazungu,* 'Europeans'); *wadosiz* (< Sheng: *wadosi,* 'rich people'), *mitiz* (< Swahili *miti,* 'trees') or *nyimboz* (< Swahili: *nyimbo,* 'songs') (Barasa and Mous 2017:9).

Chapter 8

Conclusion: the rise of a Swahili vernacular

The rise, development and apparent transformation of Sheng from a covert 'youth' language into a vernacular of wider use in Kenya within half a century is indeed a fascinating phenomenon. It adds to our understanding of language contact and change, and is linked to the massive demographic transformations that have taken place in post-colonial Kenya. In the new millennium, Sheng has received influences from across the globe, with significant contributions by Africans in the diaspora through internet-based information systems. Sheng is on the rise and increased acceptability will widen its role in all levels of communication, so it is a matter of on-going relevance to study further its impact on the language ecology of Kenya, especially the implications of its entry into domains previously restricted to English and Swahili. What is Sheng's future as its role in politics, print and broadcast media continues to grow at the current fast pace? What is the long-term impact on the two official languages – English and Swahili – and on the rest of Kenyan languages in general? Should Sheng have a place in the repertoire of existing (and contested) Kenyan vernacular languages? Is it possible to 'eradicate' Sheng, in response to a section of public opinion? Sheng is indisputably the dominant vernacular speech of the low-income estates of Nairobi (*mitaa*), but speakers also adjust their speech ('Kenyanese') according to social relations they share with their interlocutors. In trade and industry, it is the vernacular of the urban proletariat (youths, adult men and women) working in the 'informal sector' of the *jua kali* industry, street hawkers, *mitumba* sellers and market traders, and of course *matatu* public transport operators.

Sheng richly adds to the existing repertoires of Swahili broadly, and to Kenyanese in particular – the spectrum of speech codes with which Kenyans navigate around a complex and stratified multilingual ecology. Sheng innovations and its 'non-standard' features have gained widespread use and acceptability as normal features of Kenyan Swahili (KS), thus marking the addition of a new variety to the Swahili macrolanguage. The popular view of Sheng remains that of an urban youth peer language – *lugha ya mabeste* or the language of 'besties' (friends) of the lower socio-economic classes – but it is no longer restricted to that single demographic bracket of the population.

Sheng has not only widened the urban community by taking it to non-urban settings, but also added to the language resources available to Kenyans in general, and Nairobians in particular. In our sample of 935 participants in the Nairobi study, Sheng was listed as the sixth most common household 'language', and many cited it as their language of 'solidarity'. By 'language' we understand they meant that Sheng is the 'vernacular' speech form they would use in the homestead or on the street (solidarity) to chat, fight, and laugh with their siblings and cousins at home. Therefore, in terms of language ideologies and symbolic identities, Sheng is increasingly regarded by many as a 'language' equal to the approximately 60 indigenous Kenyan languages, and Swahili and English. In homesteads of Nairobi, the mother tongue of either parent may only be used by older members of the household, speaking together, or in a one-way manner whereby the older person/parent receives responses in Sheng from the younger members of the household. This implies that an indigenous language or 'mother tongue' (MT), is not always the home (nor 'first') language but rather it is Sheng, which implies that it should be included among the 'vernaculars of the catchment area', as per Kenya's language policy in early childhood development education (first years of school) (KICD 2017). Because if a student's 'home language' (vernacular) is Sheng, should they not have the opportunity to use it in the transition from home to the classroom? This consideration may be ahead of its time since the present battle is over whether to implement the use of African languages ('vernaculars') inside the classroom as media of instruction in the early stages of children's education.

This possibility of Sheng becoming a recognized vernacular of some Kenyans engenders strong feelings among its opponents, language purists, some educationists, parents and teachers, even from some of the youth. But overwhelmingly, younger Kenyans and students love to talk Sheng because they find it 'easy', that is, familiar, not requiring effort to speak 'correctly' – a vernacular. It also enjoys covert prestige – toughness and stereotyped masculinity among influential in-groups (e.g. *matatu* men) and among the urban proletarian or *masafara*. It is also an expression of social identity, as it enjoys local solidarity associations with *watu wa mtaa* (people of the hood). It is the 'language' of youth peers and friends in normal interaction on a daily basis in urban areas, or boarding schools, inside and outside of the classroom in schools (primary and secondary) or university campuses. Its prestige is also due to its urban, modern, and even global associations through contemporary music, film, social media and advertising of new products related to modern information technology, financial services, and public advocacy.

Sheng's pervasive influence among the youth inside and outside classrooms of Kenyan schools is a serious topic of frequent public discussion. Parents, educationists, legislators, and judges rally against the 'damaging' and 'illogical' nature of Sheng, and blame under-performance in general education – but more specifically, performance in English and Kiswahili composition (*insha*) – on the widespread use of Sheng. Primary and secondary school students are decried as inarticulate and unable to form grammatical sentences in 'any language' (i.e. educated Kenyan English, Standard Swahili (SS) or an indigenous African language) presumably due to the negative influences of Sheng, which makes them produce few if any, well-formed (grammatical) sentences prescribed by Standard English or Swahili. Alongside the many such voices, a senior judge noted in a public opinion piece, that Sheng is 'slowly replacing English as the medium of communication among students in institutions of higher learning, and should be given serious attention'. Speaking to students during a prize-giving event at a school in Embu, the judge publicly noted what was very close to the truth: that Sheng had 'taken root in schools and colleges to the extent that university students were better versed in it [Sheng] than in English'. That was 14 years ago, and if anything, Sheng talk has increased dramatically since, as I hope to have demonstrated in this book.

One of the repercussions of strong views against Sheng is that teachers, policymakers, and parents relieve themselves of responsibility for falling standards in academic performance due to a 'language deficit' problem. The deficit theory is not unlike that which was challenged by Labov (1972), who demonstrated that young speakers of Black English Vernacular (BEV) or African American Vernacular English (AAVE) were as logical as their Standard American English (SAE) counterparts, within the parameters of the grammar of each of the two dialects of American English. As with AAVE, Sheng talk is filled with nonstandard grammatical forms and pronunciation that indeed can interfere with reading and writing. They are objectionable in educational contexts precisely because they are non-standard and of an informal register. However, this view ignores the fact that ordinary KS is itself full of the same non-standard features, as well as extensive code-mixing. Therefore, Sheng alone is not to blame for the 'poor' speech habits in Swahili or English; it is part of a larger issue of defining 'good' Swahili or 'good' English in Kenya. It is probably more useful to first recognize the reality of Sheng as a widespread, popular variety of KS, and from that basis devise ways to help students acquire SS. Speakers of 'good' Swahili or English do not believe they speak dialects themselves, and educational and even legal repercussions arise from personal and institutional devaluing of 'incorrect' varieties such as Sheng. On the other hand, speakers of stigmatized varieties (like stigmatized groups in general) derive solidarity from their distinct cultural behaviours, in this case, linguistic ones.

The rise of Sheng is an outcome of a socially stratified, multilingual environment that disfavours the systematic use and development of African languages within the educational system. Its neutrality – and its fluidity – fills the void left by the stigmatization of indigenous languages, lack of competence in them, and the linguistic insecurity Kenyans generally have in the two official languages, English and SS. Sheng appeals as a pan-ethnic, modern variety of Swahili attuned to global (Black) culture, propelling its entry into formal domains such as media and advertising, to reflect youth-led innovation, and a modern Kenyan identity. Sheng is a linguistic response to the marginalization of the low socio-economic status Kenyans ('*masafara*') by the wielders of 'power' ('*mababi*') embodied by their insistence on an elusive or fictional 'Standard' English and Swahili.

A modern identity of Kenya is necessarily youth-oriented not only because of demographics (75 per cent are under 35 years old) but also because of their pivotal role in (linguistic) innovation, enterprise, and global interconnected-ness. This calls for a thorough understanding of the implications of Sheng for school curricula, and language policy and implementation in Kenya. The opportunities provided by Kenyan indigenous languages, SS and Sheng in media, politics and all kinds of trade and industry demonstrate that languages are resources, not a problem. These occupations provide much-needed employ-ment, and their full potential is yet to be realized, or systematically harnessed. Sheng has so far generated interest driven mainly by market forces behind cor-porate advertising, and data-mining in social media, e.g. Facebook, YouTube, Twitter, etc. Other interests will result from the applications knowledge about Sheng can yield in areas of communication, and language based analytical models such as voice recognition software, and linguistic forensics. At present, research and enterprise in Sheng is being driven by individuals, NGOs and multinationals without institutional (government) support or intervention.

The rise and rise of Sheng is an example of how a speech code or language variety can break through its restricted, low-status domain into prestigious and financially rewarding ones such as corporate advertising, music, film, and fashion. Many studies show that socio-economic status differences play a role not only in language variation across a sociolinguistic space but also in language change over time. In fact, much language change originates from social classes that are far from the elite ('change from below', Labov 2001). Change from below starts in informal speech, often that of young speakers, as a form of resistance to authority and non-conformism. But they are also upwardly mobile, and therefore in a position to spread the speech forms to broader groups – from among the *mtaa* youth, to the general public who are not initially conscious of these changes in the language (see Milroy 1980, 2004 in UK). Indeed, we have seen many speakers of KS are unaware that they at times speak what is considered Sheng, and that higher socio-economic status speakers are adopting Sheng to create a parallel, elite version based on English ('Engsh') in an on-going 'class struggle' for ownership of linguistic symbols of social identity.

Sheng speakers proudly refer to Sheng as *lugha yetu sisi vijanaa* (our language, of the youth) because it provides a sense of ownership and value to this majority section of underprivileged Kenyans. It empowers this demographic group who are otherwise excluded from eating at the 'high table' of Kenyan politics and economics. They can use Sheng to earn a living, talk loud and proudly (and fluently), and even gain political office by speaking naturally in the vernacular. The chief challenge to the greater possibilities for Sheng is posed by an older generation of policymakers who remain anchored in old beliefs that monolingualism is the ideal state of society; for this school of thought, multilingualism is a problem to be eradicated at best, or stifled by any means. They still believe that 'standard' varieties of colonial languages such as English offer the best alternative for Africa in the 21st century. They also wrongly believe that only one version of 'Standard' Swahili – *Kisanifu* – is acceptable.

Sheng has also broken its inner-city urban frontiers to become established in some rural areas of the country, and in most peri-urban metropolitan areas. Additionally, acceptable use of a 'marginal' speech code in domains not previously seen or even expected such as mainstream newspapers and radio, contradicts popular understanding of Sheng as a transient, age-graded, peer language of not much use away from the streets of inner-city Nairobi. Indeed, we noted that extreme registers of Sheng might be linked to Nairobi's marginal groups (e.g. criminals, the underground, *matatu* men and women) or youthful, prohibited activities, but negative associations or linking Sheng to those stigmatized in-groups are becoming less and less. Senior Kenyan politicians these days do not shy from using Sheng words and idiom to woo the public (and they do try very hard!) or to make campaign slogans and promises in Sheng (*'tuna-wes-make'*, *'unbwogable'*, etc.). We saw how the former US president Barack Obama, who has Kenyan origins, made a spirited attempt to greet Kenyans in Sheng during a visit to the country in 2015. Another illustrating example is that of the current governor of Nairobi, who adopted the nickname 'Sonko', a Sheng word for 'wealthy person' and later formalized it by deed poll before entering politics.[1] A 'youth' at 43 years, the Nairobi governor's popularity in Nairobi's Eastlands and birthplace of Sheng grew to the extent that in 2017 he unseated the incumbent governor, by campaigning mostly in Sheng and dressing in the appropriate style including torn jeans, tee shirts, gold jewellery and flashy accessories (*mandechu*, 'bling' in Sheng). His opponent was a pharmacist by profession and polished holder of an MBA degree who campaigned mostly in English and KS. He lost the election to Sonko whose story is the story of Sheng: emerging from the margins

---

[1] The words *sonko* (plural: *masonko*), and its other Sheng synonym, *mdosi* (plural: *wadosi*), are now part of general KS.

of the city's urban proletariat to the centre of national mainstream culture and politics, and possessing real, not only aspirational wealth.

The Sheng generation

The 'Sheng generation' is the generation of millennials, that is Kenyans who reached adulthood in the early 21st century (i.e. born circa the mid-1980s, the under 35s). They play a pivotal role in innovation, enterprise, and global inter-connectedness, innovate in response to global influences, and at the same time localize international influences of language, music, art, and popular culture. Kenyan millennials cannot imagine a world without Sheng, just as their peers around the world cannot imagine a world without the internet. Sheng serves as one of the links to global culture by fusing it with local African influences (words, transformations of grammar, music lyrics, etc.). The speed of these sociocultural processes has been increased by the fast pace of moderniza-tion in Africa during the last few decades. This particular 'youth' language has emerged from the margins and needs to be re-evaluated as an economic resource and potential contributor to national integration. A modern Kenyan identity is necessarily defined by 'youth' not only because 60 per cent of the population is under the age of 25, and 75 per cent are millennials. We have also seen that in terms of language ideologies, 'youth' in Kenya is not limited to that numerical age group alone because many older Kenyans also engage in Sheng talk in their daily lives, at least in Nairobi where we collected most of the data on this aspect of the research. By looking at Sheng as integral to Kenyan language, culture and society, we can obtain useful insights into sociocultural processes relevant to Kenya.

During a small group interview in June 2015 with 16 teenage respondents in Kayole, a section of Nairobi's Eastlands where Sheng is the vernacular, the majority of boys and girls (aged 16–18) concurred that the word *gange* is the SS (*Kiswahili Sanifu*) word for 'work, employment'. They also thought that *janta* is its Sheng equivalent. But in reality, *gange* is an older Sheng word ('work, job') dating back to the 1970s, and the SS word for 'work' or 'employment' is, in fact, *kazi*. Two interesting observations emerge from this single example: that as we already know, Sheng words sometimes change their meaning, and (more often) new words emerge, just like any other natural language. It also shows that Sheng may have greater traction, appeal or influ-ence among the young generation of speakers than SS. In many ways Sheng is the new 'standard' among millennials, especially those who are no longer in school and lack exposure or the desire to conform to the 'official' SS. This is significant because Kenya suffers very high dropout rates between primary and secondary school, and insufficient spaces are available at the university. These facts mean that millions of Kenyans are left behind after primary or secondary school; according to UIS (2018), in 2009 there was 77.72 per cent enrolment in primary school, 48.3 per cent in secondary and a mere 4.04 per cent in tertiary education (college and university). Notably, female enrolment was higher in both primary and secondary education by nearly one and half percentage points, but lower in tertiary education (3.33 per cent vs 4.74 percent male enrolment). Although the millions of unfortunate school leavers are presumed to have had 14 years of exposure to 'Standard' English and 'Standard' Swahili, it is more likely that the language variety most familiar to them, their vernacular, is Sheng or an indigenous language in the case of most rural citizens.

Sheng is appealing due to its youthful, dynamic attributes. The style shifting and code-switching, or 'translanguaging', between two high status languages, English and Swahili (and Engsh), while also embracing Kenyan indigenous languages makes Sheng both modern and authentically African. On the commercial side, the marked rise in use of Sheng is a result of its centrality to a demographically significant sector of the Kenyan market who have *chapaa* (money) to spend on bank accounts, small loans, phone credit, mobile phones, and other consumer goods. It is unsurprising therefore that this creative, innovative, youthful, savvy, modern Sheng generation is a lucrative target for local and multinational businesses and corporations. The idea of modernity embodied by Sheng is necessarily youth-oriented not only because of numbers but also because of its users' increasingly pivotal role in 21st-century business and enterprise. They are also familiar and at ease with digital and internet technology, which is crucial to 21st trade and enterprise through social media advertising and e-commerce. Bodash delivery company is an example of the intersections of Sheng and modern *jua kali*, Kenya's indigenous business enterprise and industry.

Sheng is said to have a 'damaging influence' on English and Swahili, and the cause for the fall of standards in general primary and secondary school education in Kenya (e.g. Momanyi 2009). It is also blamed for stifling the inter-generational transfer of Kenyan languages and cultures, as children shift from their parents' languages and dialects in favour of 'dominant languages such as Swahili or English, or emerging dialects such as Sheng' (Karanja 2012:115). The tenacity of Sheng among young speakers – its negative influence on standard language (Swahili and English) notwithstanding – is not unique to Kenyan youth. Research among African Americans students shows that youths persist in using the vernacular – AAVE – not because they received insufficient input or instruction on SAE. Rather they return to the vernacular in adolescence for reasons relating to social identity, or as an act of rebellion that relates to the status assigned to the various dialects and academic achievement (Fordham 1999). Similarly, Sheng continues to persist, going against all efforts to neutralize its use through prohibition. The old-fashioned 'eradicationist' approach is impractical and unfair to students who are prevented from using their vernacular as a means of acquiring knowledge or information. This attitude affects all Kenyan indigenous languages (vernaculars) which have, for all practical purposes, no role whatsoever in the education of young Kenyans within the formal educational system. It is ironic that the education system undermines the official policy of appreciating indigenous languages, and using them as tools of learning in early childhood development. It is also contrary to the constitutional rights of all Kenyans to 'have the freedom to enjoy their language and culture'. In the same ironic vein, the spread of Sheng is facilitated by the boarding school system where a great number of Kenyan youths spend a significant part of the year, away from home. It is also where they first come in contact with other Kenyan youths of different linguistic backgrounds for the first time, and during a formative period of life. It is also where they expand their personal, social and linguistic networks. In this context, Sheng plays a central role in their daily lives since group reference or 'talking like' is critical as with all other matters affected by peer pressure. Regarding personal identity, young speakers also want to use features associated with characteristics which they wish to project, such as modernity, urbanity, 'coolness' – all embodied by Sheng. For the same reasons, millennials shy away from the 'backwardness' features associated with rural life (*washamba*) and Kenyan indigenous languages.

The primary motivation for the rise of Sheng is its role as marker of identity, youthfulness and innovation, the 'peer language' factor that explains other similar ones in many parts of the world. It is also an outcome of a socially stratified society that favours speakers of 'good' English or Swahili. These ideal models are held against the popular speech (KS) of the common *wananchi*, and speakers of Sheng and indigenous Kenyan languages. In certain ways, Sheng is also a reaction to a language policy that is unwilling to dislodge the high-status position of English in education and government. It has found an important space between the high-status English and low-status Kenyan indigenous languages, with SS perceived by many Kenyans as too formal and 'difficult' to master and use comfortably as a language of ordinary conversation. Additionally, Sheng practitioners defended their rejection of SS, which they see as alien to their own social or individual identity because 'Kiswahili is the language of the Waswahili'.

Language attitudes

Language attitudes should not be ignored, as they are part of a community's linguistic culture which should inform or influence language policy. Attitudes towards a language or group of languages may affect the implementation of policy and cause it to fail. It may also produce unintended results and wasted time and resources, or the desired results may not come about, or there may even a backlash against the policy. Most Kenyans have positive attitudes towards Swahili, therefore it is unproblematic to designate Swahili as the country's 'national' language that is widely accepted in many registers. The same cannot be said of any other language in Kenya. At the same time, many say *Kiswahili ni kigumu* (Swahili is hard) usually in reference to Standard or textbook Swahili, not the KS vernacular. Some say Dholuo sounds 'nice' or 'sweet' or Somali is 'a difficult language', and many believe that the best or even only way of expressing nationalism is through Swahili and that the best language for upward mobility is English. Similar attitudes, negative as well as positive, towards different ways of speaking mean that for example, many Kenyans want to, and strive very hard, to speak good English, reflecting the positive attitudes towards this language. We saw in Chapter 3, how larger social structures determine language choice by teenage respondents. For example, secondary students were very clear that Sheng or MT are not the languages in which to engage authorities (e.g. teachers, police or at work) or representatives of government (e.g. 'when speaking with the president'). It has to be Swahili or English, the languages of power and authority in Kenya. Sheng is still regarded by Kenyans as a *lugha ya mtaa* or the language of the 'estates', referring to the multi-ethnic, low-income housing estates of Nairobi where it originated. It is also referred to as a 'youth' language (*lugha ya vijana*), but we have argued that this concept of 'youth' has to be redefined in terms of language ideologies, not numerical age. Many young Nairobians in this study believe that Sheng would make a good national language as it 'equalizes' people (when one talks in Sheng). On the flip side, most of those interviewed during this research demonstrated no desire to learn another Kenyan language, reflecting less positive or even outright negative attitudes towards Kenyan indigenous languages.

Kenyans complain of the difficulty of SS, while coastal native speakers complain that their children do not do well in national Swahili exams. Both are consequences of being held to an idealized 'standard' dialect they do not have much contact with except in books and dictionaries. But the chief marker of KS is the widespread use of Sheng talk, shifting the boundaries between restricted code and popular KS. The test of individual bilingualism showed average competence at best, or quite poor when one considers the official status of Swahili and English in Kenya, in a test group comprising teenage and adult male and female students, inside a school classroom setting. There are implications of the Sheng phenomenon for Swahili translation, school curricula, language policy and implementation in Kenya and elsewhere. Specialization will become necessary in areas of translation, interpretation, dictionary writing and new grammars of KS; these will have an impact on the teaching and learning of Swahili abroad in western universities.

Sheng in education and the question of vernacular language instruction

Kenya, like most African countries, is characterized by individual as well as societal multilingualism, yet a colonial language, English, dominates the education sector. The prevailing view is that teaching Kenyan children in MT or regional vernacular damages their prospects of mastering English, and therefore they should be taught in English only. But this merely reflects a popular misunderstanding of the reasons why students fail to master the official languages, English and Swahili, and hence perform poorly in other subjects. Language is a key to communication and understanding in the classroom, therefore it goes without saying that it is necessary for teacher and student to share a common language of instruction. Instruction in a language that students do not speak has been termed 'submersion' instruction (Skutnabb-Kangas 2000) because it is like holding learners under water without teaching them how to swim. The difficulties of this form of learning are compounded by low levels of teacher education, poorly designed, inappropriate curricula and lack of adequate facilities including books, desks, rooms, computers, etc. Between 2002 and 2007, 2.1 million children flooded ill-equipped classrooms in Kenya when universal free primary education was launched by the government. Malawi also enacted its free school reforms in 1994, well before the rest of the continent – and promptly felt the pain of overcrowding (Olopade 2014). Enrolment does not mean education because overcrowding can lead to less personal attention and less absorption of the subject material. There are strong, research-based arguments, by individual scholars and organizations such as UNESCO, demonstrating the importance of MT in early education. There are proven cognitive, psychological and pedagogical benefits of using MT at early stages of learning/schooling, not to mention the inherent value of bringing up fluent bilingual or multilingual citizens. Use of a familiar language to teach beginning literacy facilitates an understanding of sound–symbol or meaning–symbol correspondence, but learning in a foreign language makes it harder to decode the meaning of what the student is 'reading' even though they can decide on the meaning of the symbols. This is why teachers reported that students memorize texts in order to regurgitate them during exams, without fully understanding those texts. Students sit silent and repeat mechanically, leading to frustration, failure, and dropout. Bilingual instruction allows teachers and students to interact naturally and negotiate meanings together, creating a participatory learning environment that is conducive to cognitive as well as linguistic development. Once students have basic literacy skills in their first language (L1), and communicative skills in their second (L2), which is used as a medium of instruction, they can transfer the literacy skills they have acquired in the familiar language. Concerning 'affective domain', confidence, self-esteem, and identity are preserved and strengthened through the first language. Students can become bilingual and bi-literate, but this assumes that for MT-based bilingual schooling to be adequately implemented, social and political issues must be resolved for the education project to be successful.

Opponents of MT instruction in education argue that there is no general rule that primary education should be in the MT, that in fact in some language situations, primary education in the MT may not be desirable. Dasgupta (1997) for example argues that certain factors may militate against education in the MT, including: (1) difficulty in determining the MT in multilingual settings where children grow up with multiple MTs; (2) definition of 'a language', i.e. the standard variety to be taught; and (3) the social and ethnic divisiveness of MT education. He argues that in multilingual settings, the maintenance of social cohesiveness may be of more importance than the benefit of MT education. Where patterns of language use are linked to social class, MT education could further diminish access to power structures by underprivileged groups. These are fair arguments that are quite widespread in Kenya, though they may at times be articulated differently. Many argue that promoting local languages promotes divisiveness and that instead Swahili should be promoted as the language to unite all Kenyans, similarly to neighbouring Tanzania. There also are difficulties of determining the 'standard' variety of the local language be taught in schools since very few Kenyan languages have substantial reading materials (grammars, dictionaries or novels), and there are also issues and controversies about which dialect to promote as the standard variety. The selection of such a 'standard' is normally based on the numerically dominant variety, following the strategy used by Bible translators, for example 'Kalenjin', a macrolanguage, is represented by Kipsigis, while Maragoli stands for all Luyia dialects; for decades the Gikuyu language Bible translation served the whole cluster of speakers of Mt Kenya dialects and languages including Kimeru and Kiembu. The same strategy was taken for Swahili, whose standard is the Zanzibar dialect, but this can create some resentment among the minority dialect speakers (see, for example, Khalid 1977). A single response to these arguments is that the avoidance of classroom instruction in MT or Kenyan indigenous languages has not created national social cohesion. Some of the worst political violence, which results in inter-ethnic conflict, is witnessed in the most ethnically diverse parts of the country – in cities and towns, and in communities of the Rift Valley. These communities both rural and urban consist of ethnically diverse populations and Swahili is the main language of social interaction; therefore the conflicts are not linguistic or a consequence of language use. National cohesion and the avoidance of social conflict is hampered not by language but by social, historical and economic injustices, the competition for unequally distributed resources (land, mainly) which results in ethnic nationalism and related tensions.

Is Sheng the real McCoy?

As in the case of the US 'Ebonics' debate, linguists are contradicted by the strong, recurrent views of non-linguists in newspapers and members of the public for condemning Sheng and calling for the 'fight' against it. The debate around the term 'Ebonics' reached a controversial level when a school board in the city of Oakland, California, declared Ebonics an African language, not a dialect of English. Therefore, its speakers were entitled to bilingual education, and additional remuneration for teachers who were bilingual in Ebonics and SAE. The general public was outraged, but the decision was supported by linguists who pointed out that many studies have demonstrated the importance of recognizing the existence of nonstandard varieties of a language, and that using it to teach the standard variety can be useful (Wolfram 1998). There are periodic eruptions of blame games in Kenyan national debate about fallen standards especially soon after the release of national examination results. It is claimed that the overbearing influence of Sheng is a leading cause of poor performance among pupils who are unable to distinguish between the language to use in official (formal) and social (informal) settings.

'Protest language could be the bane of good performance.'

While announcing the results of the Kenya Certificate of Primary Education, Education Minister Prof. Sam Ongeri revealed that Kenyan students were lagging behind in their reading competence and comprehension achievements compared to their counterparts in Tanzania, Seychelles, Mauritius and Swaziland...he attributed the problem to Sheng which he said was leaving a negative impact on English and Kiswahili.

(*Standard Newspaper*, 7 January 2012)

Teachers, educationists, and other leaders actively and vociferously oppose any attempt by the government to enforce an indigenous language policy. Leading newspapers and powerful shapers of public opinion frequently carry the headlines, and many opinion articles reflect the continued confusion about Kenya's language policy in education, which in fact has not changed much since 1922, in that successive administrations, colonial and post-independence ones, have always recommended the use of indigenous languages as media of instruction in early childhood development – grades 1 to 3 in primary school education. Furthermore, in opposing Sessional Paper 14 of 2012, the Kenyan National Union of Teachers (KNUT) leadership described the move to use indigenous languages as 'retrogressive and difficult to implement' and that there are dangers of adopting such kind of a policy 'which will not promote national cohesion'. The union leaders also pointed out correctly, that most teachers have no training in how to teach Kenyan indigenous languages.

'Teachers and parents oppose new rule on using local language in Schools'

...of what purpose is the policy paper that has made it a requirement that teachers in public primary schools teach in the vernacular? What studies have been conducted to conclude that teaching in mother tongue will add value to the learning process for children below Class Four?

(*Daily Nation*, front page, and editorial, 28 January 2014)

But there are other important reasons why Sheng should not be blamed for students' poor performance in national exams which are conducted in Standard English and Swahili. A 2013 study (UWEZO Report 2013) revealed that a third (35 per cent) of public school teachers, for example, showed no mastery of the curriculum they teach, including language. Apparently, seniority and years of training among teachers did not correlate with better teacher competence. It can be inferred from these results and also from field observation that many school teachers of Kenya are poor in English and Kiswahili themselves, or rather, they speak non-standard varieties of the two official languages, and therefore are unable to provide appropriate linguistic role models for students. In the Nairobi schools I visited, teachers often reverted to Sheng while interacting with their students outside the classroom. In rural areas, teachers very often have to use the regional indigenous language to explain things (in and out of the classroom) for them to understand: 'It is impossible to teach without using a local language. The children do not understand the subject material because they cannot understand English, and so they rely on rote memorizing of exam questions and answers in order to pass', explained a teacher who also expressed her observation that rural students find it far easier to understand Swahili than English, in the first place. As a result, despite the emphasis on English as the medium of instruction and examination, many students are not able to use it meaningfully after completing primary school (Mberia 2002). But if Kenyan students are unable to express themselves well in either English or Kiswahili, and resort to Sheng or a regional vernacular in rural areas, or more likely, a mix of all, accommodation can be made for the use of those vernaculars (including Sheng) in certain classroom situations.

The Kenya National Adult Literacy Survey report (KNBS 2007) indicated that 61.5 per cent of the adult population attained minimum literacy level while only 29.6 per cent of Kenyan adult population had attained the desired mastery of literacy competence. In addition to high gender and regional disparities in literacy attainment in the country, the report indicated that close to 29.9 per cent of young people aged between ages 15 and 19 years, and 49 per cent of adults aged between 45 and 49 years in Kenya are illiterate. The low school transition figures we saw earlier strongly suggest, among other things, how little traction English has gained in aggregate terms, and that most Kenyans are more likely to speak a Kenyan vernacular, KS or Sheng as their primary language of use and communication, outside the classroom.

A lot of research shows that vernacular language or MT is useful when exploring the grammar of a target (i.e. second) language, to promote literacy in it (e.g. Labov 1995, Benson 2004). When using a 'contrastive analysis' approach to teach a second language, the teacher relates the grammar of the language being taught (L2) to that of the first language (L1 or MT), especially during the early years of school. Lambert (1977) argued that the 'additive bilingualism' model works for educational purposes better than the 'substractive bilingualism' model where L2 (second language) is acquired without accommodating linguistic skills already developed in the first language (L1); in other words, we throw out the baby with the birth water when we refuse to use MT to teach other things (including English and Swahili) in school; L1 skills are replaced by, instead of being added to the L2. The effect is conflict of linguistic and cultural systems at best, or the loss of L1. If Sheng is in fact the L1 of some Nairobians, as the results of this study suggest, it can be used to help students improve their competence in English and Swahili. In its simplest form, the teacher can request a translation to explain the meaning of a word, or aspect of grammar, or to correct either:

Sheng:	*Unakam saa hii*?
SS:	*Unakuja sasa hivi*?
English:	Are you coming right now?

Sheng:	*Unasemaje **mboch** kwa Kingoso/Kiswahili*?
SS:	*Unasemaje mtumishi wa kike wa nyumbani kwa Kiingereza/Kiswahili*?
English:	How do you say house help in English/Swahili?

In teaching the present perfect tense of English, one might relate Sheng to SS (L2), and English:

Sheng:	*Nimestay hapa tangu last year.*
SS:	*Nimekaa hapa tangu mwaka jana.*
English:	I have lived here since last year.

This distinction in teaching style – which some Kenyan teachers evidently use anyway, as earlier described – encourages teachers to have a 'difference' rather than 'deficit' perspective of students and the language varieties they use, instead of simply condemning the students' speech as 'wrong' language that is insufficient and unacceptable. In this model of managing multilingualism, teachers respect their students' sociolinguistic knowledge and allow them to speak in vernacular when appropriate, but increase their opportunities to practise good Swahili or English by creating those discourse conditions that call for it. Unfortunately, these conditions are few and far apart at present because many young students do not have access to good books, journals, magazines, and newspapers, or radio and television programming that provides linguistic role models in interesting, relevant ways, and in the desired 'standard' English or Swahili. Instead, Sheng is their vernacular, the language of their everyday interaction. They come into close contact with it during a formative period of life during which they rapidly expand their personal and sociolinguistic networks. Therefore, it has a central place in their socialization especially as an identity marker of solidarity and belonging to a community of practice. We have also demonstrated some gaps of grammar and meaning which makes the case for regarding Sheng as having significant differences from both Swahili (its matrix) and English (its main source of innovations). These characteristics make a case for giving it a place in the school curriculum, instead of regarding it a 'deficit' or a 'problem' and focusing on its 'eradication'. Indeed, a different response to Sheng is already emerging among educationists, some calling for Sheng to be 'nurtured in the same way as other Kenyan languages' (Mutiga 2013:12). If indeed Sheng is the vernacular or 'home language' of a large and fast-growing section of Kenyans, it is necessary to cultivate an awareness of its importance in managing students' transition from a 'primary, home language' to the desired SS and English.

Kenya continues to face challenges of national integration and cohesion as a relatively new, half-century-old nation state. The term 'negative ethnicity' has gained currency in national discourse, a term that Wamwere (2003) popularized to counter the inherently negative term 'tribalism' promoted by colonial and western scholars specifically to describe African societies. In popular (western) imagination today, 'tribe' refers to a simpler life of cultural and linguistic homogeneity, of clearly bounded, parochial and stable communities ruled by clans and chiefs. But this view does not do any justice to the complexities of language culture and society of both urban and rural Africa today. African scholars such as Ogot (1999) or myself view the word 'tribe' as simplistic, an outsider label or 'coinage of western scholars who defined African nations as static, without government, culture or history' (ibid), to justify the colonial expropriation of African land and natural resources. The outsider perspective is also reflected by the Swahili word *kabila* which is a loan from Arabic (not Bantu), and one that other Kenyan indigenous languages later borrowed from Swahili to fill in this gap. For these and other reasons, we prefer the terms 'nation' or 'community' instead of 'tribe' to describe modern Kenyans of different ethnolinguistic origins (e.g. Luo nation, Kamba community, etc). Terminology aside, the issue of *ukabila* (negative ethnocentricity or 'tribalism') retains an uneasy shadow over Kenya's national unity, and a relentless verbal 'fight' against it echoes with frequency in national discourse such as newspaper editorials, letters to the editor, news analysis and commentary. Language is crucial in this struggle because a common 'language' such as Swahili can foster wider solidarity and nationalism among Kenyans, but alone it cannot resolve the challenges of national integration and cohesion. Sheng can make a contribution in this direction because it is an important facet of Kenya's national identity at home and abroad.

Appendix

Landlord anakunyima hao juu una sura mbaya

Maisha hapa Nairobi ni noma ile mbaya. Sana sana kama wewe ni mtu umepanda nyumba ya kuishi. Hakuna watu wanakuwanga na madharau hapa mtaani kama ma landlords. Unapata landlord anasahau kuwa hao na tenants pia ni binadamu. I think 90% ya raiyah za Kenya ni wale wamerent keja na hiyo ndiyo life hukua kwa sababu hatuwezi kua sure sisi wote. Kuzaliwa yes tunazaliwa the same way, lakini after hapo life ni yako, na inakutegemea wewe mwenyewe. Landlord wengine joh hata kama keja ni zenu, msisahau mnabiitaji tenant ndio mambo ikue irie kwenu. Usidharau ule tenant amerent kwako juu akikuachia hiyokeja hautaishi hapo. Kumbuka no man is an Island, and no man stands alone. Usishinde hapo ukipija tenants makelele eti wanatumia ploti yako vibaya. Sana sana wale landlords wanaishi tiplo moja na tenants wake wanakuanga mangati ile serious na sio kwa ubaya.

Wale hunisikisha moto ni wale landlord wanajifanyanga eti ploti zao ni special hawataki wamama wazee na mtoto. Unapata mama amepigwa na jua akiwa na mtoto kwa mgongo, halafu akituliza landlord anaanza maswali ya ujinga. "Kwanza wewe umeolewa? Huyo mtoto ako kwa mgongo ni wako ama ni wa nani" na je mzee wako anafanyanga kazi gani? Yani anauliza hizo maswali zote na mwishowe anaambia huyo mama eti hakuna vacant room. Mwingine anawambia nyumba iko lakini mtoto amemharibia juu hiyo ploti hawarentishingi watu wako na mtoto ama watoto. Ma landlord wengine sarenii za oyyo.

EVICTION NOTICE

lakinikulingana na vile nimekucheki nimeona tutasumbuana. Uko sure na hii mwili yako utaweza kulipa rent? Jamaa anakunyima keja eti sura yako ni mbaya inakaa suspect eti mtasumbuana, ma landlord wengine sarenii ungati.

Lazima ukubali advice

kuna wale mavijana hawapendi kupewa advise na wazee. Eti wananona ni kama wanatoshanishwa, eti hayu buda anaimbeba aje! Vijana wengi hawafuatangi advice kwa sababu

Landlord mangati zaidi ni wale waku-judge kitabu kwa cover yake. Jamaa anaona mtu amekuja kuulizia nyumba ashaanza kum-judge, eti juu mtu ni boy boy, hawezi mpea nyumba ya kurent. Kwanza anaanzanga na kuuliza kama mtu ako na bibi. Ukisema hauna anakuwambia pole sana kwa hii ploti hatupatiangi vijana nyumba. Unapata landlord mwingine amadharao mtu eti juu ako na mwili ndogo, na kakufichi anakwambia wazi eti nyumba ziko

wanaangalia mtu mwenye anamadvise ni nani na natabia zake ziko vipi. But mimi naona hiyo sio poa. Chukua advice kutoka hata kwa mtu mdogo ama hata maskini. Usiangalie mwenye anakuadvice wala usiangalie tabia yake, fuata advice yake labda inaweza ikakusaidia.

QUOTE:
KUJIBA SIO KAZI. KAZI NI KUWATOKA RAIYAH.

NYAHUNYO NYAHUNYAHU

kwa mabibi na mabwana wale wote hupigana na kutukanana mbele ya raiya nyahunyo nyahunyahu kwenu. Mkipendana hamkiamba majirani hawataZaila iko siku. Vita ya sufuria vikombe sahani na vijiko ndio yenu mbaka mtatoana nje kutokanana, eti sita wewe ni mwanaume ngoma naingia yako ni nchie moja. Mwe anajiliu "kwenda huko wewe ndie unafanyanga oikaanikiwe nje juu hijui kuanika ikiss venye indafaa". Yaani mnajianika mambo venu eti juu mmekosana, kama unajua uko kwa hio group nyahunyo ile serious kwao na urekebishe tabia.

Sheng Glossary

The following list of words includes a few phrases and other parts of speech. It was culled from transcribed interviews and narratives collected for the Nairobi Data Set in August 2002, August 2015 and March 2017. Some notes of comparative interest are marked in the last column, e.g. source of loan word. SS stands for 'Standard Swahili' and KS for 'Kenyan Swahili.' Sheng's vocabulary keeps growing and changing, so there are many new words that are not included here. A more comprehensive Sheng dictionary compiled by GoSheng Services is available online at http://www.sheng.co.ke/kamusi/ and there is an earlier one in print published by Prof Ireri Mbaabu, *Sheng-English dictionary*. Dar es Salaam: Chuo Kikuu, 2003.

Note: dh represents IPA sound /ð/ and /ŋ/ is represented by <ng'>. IPA symbols ɛ and ɔ represent Sheng vowels which are lower and more open than the SS <e> and <o>, and correspond to Gikuyu <ĩ> and <ũ> respectively. Known source of words is indicated, and examples from natural data where available. Parts of speech etc. are abbreviated *n:* noun, *vb:* verb, *adj:* adjective, *adv:* adverb, *excl:* exclamation, *imp:* imperative verb-form; *ss:* sentence, *exp:* expression, *phr:* phrase. The symbol (<) indicates the source or origin of the Sheng word where known, and (*) means unknown or inexistent SS equivalent, otherwise noted in italics. Variants of the same word are separated with a back slash e.g. *ocha/ochaa*, and the marker for plural is provided in brackets e.g. *chali (ma-).* Where none is indicated, the word has the same form in both singular and plural e.g. *gavaa.*

Sheng	Word Category	Standard Swahili	Gloss + comment
Ach/Walach	n	*Msomali*	Somalian (person)
aire!	excl	*	iree! (<Jamaican English)
alam	n	*tatizo, shida*	trouble (<English, alarm). Also,*noma*
alele	n	*pochi*	wallet
Antono	n	*Msomali*	Somalian person
asapaa	exp	*hapa hapa*	right here. Also: *paa sasa*

Sheng	Word Category	Standard Swahili	Gloss + comment
ashara	n	*shilingi kumi*	ten shillings. Also *ashuu; kinde*
Atenɔ/Atenɔɔ	n	*Mwithiopia*	Ethiopian person
avunjaa	n	*viatu vya kijeshi*	military boots
babi (ma-)	n	*tajiri*	wealthy, high SES person (< Jamaican English 'Babylon')
bachu	n	*miraa*	miraa; khat
bamba	vb	*shika*	hold; sieze; catch; get; e.g. *bamba mwizi* = catch a thief
bamba	vb	*shika; kamata*	hold, get hold of, arrest
bandi (ma-)	n	*mwizi*	thief (<English 'bandit')
banjika	vb	*cheza ngoma*	dance to music. Also: *ku-banju*
beste/beshte (ma-)	n	*rafiki*	friend (<UK English slang, 'bestie')
bika/bika	n	*biskuti*	biscuit(s)
binja	vb	*fanya mapenzi*	have sex
bisnaa	n	*biashara*	business (< English)
bluu	n	*shilingi ishirini*	twenty shillings
bob	n	*shilingi*	shilling (<UK English slang, 'bob')
bogolo (ma-)	n	*msichana*	girl. Also: *manzi, msupuu, dɜm*
boli	n	*mpira*	(1) ball (2) pregnancy
bongo	n	*pesa*	money ('used only in Mbotela [estate]'). Also: *ganji, dɔɔ, cheda, chapaa*, etc.
bonga	vb	*ongea*	talk, speak, chat. *Kila msee anabonga Sheng* = 'Everyone speaks Sheng'.
boza	n	*bangi*	marijuana. (< Hindi) Also: *godɛ, dɔm, gushumpeng', kuchi, shada*, etc.
brathɛɛ (ma-)	n	*ndugu, kaka*	brother; mate (< English)
buda/budaa (ma-)	n	*baba*	father (< Hindi *Buda*)

Sheng	Word Category	Standard Swahili	Gloss + comment
burungo	n	*(1) bidhaa za kuiba (2) bidhaa, mzigo*	(1)stolen property (2002) (2) any package or parcel (2017)
bwenya	n	*koti*	coat, jacket.
ɔcha/ɔchaa	n	*mashambani*	upcountry (< Gikuyu gĩcagi) also: *ochaa, oshagoo, gicagi.*
ɔdee	n	*maji*	water
ɔdijɔɔ	n	*mwalimu*	teacher. also: *odich, mwode, tichoo, mtichεε, odijɔɔ, mundu.*
ɔdukɔɔ	n	*duka*	shop
ɔdush	n	*njiwe*	dove, pigeon. (< Gikuyu *ndutura*)
ɔfarɔɔ	n	*Ofafa*	Ofafa, a housing estate of the Eastlands.
ɔgambo	n	*mboga*	vegetables (<transposition of ss *mboga*)
chali/chalii (ma-)	n (male)	*kijana*	guy, bloke, youth. (< UK English slang, 'charlie') according to OED however, it means 'a fool.' e.g., 'what a bunch of charlies.'
chapaa	n	*pesa*	money. Also, *munde, mkwanja, dɔɔ, monyo, dala, kakitu, ganji, cheda, kisisa, mula, bongo (Mbotela), mathendi, mafish, mangwenyes (Mbotela), mdoo, mgunji, nduu,* etc.
chapɔɔ	n	*chapati*	chapati
chengere	n	*pingu*	handcuffs
chᴣki	vb	*angalia*	look. e.g. *chᴣki leyu dᴣm* 'look at that girl'.
chips-funga		*	a euphemism for 'prostitute.' (lit. 'take- away chips')
chizi (ma-)	n	*wazimu; kichaa*	mentally unfit; mad, crazy person
chopii (ma-)	n	*mwanafunzi*	student. Also: *studᴣᴣ*
chora noma	vb	*leta shida*	cause trouble
chuna ngoma	vb	*cheza ngoma*	play music
chwani	n	*thumuni*	fifty (old usage: fifty cent coin)

Sheng	Word Category	Standard Swahili	Gloss + comment
ɔjijɔɔ	n	*mtaa*	any low income estate. Also *area-code, mtaa, ghetto.*
ɔnyasɔɔ/ ɔrnyasɔɔ	n	*kaputula*	short trousers; shorts. Also: *orwarɔɔ*
ɔpara/oparɔɔ	n	*kipara*	bald spot
ɔpilo	n	*pilipili*	hot pepper
ɔra!	excl	*potea!nenda!*	get lost! (< Gikuyu, *ũra*)
ɔraimɔɔ	n	*shule ya msingi*	primary school. also: *praimɔɔ*
ɔrezɔɔ	n	*rais*	president (< English)
ɔrifɔɔ	n	*kiranja*	prefect (< English)
ɔrismɔ	n	*krisimasi*	Christmas (< English) e.g., *estɔɔ yondhe imekacha ɔcha juu ya orismɔ* = the entire estate has gone up-country for Christmas (source: GoSheng)
ɔs (ma-)	n	*shilingi mia moja*	one hundred shillings. (transposition of sheng *sɔɔ*
ɔtherɔɔ	n	*githeri (KS)*	*gĩtheri* (< Gikuyu)
Dagɔɔ	n	*Dagoretti*	a low-mid income southern surburb near the city. e.g., *dagɔɔ ni bɜz ya manyam chom.* 'Dagoretti is a *nyama choma* centre.' (source: GoSheng).
darɔ, darɔɔ, daro, dara	n	*darasa*	class(room)
dasɔ	n	*soda*	(transposition of 'soda')
dastee (ma-)	n	*	duster (< English)
dɔba	n	*	reggae music (< Jamaican English, 'dub' [music]
dɔɔ/doh	n	*pesa*	money (< US English slang 'dough')
dɔrɔ	vb	*lala*	sleep (< English 'doze'). Also *dulu, dɔzi*
deree (ma-)	n	*dereva*	driver

Sheng	Word Category	Standard Swahili	Gloss + comment
dɛmo, mdɛmo	n	*chakula*	food (cf. *kudema* 'to eat'). Also: *sosi; dishi; manga.*
dhanya	vb	*piga/chapa*	hit; beat e.g. *Nitakudhanya!* = 'I'll beat you up!'
dhuti (thuti)	n	*suti*	suit (< Gikuyu *thuuti*, via Swahili *suti* and English, suit)
dinga (ma-)	n	*motokaa*	motorcar. Also *ndaʒ*
dith	vb	*fundisha*	teach
duba (ma-)	n	*matako*	buttocks. Also: *madiaba*
dunga	n	*viatu*	shoes
facebook-funga	n	*	'a person that is picked up from Facebook after a few flirty message and taken home for sex.' Source: GoSheng online dictionary, http://www.sheng.co.ke/kamusi (Accessed July 12, 2018). See also, *poko, chips-funga.*
fala (ma-)	n	*mjinga*	fool, simpleton. Also: *dwanzi, tosti*
farasi	n	*Subaru car*	*Jeff alidandia farasi mbichi* = jeff bought a brand new subaru. (source: GoSheng, ibid)
fɛgi (ma-)	n	*sigara*	cigarette (< UK English slang, 'fag')
filanga	vb	*jisikia; jiona*	be vain, proud e.g. *Huyo dɛm anajifilanga sana* 'That girls is very proud.'
finjʒ	n	*shilingi hamsini*	fifty shillings
fisi (ma-)	n	*polisi*	police. lit. 'hyenas'. Also: *karao, babi*
fiyuu	n	*thumuni*	fifty cent coin (< English 'fifty'). Also: *chwani.*
fizɔɔ	n	*fizikia*	physics
fuaka	vb	*vuta bangi*	smoke marijuana
gange	n	*kazi*	job, employment, job. Also: *janta, wʒra.*

Sheng	Word Category	Standard Swahili	Gloss + comment
ganji	n	*pesa, fedha*	money. Also: *ganzi, githafu, dɔɔ, mafish (2017), mathedi (2017)*
gavaa	n	*serikali*	government authorities in general, including the police.
gesi	n	*filisika*	broke, pennyless e.g. *wee mgesi* or *uko waya* = 'you are broke.'
gɛto (ma-)	n	*mtaa*	(< English 'ghetto'). Low income housing estates, including 'slums' esp. of the Eastlands.
gidhaa (githaa)	n	*wakati*	time. (<Gikuyu *gĩthaa/ithaa*, 'hour, time') e.g. *manze hii si githaa poa na waks* = man, this is not a good time to work' (Source: GoSheng http://www.sheng.co.ke/kamusi (Accessed July 12, 2018)
gidhɛri/githeri	n	*githeri (KS)*	(< Gikuyu *gĩtheri*) also: *gith, ɔdherɔɔ, odhedhe, gidh, odheng'a.*
gishagi	n	*gishagi, oshagoo (KS)*	upcountry, rural home (< Gikuyu *gĩcagi*). Also *ocha/ɔcha, dala, oshagoo.* More recently (2017); *mashinani* (< KS 'grassroots').
gisuha	n	*mtoto*	child. Also, *mtoii*
Githare	n	*Mathare*	very low income, densely populated section of north east Nairobi.
gode (gode)	n	*bangi*	marijuana. also: *boza, shada* and *kuchi, kushumpeng'* (< Jamaican English)
gofa (gomba)	n	*salamu*	greetings
gomba (gomba)	n	*miraa*	miraa, khat
gota	n	*salamu*	greetings using knuckles of a clenched fist. The verb *gotea* means 'pass greeetings to so and so, parallell to Jamaican/US English: 'big up' e.g. *Nagotea wasee wote wa Dandɔɔ* 'Big up to all guys of Dandora [estate]'.

Sheng	Word Category	Standard Swahili	Gloss + comment
gotha	vb	*danganya*	cheat, trick (< *gũtha,* informal Gikuyu 'to hit')
guoko	n	*shilingi tano*	five shillings. (< *guoko,* Gikuyu slang)
guoko	n	*vita*	fight (< *guoko,* Gikuyu slang, 'fist fight')
gwara	vb	*anguka/ kutofaulu*	fail e.g. test
gwaya	vb	*ogopa*	be afraid
gwenje	n	*pesa*	money. Also: *dɔɔ, ganji, mangwenyes, mafish, mathedi.*
hadi	adv	*hata*	e.g. *hadi leo nilipata wengine* 'even today I found others.' Different use from SS.
hamsa	n	*hamsini*	fifty (< Arabic *'hamsa)*
handa	vb	*sumbua*	rob; harass e.g. *nilihandwa na makarao jana!* 'I was so harassed by police yesterday!
hanyahanya	vb	*tafutatafuta*	busily search
Harlii	n	*Hurlingham*	upper SES surburb close to downtown Nairobi
hasapaa	adv	*hapa*	here
hashu/ashuu	n	*shilingi kumi*	ten shillings (Arabic, *Hashu);* also *ikongo, kindε*
hasura/hasla (ma-)	n	*hasla (KS)*	hustler, wheeler dealer, or middleman ('broker').
hepi	n	*furaha*	good time. e.g., *kula hepi* ' to have a good time.'
hewa (ma-)	n	*mziki*	music
inashanura watu	phr	*inaerevusha*	(Sheng) makes people street smart. (< informal Gikuyu vb, *canũra,* 'make street smart)
isivii	phr	*ni hivi*	it's like this
jackɔɔ (ma-)	n	*koti*	jacket (<English 'jacket')
janta	n	*kazi*	work, job. Also: *jobo* (<English 'job') and *wɜra* (<Gikuyu *wĩra)*
jeve/njeve	n	*baridi*	cold

Sheng	Word Category	Standard Swahili	Gloss + comment
jifil	vb	*jiona, jigamba*	be vain, feel superior (< English 'feel' plus refelxive vb marker *ji-*)
jikata	vb	*(1)ondoka (2) kimbia; toroka*	(1) leave, go. e.g. *acha nijikate sasa* 'let me leave now' (2) escape, run away.
jo!	excl	*lo! doh!*	exclamation of surprise or suspense.
juala (ma-)	n	*kondomu*	condom (< SS *juala*, plastic bag). Also: *CD, ndomko, kondiko, ndula, mbosho*
junguu (wa-)	n	*Mzungu*	White person (< SS *mzungu*)
kaa ritho	phr	*jihadhari*	be alert. also: *kaa macho*
Kaɔɔ/Mkaɔɔ (Wa-)	n	*Mkamba*	Kamba person
kadonga (tu-)	n	*sigara*	cigarette
kago	n	*mzigo*	stolen property (< English 'cargo')
kajande	n	*mahari*	dowry
Kam niku-show	ss	*Njoo nikuonyeshe.*	'Come I show you.'
karaɔ (ma-)	n	*polisi*	police officer
kasheshe	vb	*kelele*	noise; too much talk. (SS: *kasheshe* 'troublesome'). Also: *pang'ang'a* (2017)
katia	vb	*tongoza*	seduce a girl
katia	vb	*enda*	go; e.g. *katia hɔm* (SS: *kwenda nyumbani).* Go home.
kavu (kavu)	n	*shilingi elfu moja*	1000 shillings. Also: *ngiri, thaɔɔ, brown.*
kawarosho	n	*chochoro*	alley
kɔbɔlɛ/kobole	n	*shilingi tano*	five shillings
keja	n	*nyumba*	house
kejani	n	*nyumbani*	at home
kem	n	*kemia*	chemistry
kerɔrɔ/keroro	n	*pombe*	alchoholic drink. Also: *kewowo.* (<Gikuyu, *kĩrũrũ* a traditional alcoholic brew)

Sheng	Word Category	Standard Swahili	Gloss + comment
kibao	adj	*-ingi*	many, much
kibestɛ	adv	*kirafiki*	friendly, in a friendly manner (<sheng best3/besht3)
kidi (wa-)	n	*mtoto*	kid (< English)
kidiwa	vb	*taniwa*	pull one's leg (< English 'to kid')
kijaka	n	*Kijaluo*	Dholuo language. *Mjaka (*Luo person)
kijanta	n	*kikazi*	place of work
kilami	n	*Kiingereza; Kimombo (KS: Kizungu)*	English language. Also: *Kingoso*
kindɛ/kindi	n	*shilingi kumi*	e.g., *nichute kindɛ = give me ten shillings* (SS: *nipe shilingi kumi*)
Kingoso	n	*Kiingereza; Kimombo*	English language. Also: *Kilami*
kionjee (vi-)	n	*kioski*	kiosk
kiradhi	n	*tabaka*	'class', 'posh' <Gikuyu *kĩrathi* and English 'class'
Kisapere	n	*Kikikuyu*	Gikuyu language. *Msapere* (person); *usapere* 'kikuyuness'
kitowe!	excl	*ondoka!*	get lost!
kiwaru	n	*wivu*	jealousy (<Gikuyu slang *kĩwaru*)
konkodi (ma-)	n	*makanga*	*matatu* tout. also: *manamba, mpongo.* e.g., *Ule konkodi alidondoka vidu kwa mat akadedi* = That tout missed his step while getting off the matatu, fell and died. (Source: GoSheng http://www.sheng.co.ke/kamusi (Accessed July 12, 2018)
korona	n	*malaya*	prostitute. also: *poko, luch, kuro, lanyɛɛ*
kuchi	n	*bangi*	marijuana. also: *ndom, shada, gode, boza*, etc.
kuchil	vb	*pumzika*	relax (< informal English 'chill/ chill out')
kudandia	vb	*rukia*	jump on[to]

Sheng	Word Category	Standard Swahili	Gloss + comment
kudema	vb	*kula*	eat. Also. *kudishi, kumanga, kubonya, kufyeng, kudish.*
kudish/kudishi	vb	*kula*	eat (< English 'dish')
kugoroka	vb	*enda wazimu*	go mad, crazy. (< Gikuyu *kũgũrũka*)
kukeiyo	vb	*lala*	< English 'KO' knockout.
kujaz	vb	*pendeza*	entertain e.g. *Amenijaz* = 'S/he has entertained me'.
kukoya nyakɛɛ	vb	*kula nyama*	eat meat
kula mziẓi	vb	*kutulia*	chill out
kumada/ kumoda	vb	*(1)kuua (2) maliza*	(1) kill e.g. *tulicheki motii ikimada pak*a = we saw a car killing a cat. (2) finish e.g. *tutamada hiyo chakula* = we will finish that food. (source:GoSheng) http://www.sheng.co.ke/kamusi (Accessed July 12, 2018)
kumanga	vb	*kula*	eat. Also: *kudema, kukoya*
kumanya	vb	*kujua*	know; understand (< Gikuyu *kũmenya* 'to know, learn, understand')
kumethɔka	vb	*ni kubaya*	'things are bad, tough, serious' (< Gikuyu *thũũka* 'go bad, tough, serious'.
kungenya	vb	*kufa*	to die. Also: *kudɛdi.*
kungondi	vb	*kupokonya*	steal (< *mgondii* 'gangster, thug').
kunyii	n	*matako*	buttocks Also: *madiaba*
kunyora	vb	*kukojoa*	urinate
kuro	n	*malaya*	prostitute. also: *poko, luch, lanyɛɛ*
kushut	vb	*piga risasi*	shoot (<English)
kusorora	vb	*jasusi*	spy around, be nosey
kusota	vb	*filisika*	be broke
kuukata	vb	*kufa*	to die
kuwa masaa	vb	*kuwa macho*	be alert, 'all eyes'
lanyee	n	*malaya*	prostitute. also: *luch, poko, kuro.*
kuzɔɔ (ma-)	n	*binamu*	cousin (<English)

Sheng	Word Category	Standard Swahili	Gloss + comment
lɛbo (ma-)	n	*vazi shali*	expensive clothes (<English 'label')
limaa	n	*shule*	primary school. also: *praimoo*.
loba	vb	*kosa kuelewa*	not understand e.g. *umeloba hayo maneno* = You did not understand those words.
long'ii	n	*suruali*	trousers (< English 'long' [trousers])
luch	n	*malaya*	prostitute. Also: *lanyɛɛ, poko, kuro*
luu	n	*choo*	toilet (< UK English, 'loo')
madamosi	n	*msichana*	girl
madiaba	n	*matako*	buttocks. also *madigida*.
madondo	n	*maharagwe*	bean stew
mahewa	n	*mziki*	music. Also: *hewa*
majani	n	*pesa*	money. Also: *dɔɔ, chapaa, ganji,* etc.
mamudii	n	*walimu*	teachers. also *watichɛɛ, maodijɔɔ*.
mandaoo	n	*mandazi*	mandazi (Kenyan pastry)
mang'wenyes	n	*pesa*	money (used esp in Mbotela estate)
manguatha	n	*fukara*	beggars
mangunda	n	*pombe*	alcohol
manoma	n	*shida, matatizo*	problems. Also: *mashida*
manyu	adv	*nyuma*	behind (< transposition of SS *nyuma*)
manyuitee	n	*chai*	tea (used esp. in Mbotela estate)
manzi	n	*msichana*	girl. Also, *dem, shore, chike, nyamu msupa, shauti, kasupuu,* etc.
marima	n	*baa*	drinking den (<English) (<Gikuyu *marima* 'holes')
masa	n	*mama*	mother. Also: *mathɛɛ, mthama*
mat	n	*matatu (KS)*	privately run public transport vehicle. also *mathrii, nganya*.

Sheng	Word Category	Standard Swahili	Gloss + comment
matape	n	*matajiri*	rich people. Also: *masonko, mababi*
Mathaland	n	*Kibera*	very low income residential area ('slum') of Nairobi.
mathɔɔ	n	*hesabu*	mathematics
mathɛɛ (wa-)	n	*mama*	mother. also: *mthama, masa.*
mauduu	n	*filisika*	state of being broke (moneyless) e.g. '*nimeuduu*! I am so broke!
maunenge	n	*njaa*	hunger
mawowow	n	*	hip hop [styled] youth (< US English, yo!)
mbanyu	n	*nyumba*	house (< transposiion of SS *nyumba*)
mbao	n	*ishirini*	twenty (< informal Gikuyu, *mbao*)
mboch	n	*mfanyakazi wa nyumbani wa kike*	housemaid. Also: *antii* (< English 'aunty')
mbotokoto	n	*selfie*	selfie (< Sheng *mboto*, 'photo'). e.g., *Bob Collymore aliwahi mbotokoto na Uhunye* = bob collymore took a selfie with [president] Uhuru.' (Source: GoSheng) http://www.sheng.co.ke/kamusi (Accessed July 12, 2018)
mbosho	n	*mfuko*	pocket; wallet
mbota	n	*saa*	watch
mbuja	n	*viatu vya kijeshi*	military boots. Also: *avunjaa*
mbuku	n	*kitabu*	book (< English 'book')
mbuthu	n	*busu*	kiss (< SS *busu*)
mbuyu	n	*baba; mzee*	father. Also: *mseiya, fathɛɛ, mzaɛɛ, mzɛii, muthee.*
mbwenya	n	*koti*	coat, jacket.

Sheng	Word Category	Standard Swahili	Gloss + comment
mchuda	n	*uume*	penis. Also: *mdeki, linga, mkwanju, bakora, kɛii, ndeii, msedes, mchuda, abdala, nyanga, msedes, mboli, nalinga, nyoro, rungu, shuma, etc.*
mchuma	n	*bunduki*	gun
mɔkoro/ mokoro	n	*mama/mama mzee*	elderly woman. (< Gikuyu *mũkũrũ*) also: *mnyanyɜɜ, mnyandɜɜ*
mɔzɔ	n	*sigara*	cigarette. Also: *oz, kabenga, fɛgi.*
mdemo	n	*chakula*	food (< *kudema* = eat)
mdhama	n	*mama*	mother. Also: *mathɛɛ, masa, mokoro.*
mdoo	n	*pesa*	money. Also: *ganji, dɔɔ, chapaa, mgunji, etc.*
mdosi (wa-)	n	*mkubwa*	big (rich) person, boss. Also: *sonko.*
mgondii (wa-)	n	*mkora*	gangster. Also: *mandingo, kauzi*
Mjaka (Wa-)	n	*Mjaluo*	Luo person
mjamo	n	*mmoja*	one (< transposition of SS *mmoja*)
mkadhɔɔ (mi-)	n	*mkate*	bread. Also: *bof, mkaɛɛ, oremo, oredo, omofa.*
mkambodia (wa-)	n	*mkamba*	Kamba person
mkinyoo	n	*	side cash, windfall, fruits of a con.
Mlami (Wa-)	n	*Mzungu*	White person
mlosho	n	*msichana*	girl. Also: *manzi, msupuu, kasupuu, dɛm, etc.*
Mngoso (Wa-)	n	*Mzungu*	White person
mnoma	n	*jasiri*	bad, tough guy (< Sheng *noma*)
mob	adj	*-ingi*	many, much. (< English). Also: *kibao.* e.g., *kuna vitu mob ndani ya dinga* = There are many things in the car.
mobinjo	n	*simu ya mkononi*	mobile phone. Also: *nangos*

Sheng	Word Category	Standard Swahili	Gloss + comment
mohahɛ	n	*msengenyo*	gossip (<Gikuyu *mŭhahĩ*)
morenga	n	*motokaa/gari*	car. Also: *dinga, ndaɛ*
mos mos	adv	*polepole*	slowly (< Dholuo)
mpongo	n	*makanga (KS)*	*matatu* tout or conductor. also: *manamba, makanga, konkodi.*
mradi	n	*mpango*	plan (SS *mradi* 'project')
mrɔrɔ	n	*mwanamke*	woman/girl. Also: *manzi, dɛm, msupuu, mshii,* etc.
Msapere (Wa-)	n	*Mkikuyu*	Gikuyu person
msee, mse	n	*mwanamume*	guy, man, person (male), father. Also, *mzito, buda, dabus, mzaɛɛ, sonko.*
mshandee	n	*mshahara*	salary
mshii	n	*msichana*	girl. Also: *manzi, mroro, dɛm, msupuu,* etc.
msista	n	*dada*	sister. Also: *mstasis* (transposition of *msista*)
msomo	n	*Msomali*	Somalian. Also *walach, walalo*
msororaji	n	*mjasusi*	spy, snoopy person.
msupuu/msupu	n	*mrembo*	beautiful woman. Also: *dɛm, mroro, manzi,* etc.
Mtaliban (wa-)	n	*mjaluo (wa-)*	Luo person(s)
mtiaji	n	*msaliti*	traitor.
mtichɛɛ	n	*mwalimu*	teacher. Also: *mode, odijɔɔ.* e.g., *mtichee wetu wa jiog hakam leo* = Our geography teacher is not coming today. (Source: GoSheng) http://www.sheng.co.ke/kamusi (Accessed July 12, 2018)
mtoo	n	*bunduki*	gun. Also *mchuma.*
Muarabe	n	*Mwarabu*	Arab person
Muimbaka (wa-)	n	*Mkamba*	Kamba person. also: *mkambodia.*
mung'aring'ari	n	*	boys' play wheel (< Gikuyu *mŭng'aring'ari*)
muradhi/ murathi	n	*darasa*	classroom. Also: *darɔɔ*

Sheng	Word Category	Standard Swahili	Gloss + comment
muthiru	n	*ukimwi*	HIV
mwagush (wa-)	n	*mshamba*	country (rural) person
mwebaba	n	*chokleti*	chocolate
mzaɛɛ	n	*mzee*	old man. see *buda, mseia.*
mzeles	n	*rafiki*	friend, mate. Also: *bestɛ, boi*
Naii	n	*Nairobi*	Nairobi
nangos	n	*simu ya mkononi*	mobile phone. Also: *mobite, mtambo, mobinjo.*
narɛ	n	*kibiriti*	matches/matchbox; fire (2) fig. tough
nari	n	*tairi/ gurudumu*	car tyre
nati/mnati	n	*	dreadlocks. Also: *mnati, bingi* (< Jamaican English, 'natty'). Also: *didrɛ* (transposition of 'dread[i]')
ndaɛ	n	*gari*	new car coinage elicited in 2017. (<Hyundai). Also: *motii, dinga.*
ndechu	n	*dhahabu*	gold (e.g. *amevaa mandechu* = 'S/he is wearing gold [bling].'
ndesho	n	*shonde (KS: mavi)*	excrement (< transposition of SS *shonde*)
ndeve	n	*dereva*	driver
nding'oing'o	n	*nyuki*	bee (< Gikuyu *nding'oing'o* but refers to a different creature (beetle).
ndom	n	*bangi*	marijuana. Also: *bɔza, shada, bɔza*, etc.
ndovu	n	*Shilingi 1000*	1000 shillings. Also: *ngiri, brown.*
ndula	n	*kiatu*	shoe. Also: *njumu, teke.*
ndudhi	n	*pikipiki*	motorbike (< Gikuyu *nduthi*)
nduu	n	*pesa*	money
ng'ethia	n	*zubaa*	stare; be idle (< Gikuyu *ng'ethia*)
ngale	n	*sigara*	cigarette
ngamwe	n	*mjinga; mshamba*	simpleton; country bumpkin. Also: *fala*

Sheng	Word Category	Standard Swahili	Gloss + comment
nganya	n	*gari la abiria (KS: matatu)*	privately run public transport vehicle. also *mathree, nganya, mat, mathree.*
ngeta	n	*mporo*	mugging. '*kukabwa koo na ma-thug*' ('arm hold to the neck by thugs.')
ngɛpa	n	*kofia*	hat, cap
nginyoo	n	*matako*	buttocks. Also: *madiaba*
ngiri	n	*elfu*	thousand. (< Gikuyu *ngiri*). Also: *thaɔɔ, brown, ndovu.*
Ngomosh	n	*Ngomongo*	low income estate of east Nairobi (< Gikuyu *ngomongo* 'hard rock').
ngori/ngosh	adj	*ngumu*	hard, difficult (situation). Also: *noma.*
ngosho	n	*shilingi tano*	five shillings
nguya/nguyas	pron	*yangu/zangu*	posessive pronoun 'mine' (< transposition of SS *yangu* and *zangu*)
ngware	n	*mapema*	early in the morning. (<Gikuyu *ngware*) Also: *rengwa*
niaje?	phr	*niaje?*	what's up? how is it? Also: *niasaje, nijea, nivopo, vipi, sema, hawayuni*
Nibaie	imp	*Ninunulie*	'Buy for me' (< English 'buy')
Nigɛi	imp	*Nipe*	'Give me.' (<English 'give')
Ninachop	ss	*Ninasoma*	'I am reading' (< fig. *chop* 'to eat [books]')
Ninanoki	phr	*Ninaenda wazimu*	'I am going crazy' (Sheng *noki* 'go crazy')
Nitamuja	ss	*Nitakuja*	'I'll come' (< Sheng *muja* = come). Also *nitakam.*
njeve	n	*baridi*	cold
njiva	n	*chipsi*	chips. Also *waruu, chipɔɔ.*
njumu	n	*kiatu*	shoe(s)
noii	n	*matako*	buttocks
noma	n	*tatizo, shida*	problem, trouble. Also: *genje, mwadhara, dhiambo.*

Sheng	Word Category	Standard Swahili	Gloss + comment
nudhu	n	*nusu*	half (<Gikuyu *nuthu*)
nyakɛɛ	n	*nyama*	meat
nyamchom	n	*nyama choma (KS)*	roast/grilled meat
nyiaku	vb	*kunya*	defecate (< transposition of SS *kunya*). Also *nyonda*.
nyita	vb	*shika/elewa*	to understand (Gikuyu < *nyita*, to grasp or understand)
nyita	vb	*elelewa*	understand. (Gikuyu *nyita*, 'grasp,' or fig. 'understand')
nyof	n	*penseli*	pencil
nyonda	vb	*enda haja kubwa; kunya*	to defecate (e.g. '*paka hii inanyonda hapa!*' = This cat is defecating right here! Also: *nyiaku* (transposition of *kunya*)
nyora	vb	*kojoa*	urinate
nywaku	vb	*kunywa*	drink (<transposition of ss *kunywa*)
ofee	n	*ofisi*	office (<English 'office')
okuyɔ/ɔkuyɔɔ	n	*Kikuyu*	Gikuyu (person, things, etc)
olodɔɔ	n	*ploti*	plot, tenement ie. set of rental rooms in a single, shared compound. 'yard' in Jamaican english. also: *tiplo* (transposition of *ploti*)
Ololɔɔ	n	*Kaloleni*	Kaloleni. Low income council housing estate of the Eastlands.
ongelesha	vb	*ongea na*	talk to. Overextension of SS vb *-ongea.*
Oribaa	n	*Kariobangi*	low income housing estate of the Eastlands
orush	n	*ndururu*	five cent coin (< SS *ndururu*)
otera	n	*	movie star
panɔɔ	n	*adhabu*	punishment (< English)
panch	n	*shilingi mia tano*	500 shillings

Sheng	Word Category	Standard Swahili	Gloss + comment
pang'ang'a	n	*domo*	*'pang'ang'a ni mtu ako na mdomo'* = is a loose/big mouthed person.
parɔ/pɛrɔɔ	n	*mzazi/wazazi*	parent(s). Also: *mapilo, mshotha*
pastɛɛ	n	*kasisi*	(< English 'Pastor.'
peleka honda	vb	*kuhara*	diarrhoea (lit. 'to drive a Honda')
pimbi	n	*fala(KS) mpumbavu (SS)*	simpleton. Also: *fala.*
piwa	adv	*wapi*	where (< transposition of SS *wapi*)
poa	adj	*sawa*	ok, fine, good, cool. *Ni poa.* 'it's cool/ok'
poko	n	*malaya*	prostitute
primɔɔ	n	*shule ya msingi*	primary school
punju	n	*mwizi*	thief
rada	adj	*-zuri*	fine; cool; ok.
raiyaa	n	*umati*	crowd of people (< SS *raia* 'citizen')
rasa	n	*matako*	buttocks
ridhɛɛ	n	*risasi*	bullet
risto	n	*mazungumzo*	chat (<transposition of *stori* < English 'story'). Also: *piga/chapa risto*
rora, lola	vb	*angalia*	look (< Gikuyu *'rora'* or Giriama *lola*)
rwabe	n	*mia mbili*	two hundred shillings
salɔɔ	n	*mshahara*	salary (< English)
sanse (ma-)	n	*polisi*	police. Also *karao*
sanya	vb	*iba*	steal
sasa?	phr	*habari gani?*	'hi', 'what's up.' Also: *niaje? Mambo? Vipi? Vopo?*
sembe	n	*ugali*	also: *mgotu* (<SS *sembe* 'crushed maize')
shada	n	*bangi*	marijuana. Also: *bɔza, gɔde, kuchi, ndom,* etc.

Sheng	Word Category	Standard Swahili	Gloss + comment
shakεε	n	*shamba*	small farm
shamba	n	*miraa*	miraa
shore	n	*msichana*	woman
shuu	n	*viatu*	shoes (< English). Also: *njumu, dunga.*
sistεε	n	*dada*	sister (< English). Also: *siz.*
soo	n	*mia*	hundred. Also: *oz.*
sota	vb	*filisika*	be broke
shugεε	n	*sukari*	sugar (< English)
supuu/msupuu	n	*msichana*	pretty girl. also: *msupa, kasupuu, manzi, dεm,* etc.
taɔɔ	n	*mjini/jijini*	town (< English), downtown Nairobi
tegea	vb	*ngojea*	wait for (< SS *tega* 'trap)
tenga	n	*elfu moja*	one thousand (shillings)
tenje	n	*(1) ala za mziki (2) nyumba*	(1) music sound system (2) house
teo	n	*mtihani*	exam
tεii	n	*bia/pombe*	beer
thaɔ/thaɔɔ	n	*elfu*	one thousand. Also: *ngiri, brown, ndovu, tenga.*
thomed	n	*mtaalamu*	learned, educated (< Gikuyu *thoma* + English gerund, *-ed*).
thong'	n	*nguo ya ndani*	underwear (any type)
tibe/tiabe	n	*chai*	tea (< English)
tinge	n	*redio*	radio
tishɔɔ	n	*t-shirt*	tee shirt (< English)
todhi	n	*tosti*	toast/slice of bread (<Gikuyu; Swahili)
toka tara	vb	*kukimbia*	run e.g. *tulitoka tara* = we ran off
tomisha	vb	*kuwa mchoyo*	be stingy
tuende juu	phr	*sema ukweli*	tell the truth
tuishie	imper	*twende*	let's go (Sheng *ishia* 'go, leave')

Sheng	Word Category	Standard Swahili	Gloss + comment
tuliza	vb	*tulia*	relax
tuna	vb	*kulala*	sleep
tunajilive	ss	*tunaondoka*	'we are leaving'
tunakwendako	ss	*tunakwenda*	'we are going' (< Luyha -*ko* suffix)
tutachekiana	ss	*tutaonana*	'see you later' (< Sheng *cheki* 'look, see')
twende kaslambo	ss	*twende tukalale*	'let's go sleep'
ubao	n	*njaa*	hunger
udu	n	*utoto*	childhood
uduu	adv	*hakuna*	there's none
ufa	n	*wimbo*	song
ugangaa	n	*ugali*	ugali
umera	vb	*ondoka*	go, leave (< Gikuyu *umĩra* 'get out')
umeshona		*umenona*	you're fat
usukɔɔ	exp	*pale*	over there
utadu?	phr	*utafanyaje?*	what are you gonna do? (< English 'do')
vako/vakɔ (1)	n	*subira*	wait i.e. *kula vako*
vako/vakɔ (2)	n	*uwongo*	*hiyo ni vako!* that is a lie!
veka!	imp	*njoo! (SS) kuja! (KS)*	come [here]!
veve	n	*miraa*	miraa, khat
vingipi?	excl	*vipi?*	'how are you?'
vuta waya	vb	*piga simu*	*kesho nivutie waya toungee* 'call me tomorrow we talk.'
wacha kudoro manze	ss	*wacha kulala bwana*	stop sleeping, man!
wacha ufala	ss	*wacha ujinga*	stop being dumb
wadhii	n	*abiria; wasafiri*	travellers (< Gikuyu *athii* 'travellers, passengers'
Walaluu/ Walalɔɔ	n	*Msomali*	Somalian (< *Wariahe!* a salutation in Somali)
walige	n	*pochi*	wallet. Also *mbosho*.

Sheng	Word Category	Standard Swahili	Gloss + comment
warosho	n	*chochoro*	alley
waruu	n	*viazi*	potatoes, usually in reference to 'chips' (french fries) (< Gikuyu *waru*). Also *njiva, wanjiva, chipɔɔ, chibɔ*. e.g. *twende tukamange waruu* ' let's go eat some chips'
wasapii	phr	*ni wapi?*	where is it?
wotɛɛ	n	*maji*	water (< English 'water'). Also *wati, mode.*
zii	adv	*hakuna*	none (< zero)

Bibliography

Abdulaziz, M.H. Mkilifi. 1972. 'Triglossia and Swahili-English bilingualism in Tanzania', *Language in Society*. 1: 97-213.

Abdulaziz, M.H. & K. Osinde. 1997. 'Sheng and Engsh: Development of mixed codes among the urban youth in Kenya.' *International Journal of the Sociology of Language*. 125: 43-63.

Agongo, Rachel Msimbi. 1980. 'Linguistic and attitudinal factors in the maintenance of Luyia group identity'. Ph.D. dissertation, University of Texas, Austin.

Allen, J. de V. 1993. *Swahili Origins: Swahili Culture and the Shungwaya Phenomenon*. London and Athens: Ohio.

Anderson, Benedict. 1991. *Imagined Communities: Reflections on the Origins and Spread of Nationalism*. London: Verson.

Austin, D. 1984. *Urban Life in Kingston, Jamaica*. New York: Gordon & Breach.

Barasa, Sandra & Maarten Mous. 2017. 'A Kenyan middle class youth language parallel to Sheng'. *Journal of Pidgin and Creole Languages*. 72(1):48-74.

Barber, Karin. 2018. *A History of African Popular Culture (New Approaches to African History)*. Cambridge: Cambridge University Press.

Barrett, Leonard. 1997. *The Rastafarians*. Boston: Beacon Press.

Batibo, Herman. 2005. *Language Decline and Death in Africa: Causes, Consequences and Challenges*. Cleveland: Multilingual Matters Ltd.

Bell, Allan. 1984. 'Language style as audience design'. *Language in Society*. 13(2):145–204.

Benson, TG. 1964. *Kikuyu-English Dictionary*. Oxford University Press East Africa.

Bir, F. C. 1902. *English-Hindustani-Konkani-Swahili Glossary and Phrase Book.*. Nairobi: [s.n.].

Bokamba, Eyamba. 1989. 'Are there syntactic constraints on code-mixing?' World Englishes 83. *Current Issues in Language Planning*. 51:34-50.

Broomfield, G. W. 1931. 'The re-Bantuization of the Swahili language'. *Africa*. 4(1):77–85.

Brown & Gilman. 1960. 'Pronouns of power and solidarity'. In Sebeok (ed). *Style in Language*. Cambridge, MA: MIT Press.

Buregeya, Alfred. 2006. 'Grammatical features of Kenyan English and the extent of their acceptability'. *English World Wide*. 26:199-216.

CAK (Communications Authority of Kenya). 2017. 'Third Quarter Sector Statistics Report for the Financial Year 2016/17 (January-March, 2017)'. *Tariffs and Markets Analysis*. www.ca.go.ke, accessed 10 February 2018.

Campbell, Horace. 1985. *Rasta and Resistance: From Marcus Garvey to Walter Rodney*. NJ: Africa World Press.

Cassidy, Frederic. 1961. *Jamaica Talk: Three hundred years of the English language in Jamaica*. MacMillan Carribean: London and Basingstoke.

CBK (Central Bank of Kenya). 2017. 'Diaspora remittances'. https://www.central-bank.go.ke/diaspora-remittances/, accessed 20 June 2018.

Chimerah, Rocha. 1998. *Kiswahili: Past, Present and Future Horizons*. Nairobi: University of Nairobi Press.

Chomsky N. 1965. *Aspects of the Theory of Syntax*. Cambridge, MA: MIT Press.

Chomsky, N. & M. Halle. (1968). *The Sound Pattern of English*. Cambridge, MA: MIT Press.

CKRC (Constitution of Kenya Review Commission). 2002. 'The Main Report of the Constitution of Kenya Review Commission'. http://katibainstitute.org/, accessed July 12, 2018.

Daily Nation, 28 January 2014: 'Teachers and parents oppose new rule on using local language in schools.' Front page, and editorial.

Dasgupta, P. 1997. 'Foreword'. *Revisualizing Boundaries: A Plurilingual Ethos*. New Delhi/ London: Thousand Oaks/Sage.

Duranti, A. 2012. 'Socialization and improvisation.' In A. Duranti, E. Ochs, and B.B. Schieffelin (eds). *Handbook of Language Socialization*. Malden, Mass.: Wiley-Blackwell.

Fishman, J. A. 1965. 'Who speaks what language to whom and when?' *La Linguistique*. 1: 67–88.

Fishman, J. A. 1972. *Language in Sociocultural Change* (Essays by Joshua A. Fishman introduced and edited by Dil, Anwar). California: Stanford University Press.

Fordham, S. 1999. 'Dissin' "the standard": Ebonics as guerrilla warfare at Capital high'. *Anthropology and Education Quarterly*. 303:272-93.

García, Ofelia & Li Wei. 2015. 'Translanguaging, bilingualism, and bilingual education'. In Wayne E. Wright , Sovicheth Boun & Ofelia Garcia (eds.). *The Handbook of Bilingual and Multilingual Education*: 223-240. Malden, MA: Wiley-Blackwell.

Githinji, Peter. 2007. '*Mchongoano* verbal duels: A risky discourse'. In Kimani Njogu, and G. Oluoch–Olunya (eds.). *Cultural Production and Social Change in Kenya: Building Bridges. Art, Culture & Society*: 89-109). Nairobi: Twaweza.

Githinji, Peter. 2008. 'Sexism and misrepresentation of women in Sheng'. *Journal of African Cultural Studies*. 20 (1):15–32.

Githiora, Chege. 2002. 'Sheng: Peer Language, Swahili Dialect or Emerging Creole?'. *Journal of African Cultural Studies JACS*. 15(2): 159–83.

Githiora, Chege. 2008. 'Kenya: language and the search for a coherent national identity'. In A. Simpson (ed). *Language and Nationalism in Africa*: 235–51. New York: Oxford University Press.

Githiora, Chege. 2018a. 'Sheng: the expanding domains of an urban vernacular'. *Journal of African Cultural Studies*. 30(2):105–20.

Goffman, Ervin. 1981. *Forms of Talk*. Philadelphia: University of Pennsylvania Press.

Government of Kenya. 2001. Population and Housing Census. Vol 1, 2001. Nairobi: Government Printer.

Goyvaerts Didier, 1996. 'Kibalele: Form and function of a secret language in Bukavu (Zaire)'. *Journal of Pragmatics*. 25(1):123–43.

Gumperz, J.J. 1982. *Discourse Strategies*. Cambridge: Cambridge University Press.

Halliday, M.A.K. 1976. 'Anti-languages'. *American Anthropologist*. 78(3):570–84 .

Hamilton, R. 1995. *Towards a Conceptualization of the African Diasporas: Exploring Contours of African Diaspora Social Identity Formation*. East Lansing: Michigan State University Press.

Heine B. & W. Möhlig. 1980. *The Atlas of the Languages and Dialects of Kenya*. Berlin: Dietrich Reimer Verlag.

Hurst Ellen & Rajend Mesthrie. 2013. ' "When you hang out with the guys they keep you in style": The case for considering style in descriptions of South African tsotsitaals'. *Language Matters*. 44(1): 3–20

Hymes, Dell. 1974. *Foundations In Sociolinguistics: An Ethnographic Approach*. London: Longman.

Iraki, F.K. 2004. 'Cognitive efficiency: the Sheng phenomenon in Kenya'. *Pragmatics*. 14(1):55–68.

Irvine, Judith. 2009. 'Language ideology and linguistic differentiation'. In A. Duranti (ed). *Linguistic Anthropology: A Reader*: 402–434. Oxford: Wiley-Blackwell.

Kachru, B. 1985. 'The English Language in the Outer Circle'. In Randolph Quirk and HG Widdowson (eds). *English in the World: Teaching and Learning the Language and Literatures*. Cambridge: Cambridge University Press.

Kamusi ya Kiswahili Sanifu (Standard Swahili Dictionary), 2004 (2nd edition), Nairobi: Oxford University Press.

Kamusi, 2018. (Swahili Oxford Living Dictionaries). https://sw.oxforddictionaries.com, accessed July 12, 2018.

Karan, M. 2001. *The Dynamics of Sango Language Spread*. Dallas, Texas: SIL International.

Karanja, Peter. 2012. 'Kiswahili Dialects Endangered: The Case of Kiamu and Kimvita'. *International Journal of Humanities and Social Science* 2(17):95–117.

Kariuki, Annah, Fridah Erastus Kanana & Hildah Kebeya. 2015. 'The growth and use of Sheng in advertisements in selected businesses in Kenya'. *Journal of African Cultural Studies*. 27(2): 229–46.

Kaviti, L., Rebecca Oladipo & Mwaniki Ndung'u. 2016. 'African adaptation processes in English: a comparative analysis of Nigerian Pidgin English and Kenyan "Engsh"'. *International Journal for Innovation Education and Research*. 4(6):50–66.

Khalid, A. 1977. *The Liberation of Swahili*. Nairobi: East African Literature Bureau.

KICD (Kenya Institute of Curriculum Development), 2017. *Basic Education Curriculum Framework*. Nairobi: KICD.

Kießling, Roland & Maarten Mous. 2004. 'Urban youth languages in Africa'. *Anthropological Linguistics* 46(3):303–41.

King, Kenneth. 1996. *Jua Kali Kenya: Change and Development in an Informal Economy 1970–95*. London/Nairobi/Athens, Ohio: James Currey/EAEP/Ohio University Press.

Knappert, J. 1983. 'Persian and Turkish loan words in Swahili'. *SUGIA, Sprache und Geschichte in Afrika*. 5:11–143.

KNBS (Kenya National Bureau of Statistics). 2007. *Measuring Literacy: The Kenya National Adult Survey KNALS Report*. Nairobi. KNBS.

KNBS (Kenya National Bureau of Statistics). 2012. *Analytical Report on Population Projections*, Volume XIV, March 2012. Kenya National Bureau of Statistics. KNBS.

KNBS (Kenya National Bureau of Statistics). 2015. 'Population distribution by political units'. https://www.knbs.or.ke/, accessed 19 June 2018. KNBS.

KNBS (Kenya National Bureau of Statistics). 2017. *Economic Survey 2017. KNBS.*

Kouega, Jean-Paul. 2008. 'The language situation in Cameroon'. *Current Issues in Language Planning.* 8(1):3–93.

Labov, William. 1966. *The Social Stratification of English in New York City.* Washington, D.C.: Center for Applied Linguistics. (2006) Second edition: Cambridge University Press

Labov, William. 1972. *Language in the Inner City: Studies in the Black English Vernacular.* Philadelphia: University of Pennsylvania Press.

Labov, W. 1995. 'Can reading failure be reversed? A linguistic approach to the question'. In V. Gadsen & D. Wagner (eds). *Literacy among African-American Youth:* 39–68. Cresskill, NJ: Hampton Press.

Lambert, W.E., R. C. Hodgson, R. C. Gardner, & S. Fillenbaum. 1960. 'Evaluational reactions to spoken languages'. *Journal of Abnormal and Social Psychology.* 20(1):44–51.

Lambert, W. E. (1977). 'Effects of bilingualism on the individual: cognitive and sociocultural consequences'. In P. A. Hornby (ed). *Bilingualism: Psychological, Social and Educational Implications:* 15–28. New York: Academic Press

Lewis, P. (ed) 2016. *Ethnologue: Languages of the World.* 19th edition. Dallas, Texas: SIL International. http:www.ethnologue.com.

Lipski, John. 2008. *Varieties of Spanish in the United States.* Washington DC: Georgetown University Press.

Lodhi, Abdullaziz. 2000. *Oriental Influences in Swahili: A Study in Language and Culture Contacts.* Göteborg: Acta Universitis Gothoburgensis.

Lüpke, Friederike & Anne Storch. 2013. *Repertoires and Choices in African Languages.* Berlin: De Gruyter Mouton.

Lüpke, Friederike. 2016. 'Uncovering small-scale multilingualism.' *Critical Multilingualism Studies.* 4(2): 35–74.

Maho, J. & B. Sands. 2003. *The Languages of Tanzania: A Bibliography.*: Acta Universitatis Gothoburgensis.

Maloba, Wunyabari. 1989. 'Nationalism and Decolonization 1947–1963'. In W.R. Ochieng (ed). *A Modern History of Kenya 1895–1980*: 173–201. Nairobi: Evans Brothers.

Martin, Gayle H. 2013. *Education and Health Services in Kenya Data for Results and Accountability: Service Delivery Indicators.* Washington DC: The World Bank. www.SDIndicators.org , www.worldbank.org/SDI, accessed 10 January 2018.

Massamba, David. 2002. *Historia ya Kiswahili 50 BK hadi 1500BK.* Nairobi: Jomo Kenyatta Foundation.

Mazrui, Ali & Alamin Mazrui. 1995. *Swahili State and Society: The Political Economy of an African Language.* Nairobi/London: East African Educational Publishers/ James Currey.

Mazrui, Alamin M. 1995. 'Slang and code-switching: the case of Sheng in Kenya'. *Swahili Forum*. 2:168–256.

Mbaabu, Ireri. 1991. *Historia ya Usanifishaji wa Kiswahili* (A History of Kiswahili Standardization). Nairobi, Kenya: Longman Kenya Ltd.

Mbaabu, Ireri. 2003. *Sheng-English Dictionary*. Dar es Salaam: Chuo Kikuu.

Mberia, H.K. 2002. 'A survey of the teaching of reading English in lower primary school of Gatundu District of Rural Thika District'. Unpublished MA thesis. Kenyatta University.

McLaughlin, Fiona. 2008. 'The Ascent of Wolof as an urban vernacular and national lingua franca in Senegal'. In Cecile B. Vigouroux and Salikoko S. Mufwene (eds). *Globalization and Language Vitality: Perspectives from Africa*. London: Continuum International Publishing Group.

McLaughlin, Fiona. 2009. 'Senegal's early cities and the making of an urban identity'. In McLaughlin, Fiona (ed). *The Languages of Urban Africa*. London: Continuum.

McWhorter, J. 2003. *Doing Our Own Thing: the degradation of language and music, and why, we should, like care*. New York: Gotham Books.

Mesthrie, Rajend. 2009. 'Differentiating pidgin from early interlanguage — a comparison of Pidgin Nguni (Fanakalo) and interlanguage varieties of Xhosa and Zulu'. *Southern African Linguistics and Applied Language Studies*. 25(1):75–89.

Middleton, J. 1994. *The World of the Swahili: An African Mercantile Civilization*. New Haven, CT: Yale University Press.

Miller, Noah. 2017. 'The tyranny of numbers on social media during Kenya's 2017 Elections'. *Daily Archives*. 4 September. LSE *Firoz Lalji Centre for Africa Blog*. http://blogs.lse.ac.uk/africaatlse/2017/09/04/, accessed 19 June 2018.

Milroy, L. 1980. *Language and Social Networks*. Blackwell: Oxford.

Milroy, L. 2004. 'Language ideologies and linguistic change'. In Carmen Fought (ed) *Sociolinguistic Variation: Critical reflections*: 161–77. New York: Oxford University Press.

Milroy J. & L. Milroy, 1985. *Authority in Language*. London: Routledge and Kegan Paul.

Möhlig, Wilhelm, Lutz Marten & Jekura Kavari, 2002, *A Grammatical Sketch of Herero*. Köln: Köppe.

Mohr, S. & D. Ochieng. 2017. 'Language usage in everyday life and in education: current attitudes towards English in Tanzania'. *English Today*. 33(4):12–18.

Mol, Frans. 1996. *Maasai Dictionary: language & culture* (Maasai Centre Lemek). Narok: Mill Hill Missionary.

Momanyi, Clara. 2009. 'The effects of 'Sheng' in the teaching of Kiswahili in Kenyan schools'. *The Journal of Pan African Studies*. 2(8).

Mose, Caroline. 2012. 'Hip Hop in Nairobi: Interrogating popular culture and its socio-political intersections in urban Africa'. SOAS PhD dissertation: London.

Mufwene, Salikoko. 2001. *The Ecology of Language Evolution*. Cambridge: Cambridge University Press.

Mutiga, Jayne. 2013. 'Effect of Language spread on a people's phenomenology: the case of Sheng in Kenya'. *Journal of Language, Technology and Entreprenuership in Africa*. 4(1):1–14.

Mutonya, M. & Timothy Parsons. 2004. 'KiKAR: A Swahili variety in Kenya's colonial army'. *Journal of Language and Linguistics.* 25(2):111–25.

Mutonya, Mungai. 2008. 'Swahili advertising in Nairobi: innovation and language shift'. *Journal of African Cultural Studies.* 20(1):23–49.

Myers-Scotton, Carol. 1993. *Dueling Languages: Grammatical Structure in Code-Switching.* Oxford: Clarendon.

Nassenstein, Nico. 2015. *Kisangani Swahili: Choices and Variation in a Multilingual Urban Space.* Muenchen: LINCOM Academic Publishers.

Nchare, Abdoulaye Laziz. 2010. 'The morphosyntax of Camfranglais and the 4-M model'. New York University. http://ling.auf.net/lingbuzz/001448, accessed 19 June 2018.

NCIC (National Cohesion and Integration Commission). 2018. http://www.cohesion.or.ke, accessed 19 June 2018.

NCPD (National Council for Population and Development). 2013. *Kenya Population Situation Analysis (KPSA).* Nairobi: NCPD.

Ngala, Kijana. 2010. *Mapinduzi* (Revolution). In *Kwani?.* Nairobi: Kwani Trust.

Ngugi wa Thiong'o. 1981. *Decolonising the Mind: The Politics of Language in African Literature.* Nairobi/London: EAEP/James Currey.

Ng'weno, H. 1968. 'Nairobi'. *African Arts.* 1(2):66–9.

Nurse, Derek & Thomas J. Hinnebusch, 1993. *Swahili and Sabaki: a linguistic history.* Berkeley: University of California Press.

Ogechi, Nathan Oyori. 2003. 'On language rights in Kenya'. *Nordic Journal of African Studies.* 12(3):277–295.

Ogechi, Nathan Oyori. 2005. 'On lexicalization in Sheng'. *Nordic Journal of African Studies.* 14(3):334–55.

Ojal, Were. 2015. 'The status of the vowel [A] in Dholuo: a phonological look at the vowel in terms of [ATR] values'. *Journal of Humanities And Social Science* (IOSR-JHSS). 20(5):76–80.

Okoth, Duncan. 1997. *A Functional Grammar of Dholuo.* Köln: Rudiger Köppe Verlag.

Olopade, Dayo. 2014. *The Bright Continent: Breaking Rules and Making Change in Modern Africa.* New York: Houghton Mifflin Harcourt Publishing Company.

Owuor, S.O. 2007. 'Migrants, urban poverty and the changing nature of urban-rural linkages in Kenya'. *Development Southern Africa.* 24(1):109–22.

Parsons, Timothy. 1997. ' "Kibra is our blood": The Sudanese Military Legacy in Nairobi's Kibera Location. 1908-1968'. *The International Journal of African Historical Studies.* 30(1):87–122.

Pfaff, Carol. 1979. 'Constraints on language mixing: intrasentential code-switching and borrowing in Spanish/English'. *Language.* 55(2).

Preston, Dennis. 1989. *Sociolinguistics and Second Language Acquisition.* Oxford: Basil Blackwell.

Preston, Dennis. 1993. 'The uses of folk linguistics'. *International Journal of Applied Linguistics.* 3(2):181–259.

Preston, Dennis. 1998. 'They speak bad English in the South & New York City, don't they?'. In L. Bauer & P. Trudgill (eds). *Language Myths*: 139–49. Harmondsworth, Middlesex: Penguin.

Republic of Kenya. 1964. *Kenya Education Commission Report.* The Ominde Report. Nairobi: Government Printer.

Republic of Kenya. 1976. *Report of the National Committee on Educational Objectives and Policies.* The Gachathi Report. Nairobi: Government Printer.

Ruzza, C. 2000. 'Language and nationalism in Italy: language as a weak marker of identity'. In Babour & Carmichael (eds). *Language and Nationalism in Europe.* Oxford: Oxford University Press.

Samper, David Arthur. 2002. 'Talking Sheng: the role of a hybrid language in the construction of identity and youth culture in Nairobi, Kenya'. PhD dissertation, University of Pennsylvania.

Myers-Scotton, Carol. 1976. 'Strategies of neutrality: language choice in uncertain situation'. *Language*. 52(4): 919–41

Shuy, Roger W. & Ralph W. Fasold (eds). 1973. *Language Attitudes: Current Trends and Prospects.* Washington DC: Georgetown University Press.

Singh, Makhan. 1969: *History of Kenya's Trade Union Movement to 1952.* Nairobi: East African Publishing House .

Skutnabb-Kangas, Tove. 2000. *Linguistic Genocide in Education – or Worldwide Diversity and Human Rights?* Mahwah, NJ & London, UK: Lawrence Erlbaum Associates [now Routledge].

Spitulnik, Deborah. 1998. 'The language of the city: town Bemba as urban hybridity'. *Journal of Linguistic Anthropology*. 8(1):30–59.

Spyropoulos, Mary. 1987. 'Sheng: some preliminary Investigations into a recently emerged Nairobi street language'. *Journal of the Anthropological Society of Oxford*. 18(1):125–36.

Swahili Oxford Living Swahili Dictionaries. 2018. https://sw.oxforddictionaries.com/, accessed on 20 June 2018.

Taifa Leo. 2017. *'Mambo ni dabo dabo'*, 24 February.

Thuku, Harry. 1970. *Harry Thuku: An Autobiography.* Nairobi: Oxford University Press.

Topan, Farouk. 1992. 'Swahili as a religious language'. *Journal of Religion in Africa*. XXII.

Trivedi, Harish. 2007. 'Translating culture vs. cultural translation'. Paul St-Pierre & Prafulla C. Kar (eds). In *Translation – Reflections, Refractions, Transformations*: 277–87. Amsterdam: John Benjamin.

Trudgill, Peter. 1979. *The Social Differentiation of English in Norwich.* Cambridge University Press.

Trudgill, Peter. 1994. *Dialects.* Routledge.

UN. 2018. *United Nations Demographic Yearbook 2016: Sixty-Seventh Issue.* New York: United Nations. <http://dx.doi.org/10.18356/bad341b3-en-fr, accessed 18 June 2018.

UIS (UNESCO Institute for Statistics). 2018. 'Data for the Sustainable Development Goals (Kenya)'. http://uis.unesco.org/country/KE, accessed 18 June 2018.

UNESCO. 1990. *General History of Africa*, Abridged edition, v.1: *Methodology and African Prehistory*. J. Ki-Zerbo (ed.). Paris/LondonNairobi: UNESCO/James Currey/EAEP.

UNESCO. 1999. *General History of Africa*. Abridged edition, v.5: *Africa from the Sixteenth to the Eighteenth Century.* B.A. Ogot (ed.). Paris/London/Nairobi: UNESCO/James Currey/EAEP.

UNESCO. 2000. Adu Boahen (ed). *Historia Kuu ya Afrika (General History of Africa Vol VII: Africa under colonial rule 1880-1935)*. Dar es Salaam: TUKI

UWEZO Report. 2013. *Are Our Children Learning? The State of Literacy and Numeracy Across East Africa*. https://www.scribd.com/document/223010944/UWEZO-REPORT-2013-The-state-of-Literacy-and-Numeracy-Across-East-Africa, accessed 19 June 2018.

Vitale, Anthony. 1980. 'Kisetla: Linguistic and Sociolinguistic Aspects of a Pidgin Swahili of Kenya'. *Anthropological Linguistics*. 22(2):47–65.

Wa Mũngai, Mbũgua. 2013. *Nairobi's Matatu Men: Portrait of a Subculture*. Nairobi: Contact Nairobi Zones.

Wamwere, Koigi. 2003. *Negative Ethnicity: From Bias to Genocide*. New York: Seven Stories Press.

Wasike, Chris. 2011. 'Jua Cali, *genge* rap music and the anxieties of living in the glocalized city of Nairobi'. *Muziki*. 9(1).

Webb, Vic & Kembo-Sure. 2000. *African Voices; An Introduction to the Languages and Linguistics of Africa*. Cape Town: Oxford University Press Southern Africa.

Wei, Li. 2018. 'Translanguaging as a practical theory of language'. *Applied Linguistics*. 39(1): 9–30.

Weinreich, Uriel, William Labov & Marvin Herzog. 1968. *Empirical Foundations for a Theory of Language Change*. University of Texas Press.

Wenger, E. 2000. 'Communities of practice and social learning systems'. *Organization*. 7: 225–46.

Werlin, Herbert H. 1963. 'Nairobi in the time of Uhuru'. *Africa Today*, in *East Africa in Transition*. 10(10):7–10.

Werlin, Herbert H. 1974. *Governing an African city: A Study of Nairobi*. New York: Africana Publishing Co.

Whitely, W. 1969. *Swahili: The Rise of a National Language*. Methuen and Co.

Whitely, W. 1972. *To Plan is to Choose*, Hans Wolff Memorial Lecture, 7 April. Indiana University, Bloomington.

Whitely, Wilfred (ed). 1974. *Language in Kenya*. Nairobi: Oxford University Press.

Wolfram, Walt. 1998. 'Language Ideology and Dialect: Understanding the Ebonics Controversy.' *Journal of English Linguistics*. Vol. 26, Issue 2.

World Fact Book. 2018. https://www.cia.gov/library/publications/resources/the-world-factbook/geos/ke.html,. accessed 6 June 2018.

Xavier, Luffin. 2014. 'The influence of Swahili on Kinubi'. *Journal of Pidgin and Creole Languages*. 29(2): 299–318.

Zawawi, S.M. 1979. *Loan Words and Their Effect on the Classification of Swahili*. Leiden: Brill.

Index